Canada and the OAS

Canada and the OAS:
From Dilettante to Full Partner

Peter McKenna

Carleton University Press

Canadian Cataloguing in Publications Data

McKenna, Peter, 1961-
    Canada and the OAS : from dilettante to full
partner

Includes bibliographical references.
ISBN 0-88629-258-1

    1. Canada — Foreign relations — Latin America.
2. Latin America — Foreign Relations — Canada
3. Organization of American States   I. Title

FC244.07M35 1995   327.7108   C95-900037-2
F1029.M35 1995

Carleton University Press   Distributed in Canada by
Carleton University   Oxford University Press Canada,
1125 Colonel By Drive   70 Wynford Drive,
Ottawa, Ontario   Don Mills, Ontario
K1S 5B6   M3C 1J9
(613) 788-3740   (416) 441-2941

Cover paintings by Annalee Davis. "When Cane Was King" series:
Gold Fingers #1, Cane Arrow #2, Fire #3, At Sea #4. Acrylic, 1993.
Collection of Glenn and Barbara McInnes. The Press is grateful to
Dennis Tourbin for helping to locate the work.
Cover concept/execution: Carleton University Press
Interior: Cover to Cover, Ottawa

Carleton University Press gratefully acknowledges the support extended
to its publishing program by the Canada Council and the financial
assistance of the Ontario Arts Council.

The Press would also like to thank the Department of Canadian
Heritage, Government of Canada, and the Government of Ontario
through the Ministry of Culture, Tourism and Recreation, for their
assistance.

This book is dedicated to the memory of Mrs. Helen Heron, unquestionably a woman of incredible strength and courage. While the road from outline to manuscript has been long, and occasionally bumpy and dark, memories of her have been an indispensable and unfailing source of inspiration and light. Even though she endured tremendous pain and suffering, she still managed to touch those around her in a very special way. Her heartfelt kindness and genuine interest in me, even when she was facing the most difficult challenge of her own life, is something I can never forget. Throughout, my frequent thoughts of her have provided me with a seemingly unending reservoir of encouragement, determination and comfort. I know in my heart that she has made the most important contribution to the completion of this study.

Contents

ACKNOWLEDGMENTS

This book, without question, represents a collaborative and community effort. It would take several pages to include everyone who contributed, in some form or another, to the completion of this manuscript. My family, friends, and colleagues all made valuable contributions — for which I am most grateful. Through their support, comments and suggestions, Dan Middlemiss, Bob Boardman, David Murray, Richard Gorham, Edgar Dosman, Jack Ogelsby, and David Black have strengthened the intellectual content of the work. Special thanks are in order for John Kirk, my mentor and good friend, for believing in me, and this project, from the very beginning. John, saying thank you hardly seems sufficient. May our wonderful friendship, which I so much value, continue!

Ted Kelly, at the Academic Relations Division within Foreign Affairs, was instrumental in my archival research—along with Paulette Dozois at the National Archives in Ottawa. The flow of information from OAS Affairs in Ottawa and Canada's OAS mission in Washington should not go unnoticed. In this regard, special thanks should go to Harold Hickman, John Graham, Karen MacDonald, and Sarah Fountain. I was also blessed with the support of Dr. John Flood, and his staff, at Carleton University Press and the wonderful copy-editing of Ms. Maggie Keith, who certainly deserves credit for smoothing out many of the rough edges. Lastly, I would like to express my gratitude to those who supported this project financially, especially the Senate Research Committee at Saint Mary's University.

Introduction

"Canada is not a Greta Garbo among the nations:
we do not want to be alone." [1]

SINCE THE FOUNDING OF THE ORGANIZATION OF AMERICAN STATES (OAS) in 1948, successive Canadian governments have—until only recently—opted consistently for a distinct but aloof role from the body.[2] Prior to the Conservative government's announcement of its intention to seek admission to the "club" in late 1989, the official file on the OAS had been opened and closed on several occasions. While Parliament mused over possible advantages and disadvantages of membership in the hemispheric forum for decades, the answer was almost invariably that Ottawa was not prepared to drop its remote Garboesque mentality and become one of a "cast of dozens."

In the summer of 1989, however, the Department of External Affairs (DEA), after reviewing Canada's policy toward Latin America, recommended that the Canadian government should join the OAS as a full-fledged member. While Prime Minister Mulroney and U.S. President Bush first broached the subject in late August, the actual policy change itself was not made public until the end of October.[3] During his address to seventeen hemispheric leaders—gathered in San José to celebrate one hundred years of Costa Rican democracy—the Prime Minister noted: "Our government has concluded that the time has come for Canada to occupy the vacant chair at the OAS that has been reserved for us all these years."[4] This announcement was followed by the 13 November signing of the OAS ceremonial documents by the then External Affairs Minister Joe Clark in Washington. On 8 January 1990 Canada officially became the thirty-third member of the organization, when it formally ratified its signature of the OAS Charter.[5]

It is instructive to remember, though, that the road to occupying the so-called "empty chair" was a long and often difficult one. Indeed, as this book indicates, Canada has had a lengthy and varied history with inter-American political institutions—specifically, the Pan-American Union (PAU) and the OAS. Canadian political leaders, for their part, have traditionally skirted the issue of membership in these bodies, but they did not seek to isolate Canada totally from these hemispheric institutions. Over the years, then, Canadian governments have opted for full participation in a handful of specialized OAS organizations. By the early 1970s Canada had obtained "permanent observer" status in the hemispheric forum, joined the Inter-American Development Bank (IDB), and had begun playing a larger role in various other inter-American bodies.

Broadly speaking, this book examines Canada's association, or lack thereof, with both the PAU and the OAS. In other words, it intends to situate the membership issue within the context of Canadian foreign policy. More specifically, it looks at how Canadian governments, over the years, have approached the oft-repeated notion of full membership in these bodies. It also discusses the reasons why these particular institutional entities were viewed in a cautious manner by officialdom in Ottawa.

Given Canada's proclivity for a liberal-internationalist foreign policy, this reluctance to join the OAS seems somewhat odd. Traditionally, Canadian governments in Ottawa—true to their embrace of "middlepowermanship"—have engaged in a particular form of foreign policy or middle-power behaviour.[6] Indeed, they demonstrated a penchant for promoting actively such liberal ideas as community-building, trade liberalization, and multilateralism (or international organization). Within this context, the calling cards of Canada's middle-power internationalism were unquestionably bridge-building, mediation, and peacekeeping.

Interestingly enough, these same governments tended not to apply—at least to its fullest extent—the tenets and behaviours of liberal internationalism to the inter-American system. Initially, U.S. opposition to Canada's participation in inter-American affairs worked against possible Canadian involvement. In later years, beginning ostensibly with the end of World War II, Canadian governments preferred to keep their distance from inter-American political institutions and entanglements. This conscious decision to remain outside these institutions was done for a number of reasons, including the lack of official government interest in the region, a concern about possible negative implications for the Canada-U.S. relationship, a preference for cultivating Canada's European or North Atlantic connection, and a belief that the UN was more institutionally palatable to Canada. This raises the question, of course, of why the Mulroney government opted for full membership in the OAS in late 1989.

The purpose of this book is, in part, to show that the Mulroney government's reversal of Canada's previous position toward the OAS was not a significant redirection of Canadian foreign policy. In other words, the decision itself signified less a fundamental shift in Canada's policy toward the hemisphere; rather, it was more of a change in the "means" of executing that policy. And a change, moreover, that represented the culmination of years of drawing closer to the inter-American system. To be sure, by seeking greater involvement in hemispheric affairs and by signalling a serious commitment to cultivating closer relations with Latin American countries, successive Canadian governments were essentially preparing the groundwork for Canada's entry into the OAS family. While that preparation was often incremental and notably unenthusiastic, it still represented steady (if somewhat sluggish) movement in the direction of full membership. In short, this study illustrates that the decision to join the hemispheric body was not so much a bold or dramatic initiative as it was the final piece in the evolving Canada-OAS puzzle.

It is important, then, to look at the membership decision for a number of reasons. First, the issue had been the subject of lengthy debate and discussion in Canada in particular and, for decades, a sore point in Canadian-Latin American relations in general. Secondly, the decision to join was a key component in a larger, long-term strategy to broaden Canada's ties with Latin America. Thirdly, Latin America itself is rapidly becoming an important area in Canada's external relations—as symbolized by the recent Liberal government appointment of Christine Stewart as a "junior minister" responsible for Latin America and Africa.[7]

Clearly, the negotiation and coming into force of the North American Free Trade Agreement (NAFTA), and the possibility of a wider hemispheric free trade area, point to the region's growing importance to Canada. (This may or may not be reflected in the Liberal government's ongoing review of Canadian foreign policy).

Other issues, such as democratic development, human rights, the environment, drug-trafficking, and population movements—which all fall within the purview of the hemispheric body—cannot but have implications for Canada. With these and other issues looming on the horizon, this seems an opportune time to reexamine the state of Canada-OAS relations. But in order to grapple with such issues as Canadian membership in the OAS, the Mulroney government's decision to join the body in late 1989, and what potential roles Canada can perform as member of the "club," it is useful to recognize Canada's myriad linkages with the wider hemispheric community.

CANADIAN LINKAGES WITH THE INTER-AMERICAN COMMUNITY

In addition to the above-mentioned institutional attachments, Canada has maintained a number of ties with the wider inter-American community.[8] And Canada is well-positioned as a Western industrialized nation, a member of the Group of Seven, and a sizeable foreign aid donor to play a leading role in hemispheric affairs. Moreover, its willingness to work assiduously within the confines of other international organizations bodes well for Canada's involvement in inter-American institutional life.[9] Perhaps more important, though, is Canada's unique situation with regard to the Western hemisphere itself. Not only is it a trusted ally of Washington and a leading member of the Commonwealth, but it also has extensive commercial relations with Latin America—as well as the distinction of never having invaded any country in the region.

Canada's long-standing role in the Caribbean is well documented, underscored by the fact that it has received a considerable amount of attention from successive governments in Ottawa—reflected, over the years, in their significant disbursements of aid, and even debt-forgiveness.[10] By the late 1980s Canada's relations or linkages with the Commonwealth Caribbean were becoming increasingly solidified. Although commercial relations between Canada and the Commonwealth Caribbean were, for many years, disappointing, the trade picture in 1989 showed signs of improvement, with two-way trade totalling some $632 million, and a Canadian surplus of some $48 million.[11]

While the trade statistics are less than spectacular, Canada's development assistance to the area has been noteworthy, and is respected throughout the region. In fact, the Caribbean Commonwealth, on a *per capita* basis, has been the largest regional recipient of Canadian aid. In March of 1990 Prime Minister Mulroney participated in a meeting of Commonwealth Caribbean heads of state in Barbados, at which he promised to increase aid to the region—which amounted to $100 million in 1989—by 5 per cent annually over the next two years.[12] At the same gathering, he announced, with much fanfare, the "forgiveness" of some $182 million in debt owed to Canada by Commonwealth Caribbean nations.[13]

Like the Commonwealth Caribbean, the countries of Latin America have been witness to a number of prime ministerial promises over the years.[14] Unlike the Commonwealth Caribbean, though, Latin America has found that those promises have tended to be long on rhetoric and short on substance. Indeed, it would not be a terrible flight of fancy to suggest that Canadian-Latin American relations, particularly during the 1970s, have been characterized by more "pop" and less "sizzle."[15] Nonetheless, Canada has managed, over the years, to establish a host of linkages with many Latin American countries, and has recognized the importance of substantially developing these ties.

Throughout the 1980s Canada has sought to cultivate favourable trade relations with the major players in the region—namely, Brazil, Mexico, Cuba, and Venezuela. By 1983 the region as a whole, and these countries in particular, represented Canada's most important export market after the United States, Western Europe, and Japan.[16] Five years later, two-way trade was still in excess of $7 billion—greater than Canada's trade with Asian countries and China combined—with Canadian exports to the region totalling close to $2.9 billion.[17]

In terms of aid to the region, successive Canadian governments have been less than forthcoming. Traditionally, a large portion of assistance was channelled through the Inter-American Development Bank. As late as the mid-1970s, however, only 4 per cent of Canada's overall budget for development assistance went to Latin America.[18] In 1981-82, by comparison, Ottawa's contribution had increased to 11 per cent, with a total disbursement to the region of some

$79 million. Four years later, aid to the region was projected to reach approximately $123 million.[19] By 1987-88 Canada's development assistance contribution to the region was increasing, with aid to the region amounting to some $375 million.[20] However, by the early 1990s, there were some signs that Canada's aid commitment to the region was in decline—dropping to $160 million in 1989-1990; increasing to $181 million in 1990-1991; decreasing to $178 million in 1991-1992; and then falling to $171 million in 1992-93.[21]

Canada's linkages from an official standpoint, in contrast to the foreign aid dimension, have been more troublesome. In fact, it was not until the early 1970s that Canada finally "discovered" Latin America on an official level. Prime Minister Trudeau's high-profile state visit to Mexico, Venezuela, and Cuba in 1976 seemed to engender a reservoir of goodwill toward Canada.[22] Moreover, during the 1980s, a number of cabinet ministers, including Allan MacEachen and Joe Clark, visited various parts of the region in hopes of solidifying Canada's presence and interest in Latin America. By the early 1990s diplomatic activity was on the rise, with prime ministerial visits to Costa Rica and Mexico,[23] ministerial visits to Paraguay and Mexico, and a visit to Cuba by Louise Fréchette, former assistant deputy minister in DEA's Latin America and Caribbean bureau.[24] Ministerial visits and contacts between officials continued to the end of Mulroney's years in office. For the most part, his last few years in power were dominated by the crisis in Haiti and the negotiation of a trilateral free trade agreement.[25]

More recently, Canada, the United States, and Mexico experienced the coming into force of the NAFTA on 1 January 1994, which creates a combined GDP of more than $5 trillion and encompasses almost 400 million people.[26] In accepting the NAFTA, and by expressing a firm interest in having new members join (e.g., Chile and Argentina), the new Liberal government of Jean Chrétien has signalled a continuing interest in expanding Canada's relations with the Americas.[27] In fact, it was significant that PM Chrétien chose Mexico as the site of his first official foreign visit abroad, rather than the United States. His March 1994 visit indicated his commitment to increasing Canadian-Mexican political and trade linkages, as well as trying to put some symbolic distance between Ottawa and Washington. In addition, Secretary of State Stewart and International Trade Minister Roy MacLaren have both paid a number of visits to various Latin

American countries—including Mexico, Cuba, Chile, Colombia, Ecuador, Argentina, and Brazil.

Although relations with Latin America have become more important lately, they do not, of course, approach the scope and depth of the overall Canada-U.S. relationship. As this book will illustrate, the Ottawa-Washington axis is a major component of Canada's hemispheric relations. It is important, therefore, to understand fully the dynamics of that axis. A striking feature is the nature and extent of commercial interactions between the two countries, not to mention the wide range of private-sector ties. These two countries maintain the largest trading relationship in the world, amounting to more than $200 billion annually. Roughly 25 per cent of all U.S. exports are sent across the Canada-U.S. border.[28] On the other hand, Canada exports approximately 80 per cent of its total exports to the U.S. market.[29]

Accompanying this intertwining of economic as well as investment interests is a long-standing network of intimate intergovernmental or bureaucratic interactions. This unique component of the Canadian-American "diplomatic culture" largely consists of extensive day-to-day working-level contacts, hundreds of face-to-face meetings, and literally thousands of telephone conferences each year. In addition to saving enormous time and effort, this familiarity with those comprising the Washington policy community also provides Ottawa with an opportunity to actually influence or moderate the direction in which U.S. policy is heading.

Clearly, these connections with the United States, and indeed with the Commonwealth Caribbean and Latin America, establish Canada as a hemispheric "actor." Its wide range of linkages and ties have furnished Ottawa with a stock of diplomatic goodwill. It has a solid reputation not only for working diligently within international organizations, but also for espousing pragmatic solutions and shunning ideologically-tainted positions (witness Canada's constructive relations with Castro's Cuba and with the former Sandinista government in Nicaragua; indeed, Canada and Mexico were the only countries of the Americas not to break diplomatic relations with Cuba in 1962). Simply put, the nature and extent of these linkages place Canada in a unique position with regard to hemispheric affairs. They provide Ottawa with a certain degree of influence, which Canadian officials will have to use judiciously.

Within this contextual environment, however, the issue of joining the OAS almost invariably seemed to be foremost in the minds of politicians, political pundits, and Latin Americanists. The membership question had, for decades, spurred intense debate and discussion in Canada. Those individuals espousing support for admission, as well as those who advocated non-membership, proffered a series of pros and cons concerning this issue. Foreign policy reviews, along with specific examinations of the membership issue itself, were undertaken on several occasions by officials in External Affairs. In 1982 a parliamentary sub-committee—which focused on Canada's overall relations with Latin America and the Caribbean—looked specifically at the membership question. Simply put, the issue of joining the OAS, while only occasionally a leading concern, never seemed to disappear completely from the Canadian political landscape. Still, Canadian governments were—for decades—reluctant to seek full membership and settled instead for a firm posture of aloofness toward the organization.

Not surprisingly, over the last fifty years or so, interested observers and students of inter-American affairs have looked at Canada's involvement in hemispheric life.[30] In the main, these analysts have tended to focus on Canada's linkages with the inter-American system as a whole. For example, they have examined the nature and extent of Canada's political, economic, diplomatic, and security ties with the hemisphere. Within this context they have pointed to Canada's sporadic participation in various inter-American conferences or to its establishment of diplomatic relations with various Latin American countries.

This same group of specialists has normally advanced two very distinct and different viewpoints. On the one hand, there were those who advocated closer ties with Latin America, arguing that this region was going to become politically and economically important to Canada in the years to come. On the other hand, there were those who opposed strengthening relations with this region of the world—in part, because it was thought insignificant to the Canadian public and more likely to bring Canada into conflict with the United States. At some point or another, each of these observers usually came out either in favour of or against Canadian membership in inter-American political institutions.

Such pundits attempted to buttress their respective positions by outlining a bevy of arguments and observations. Analysis of the subject area was basically confined to detailing the advantages and disadvantages of closer relations with Latin America. Some of the arguments for and against stronger ties were emotional in nature (e.g., that Canada was a true nation of the Americas and that French-speaking Canadians shared a certain affinity with their Spanish-speaking brethren or that Canadians would not be able to get along with the loquacious Latins) rather than substantive. In any event, the analysis normally revolved around how greater involvement in the hemisphere would either advance or damage Canadian interests. For the most part, it did not deal specifically—or in a comprehensive fashion—with Canada's attitude toward the Pan-American Union (PAU) or the Organization of American States (OAS).

The undertaking of this book was, in part, spurred on by this glaring lack of available works, published or unpublished, on the topic. With the exception of an occasional graduate study, one is left only with John P. Humphrey's 1942 *The Inter-American System: A Canadian View* or Marcel Roussin's 1958 *Le Canada et le système interaméricain*.[31] Moreover, much of the scholarly work on Canada's involvement in hemispheric affairs has focused primarily on Canadian-Latin American relations or on Canada's association with the inter-American system or community. Within this context, some analysts have examined a variety of linkages—political, economic, diplomatic, strategic, and cultural—existing between Canada and a host of Latin American states. From a thematic standpoint, they have essentially limited their studies to outlining Canada's various interests in Latin America, indicating possible roles that Canada could play in the region, and detailing the advantages or benefits to Canada of strengthening its ties with a number of Latin American countries.

This book is not intended to focus specifically on the dynamics of Canadian-Latin American relations. Of course, it does touch upon several aspects of Canada's relations with the region, but not in any detailed or in-depth fashion. Such an undertaking might have created problems of clarity and manageability as well as produced a more unwieldy and diluted focus. For these reasons, this study restricts itself to examining the nature and extent of Canada-OAS relations.

A huge lacuna exists in the literature on this topic. Little material is available on the various debates surrounding the issue, and on why successive Canadian governments refrained from joining the hemispheric body. Put simply, scholarship needs not only to fill this literature-vacuum, but also to update the available information on the subject by incorporating recent developments in Canada-OAS relations.

Examining the OAS decision also has implications for the study of political science. While this study does not attempt to break new theoretical ground, it does contribute to a better understanding of the conduct of Canadian foreign policy. Indeed, focusing on Canada's long association with hemispheric political institutions, and on the actual decision itself, helps to shed some explanatory light on how Canadian foreign policy is formulated.[32] It may even provide some insights into how and why other foreign policy decisions were taken (i.e., Canada's position on the 1989 U.S. invasion of Panama).

To begin with, an analysis of the OAS decision reveals the key actors—such as the central political figures and senior bureaucrats—who were intimately involved in the making of Canadian foreign policy. Additionally, it illustrates the reasons why this particular decision was made. In this context, it outlines the various factors—political, economic, social, bureaucratic, and external—which influence the formulation of Canadian foreign policy. Above all, however, it demonstrates clearly that the decision to join the OAS was the product of a long, complex governmental process that entailed widespread discussion and consultation between high-level politicians, foreign policy officials, other government departments, outside groups, and foreign leaders. The Mulroney government's decision to join the OAS, then, was not merely the product of prime ministerial whim, a means of generating domestic political support, or blind acquiescence to foreign (read U.S.) pressure. Rather, it was the end result of a lengthy process of internal and external governmental analysis, consultation, and deliberation.

The decision to opt for a "case study" methodology was based on two essential factors. First, it was consistent with an interest in the topic primarily for analytical as opposed to theoretical purposes.[33] Secondly, this type of methodology provided a useful approach in terms of facilitating a thorough and extensive examination of the subject area. This, in turn, helped to produce a greater knowledge of Canada's relations with the inter-American system and to suggest some generalizations about the foreign policy-making process in Canada. In short, utilizing the case study method offered a comprehensive means of looking at Canada-OAS relations and the dynamics of Canadian foreign policy.

Some of the research for the case study was drawn from governmental publications (and pertinent documents), interested academics, correspondence with politicians, and newspaper reports. A large body of information, however, was gleaned from a number of confidential interviews with high-ranking past and present DEA and Foreign Affairs officials. Indeed, included among those interviewed were four of the five Canadian permanent observers to the hemispheric body. Also interviewed were a number of the key players—both in Canada and the United States—who were intimately involved in the policy process that preceded the Conservative government's decision to join the OAS. Given the limited number of individuals involved directly in Canada-OAS affairs, these interviews were a particularly integral source of information. Moreover, a significant portion of information was obtained through archival research at the National Archives of Canada and the Department of External Affairs (now Foreign Affairs) in Ottawa. Most of the remaining text was largely based on secondary sources, including books, journal articles, and book chapters.

Accordingly, this book seeks to explore the nature and extent of Canada-OAS relations in general and the 1989 decision to join the hemispheric body in particular. In order to facilitate a thorough explanation and better understanding of the subject area, the study is divided into eight chapters. Chapter one provides a historical account of how the OAS has evolved as well as a discussion of the main legal "pillars" that underpin the body. Chapter two concentrates on the successes and failures of the organization since its inception. Chapter three, for its part, examines Canada's early association with inter-American institutional life. It also discusses the positions of successive Canadian governments—from 1931 to the late 1960s—toward the OAS, and why they steadfastly opposed joining the organization. Chapter four looks specifically at the Trudeau government's view of the OAS, and its reasons for remaining aloof from the body. (By looking at the Trudeau years, and the state of Canada-OAS relations during that period, one gets a sense of the slow movement toward full membership in the hemispheric forum). Chapter five, drawing on the two preceding chapters, outlines the various actors, and the positions which they espoused, on Canadian membership in the hemispheric forum.

Chapter six, and perhaps the most important, focuses directly on the actual decision of the Mulroney government to seek membership in the OAS. It details the various reasons and factors which underlay the decision to opt for full membership. Chapter seven outlines and discusses Canada's "performance record" for the first few years of its OAS membership. The study concludes with a number of observations on Canada-OAS relations, the constraints acting upon Canada's "OAS policy," and the likely direction of Canada's approach toward the Americas under the new Liberal government.

The dynamics of Canada-OAS relations have been both challenging and enlightening to examine, as an area of study that needs clear and comprehensive explanations. Obviously, some questions may never be answered satisfactorily—such as the precise role of Prime Minister Mulroney and the Prime Minister's Office (PMO). But as Marcel Roussin, a long-time student of Canadian-Inter-American relations, once remarked:

As far as Canada is concerned, so many things have been said about the possible participation of Canada in the O.A.S. that it might seem both fastidious and presumptuous to try adding any new views on the subject. Nevertheless, our country has reached a turning point in its relations with the other nations of the continent and in the planning of its policy within the framework of the Inter-American System.[34]

I

The Evolution of Inter-American Institutions

It is a grand conception to consolidate the New World into a single nation with a single bond uniting all its parts. Since the different parts have the same origin, language, customs, and religion, they ought to be confederated into a single state; but this is not possible because differences of climate, diverse conditions, opposing interests and dissimilar characteristics divide America. How grand it would be if the Isthmus of Panama should become for us what the Isthmus of Corinth was for the Greeks! God grant that we may have the fortune some day to install there an august congress of representatives of the republics, kingdoms, and empires to deliberate upon the high interests of peace and of war with the nations of the other three-quarters of the world. — Simón Bolívar[1]

THE HISTORY OF HISPANIC-AMERICAN RELATIONS, TO WHICH Bolívar alludes, records times of indifference and distrust as well as periods of harmony and co-operation. Not surprisingly, the movement toward Pan-Americanism—originating officially in the late 1800s—has oscillated in a similar way. We must first grapple with the unfolding of this movement to gain a better understanding of inter-American affairs, both past and present. It not only sets out the dynamics at work in hemispheric interactions, but also establishes how and why the inter-American system evolved the way it did. This is crucially important because too often analysts tend to reduce Latin American, and indeed inter-American, events with an over-simplified explanation, when it is truly an extraordinarily complex multilateral reality.

Clearly, a proper historical grounding is important to provide a sense of perspective and context. The purpose of this chapter, then, is two-fold: to examine and explain the evolution of Pan-Americanism from 1889 to 1948; and to delineate the major principles, functions, and organs of the three pillars of the inter-American system—the Rio Treaty, the Charter of the Organization of American States (OAS), and the Pact of Bogotá. The chapter concludes with some general comments and observations about the nature of Pan-Americanism.

THE EVOLUTION OF PAN-AMERICANISM

As early as 1815, Simón Bolívar, who is often (perhaps mistakenly)[2] referred to as the "father of Pan-Americanism," issued a clarion call for Spanish-American unity and co-operation. More specifically, the celebrated revolutionary envisioned a Spanish-American league or confederation, operating under the protective umbrella of Britain.[3] Such an arrangement, he believed, would inspire respect and allow Hispanic America to resist any attempt on the part of Spain to restore its colonial grip. In addition to common defence, Bolívar saw the possibility of establishing a firmer peace within the hemisphere as well as furthering mutual development.

However, it was the United States, in the early 1880s, which actually assumed the leadership of the incipient Pan-American movement. Indeed, under the stewardship of U.S. Secretary of State James G. Blaine, the first full-fledged International Conference of American States was convened in Washington in October of 1889.[4] This initial gathering of hemispheric countries marked the beginning of what was to become a long, and frequently acrimonious, process of inter-American dialogue.

For the United States, hemispheric dialogue and interchange, which was consistent with the notion of the "Western Hemisphere idea,"[5] was important from both an economic and a politico-strategic standpoint. Economically speaking, U.S. production levels had soared in the 1880s and thereby precipitated a great demand for foreign export markets.[6] Naturally, Latin America presented itself as an attractive focal point for overseas economic expansion. Some political and business leaders even had ambitions of supplanting the trade activities of certain European countries within the region.[7] Latin America also offered tremendous investment opportunities and potentially large profit margins for U.S. capital. In fact, U.S. investment over the course of the next twenty-five years climbed from a minuscule amount to some $1.5 billion.[8]

Hence, the U.S. Congress, in enthusiastically endorsing the first conference of American republics, recognized the likelihood of such a meeting "considering questions relating to the improvement of business intercourse and means of direct communication between said countries." Congress also hoped it would encourage "such reciprocal commercial relations as would be beneficial to all and secure more extensive markets for the produce of each of the said countries."[9] Clearly, officialdom in Washington hoped to convert inter-American collaboration into an increase in foreign trade, especially since the United States had an unfavourable trade balance with its hemispheric neighbours. To be sure, imports to the region in 1875 totalled some $78 million, while U.S. exports to Latin America were only $28 million.[10]

The U.S. government also attached considerable significance to the geo-strategic import of Latin America. It would be pure folly not to emphasize the importance of the Monroe Doctrine, which was enunciated in 1823, in shaping inter-American affairs. Some writers have even gone as far as to suggest that "the story of the Monroe Doctrine is the story of inter-American relations."[11] In any event, it was the organizing framework for U.S. policy toward Latin America, embodying both the strategic and ideological wellsprings of that policy. More specifically, it was intended to prohibit untoward European or any other foreign political influence from intervening in the internal political affairs of Latin America. The United States was, in effect, staking out its claim to be the self-proclaimed guardian of the hemisphere. According to Jerome Slater, the doctrine established the basis for the United States to profess that it had "both the moral right and the imperative national interest to continue to treat the Western hemisphere as its sphere of influence."[12]

Successive administrations in Washington—true to the precepts of the Monroe Doctrine—have been preoccupied with preserving U.S. hegemony over Latin America.[13] Consistent with this concern has been the long-standing goal of excluding European influences from the hemisphere—and from what the United States has considered to be its own "backyard." Intervention from Europe, it was argued, would only serve to call into question the axioms and dictates of the Monroe Doctrine.

Senior U.S. officials, including Secretary Blaine, were thus concerned about the nature and extent of a Western European (primarily English, French, and Spanish) presence in the region. Great Britain had greatly penetrated Argentina, while France, Germany, and a number of other European states touched—in some form or another—almost every country in Latin America. The European powers were also resorting more frequently to armed intervention, in hopes of protecting their growing interests in the area. Napoleon III's five-year intrusion into Mexico in the 1860s and the Spanish government's reannexation of the Dominican Republic in 1861 were pointed reminders of European meddling and interference.

Moreover, officialdom in Washington believed that European economic and financial penetration of Latin America would inevitably pose a number of difficult commercial and political problems for American policy-makers.[14] For instance, the fact that Argentina refused to support the movement for Spanish-American union, largely because of pressure from European commercial interests, was a disturbing precedent. Furthermore, European involvement in the construction of an interoceanic canal at Panama, which possessed strategic as well as commercial importance for the United States, shocked and alarmed the Americans. According to Arthur P. Whitaker, this was "striking proof of the way in which European private enterprise as well as government action could effect a penetration of Latin America to the direct injury of the United States."[15]

Similarly, U.S. policy-makers feared that continued conflict in the area (such as the Paraguayan War of 1864-70 and the War of the Pacific of 1879-83), coupled with Europe's growing economic stake in the region, would only precipitate additional European intervention. However, the establishment of a foundation for hemispheric economic co-operation, along with a plan for arbitrating disputes peacefully, could serve as an effective hedge against future extra-continental involvement. Put another way, inter-American collaboration would not only function to keep in check further European intervention, but it would also foster a friendly environment wherein U.S. trade and investment in the region could be increased. In short, this collaboration, if realized, was seen as a useful means of ensuring and solidifying Washington's economic and political grip on the region as a whole.

Latin American representatives, for their part, saw the movement toward hemispheric collaboration in slightly different terms. From a juridical standpoint, they viewed the inter-American conference as an excellent forum within which to state their firmly held position that all hemispheric countries, according to the precepts of international law, were equal.[16] Latin American states, for the first time, had an opportunity to stress the fact that all hemispheric countries, irrespective of size, population, wealth, and military power, were equal before the court of international law. Stated differently, it made absolutely no difference whether a state was a great or weak power; it would still have to operate within the norms of acceptable international conduct. The codification of international law, then, was viewed by many Latin American delegations as a potential equalizer in what was essentially an asymmetrical Pan-American arrangement.

There was also a general feeling among Latin American political and economic elites that alignment with an emerging world power—the United States—would be both prudent and beneficial.[17] Economically speaking, they thought that the burgeoning Pan-American Movement would better enable a bevy of struggling Latin American countries to secure higher prices for their products, to gain better access to new technologies and valuable skills, and to obtain substantial U.S. government loans to spur economic development.[18] Of course, closer ties with the United States also provided these same elites with an excellent opportunity to further their own personal interests and standing. Moreover, they believed that co-operation among all the American republics held out the possibility of altering, or at least modifying, U.S. policy and behaviour toward Latin America. The thinking here revolved around the notion that a United States committed to the concept of Pan-Americanism would be more amenable and susceptible to Latin American persuasion and entreaties. In other words, this movement would serve as a potential counterpoise—or, at least to some extent, as an equalizer—to the Colossus to the North. Similarly, they hoped that more formalized inter-American interaction would provide Latin American governments with a useful means of influencing—if only tangentially—the U.S. policy-making process.

The grandiose expectations of the participating American

governments, however, were not satisfied by the results of the first conference. Not only was the customs-union proposal rejected— a chief objective of the conference—but the plan to conclude a firm treaty of pacific settlement of inter-American disputes never reached fruition either. Instead of dealing in a meaningful fashion with the principal items on the conference agenda, the delegates merely engaged in platitudes and agreed upon a series of non-binding recommendations.

The customs union was viewed by most Latin American delegations as impractical and detrimental to their interests.[19] They saw little value in the idea of weakening traditional ties with Europe in exchange for promised U.S. tariff reductions. Argentina, in particular, was not prepared to give preferential market treatment to the United States—over European countries—while Washington reciprocated with only minor trade concessions.[20] More important, a committee studying the question suggested that such a union would inevitably involve a loss of national sovereignty and independence.[21] Not surprisingly, Latin officials were loath to allow the United States to add economic domination to its growing political hegemony over the hemisphere.

Concerning the arbitration of disputes, the proposed treaty elicited a number of opposing views. Since it called for disputes to be settled by a tribunal in Washington through a process of binding arbitration, Latin American officials regarded the proposal as basically one-sided and entailing an unacceptable surrender of sovereignty.[22] While the United States was prepared to accept binding arbitration, the Chilean delegation, in particular, had strong reservations about the plan. It was concerned about the possibility of the proposal jeopardizing recent territorial claims in Bolivia and Peru— stemming from the War of the Pacific.[23]

Notwithstanding these objections and shortcomings, the conference did produce some tangible results. First, the firm commitment to regularize the holding of inter-American conferences was clearly a significant development. Secondly, because this conference was the best attended of any hemispheric gathering so far (with only the Dominican Republic failing to send a representative), it provided an excellent opportunity to foster important human relationships. Thirdly, it produced the first genuine manifestations of inter-American institutional life, with the establishment of the

International Union of American Republics. (Composed of all those countries represented at the conference, it was to be responsible for organizing future conferences.)

The permanent organ of the newly-created "Union" was labelled the Commercial Bureau of the American Republics, which had its seat in Washington. Evidently, it functioned—albeit with some discomfort on the part of Latin American officials—under the watchful eye of the acting U.S. Secretary of State. Moreover, the appointment of American William E. Curtis as acting Director General, coupled with the fact that the organization had its headquarters in Washington, clearly reflected U.S. domination of the Bureau. According to Connell-Smith, it "gave that institution the appearance of a colonial office and was the cause of rising Latin American dissatisfaction."[24] In any event, when it finally gained official existence in November 1890, the Bureau concerned itself primarily with the publication of the *Bulletin of the Bureau of the American Republics*—which contained a compilation of trade statistics. However, in the aftermath of an investigative committee report on the Bureau's future, its activities were enlarged "to cover all matters concerned with the economic life and growth of the American republics instead of the mere collection and dissemination of commercial information."[25]

While it is fair to say that the conference itself was perhaps most notable for what it failed to produce, it did provide the initial building blocks for future institutional development. For this reason, and as a harbinger of things to come, it must be regarded as a major event in hemispheric political life. For instance, the general tenor and dynamics of the conference clearly revealed the major players and driving forces underpinning inter-American affairs. It also captured vividly the diverging interests of the rising great power (with expansive ambitions) and the weaker Latin American countries (with designs of invigorating economic development). In turn, these disparate interests, varying issue-agendas, and the nature of international political/state relationships all help to explain why effective international organization in the Western hemisphere was so problematic.

Although there were serious misgivings about the concept of international organization, hemispheric conferences continued apace. The next significant gathering, at least in terms of institutional development, was held in Buenos Aires in 1910.[26] This fourth major meeting of inter-American officials, though skirting most of the controversial matters, still managed to reach a consensus on re-naming the two original institutional entities. The International Union of American Republics dropped the "International" to become the Union of American Republics. And the Commercial Bureau, undergoing a similar facelift, became the Pan American Union (PAU).

In addition to a change in appellation, the Pan American Union experienced a number of other modifications. While it still maintained its seat in Washington, it took up residence in the Building of the American Republics.[27] (It was to continue to exist for another ten years.) Furthermore, it was authorized by the participating delegates to execute all resolutions flowing from inter-American conferences. This, in turn, meant that the PAU would have its original commercial responsibilities expanded to include cultural as well as archival matters, with a corresponding increase in internal administration, influence, and experience. Simply put, the PAU was beginning to emerge as a permanent secretariat, albeit one restricted in its powers.

Latin American political elites especially perceived that the PAU was essentially dominated by the United States. The fact that it was financed mainly by the State Department did little to diminish this view. And with its headquarters in Washington, a U.S. citizen as its Director General, and the U.S. Secretary of State as chairperson of the Governing Board, Latins were concerned about the decidedly U.S. complexion of the institution. Moreover, the other members of the Governing Board were Latin American diplomats, whose chief function was to cultivate friendly relations with the host country. Faced with this reality, it was understandable why Latin American governments—irrespective of organizational claims of absolute equality of states—began to see themselves in an unenviable position. As a result, they vigorously opposed any suggestion of investing the PAU with expanded functions of a purely political nature.[28]

By the time of the fifth conference in Santiago in 1923, interest in changing the PAU had reached a crescendo. As a result, two key amendments were introduced: the chair of the Governing

Board would now be an elective position, and an American republic with no diplomatic representation in Washington would be permitted to make a special appointment to the Board. Five years later, at the Havana Conference, a resolution was passed to organize the PAU on the basis of a convention prepared by the Governing Board.[29] There were also musings about the possibility of having the Board composed of representatives appointed by the American republics themselves.

Despite the positive atmosphere engendered by these changes to the PAU,[30] subsequent inter-American conferences produced only meagre results.[31] And when this was coupled with mounting dissatisfaction with a perceived U.S. domination of hemispheric affairs, the future of the inter-American system appeared bleak.[32] However, the Inter-American Conference for the Maintenance of Continental Peace and Security, staged in Rio in 1947, proved to be particularly eventful. It was there that the Inter-American Treaty of Reciprocal Assistance, popularly referred to as the Rio Treaty, was cobbled together and officially proclaimed.

Before examining the Rio Treaty, as well as the other two legal pillars of the inter-American system, it is important to understand the international climate prevalent during the period 1945 to 1948. Arguably, the years 1945 through to 1948 represent the most important period in the history of hemispheric affairs. It was in these years that inter-American interchange, particularly from a Latin American standpoint, seemed to reflect a sense of immediacy and urgency. Indeed, hemispheric discussions took on added significance and momentum, culminating in the forging of all three pillars of the inter-American system.

In the immediate postwar period, the political leadership in Latin America was concerned about developments in the sensitive security/strategic realm. World War II had painfully illustrated how vulnerable the region actually was to extra-continental intervention (e.g., German U-boats). In addition, the leadership generally feared an expansionist Soviet Union and distrusted Moscow and its communist system.[33] Furthermore, Latin American governments themselves felt a strong sense of insecurity and suspicion from a regional standpoint (especially during Juan Perón's reign in Argentina).[34]

Put simply, security considerations—both internal and external—were beginning to make their way to the top of the Latin American policy agenda.

But economic and social questions were still foremost in the minds of Latin American leaders. They were very much concerned about the socio-economic hardship and disruption that a transition from wartime to peace would bring. As a Chilean official opined at the time:

There loom two dramatic question marks that beset the man who likes to think ahead: (1) what will be done with the millions of men who will lose their employment upon the advent of peace, and (2) how will readjustment be made of raw materials upon termination of the requirements of war industries? [35]

To help soften the readjustment period, they requested a massive influx of financial assistance for the region. Realizing, of course, that a war-devastated Western Europe was in a state of virtual economic ruin, they focused their attention on the United States.

In the wake of World War II, the United States emerged as a *bona fide* world power. In addition to a population and a country largely intact, the United States could boast of a military machine second to none. On the economic side, the war effort furnished it with a finely tuned industrial complex, voracious in its appetite for raw materials, export markets, and investment opportunities. Simply put, the United States was in a position to assume a leading and commanding role in shaping the emerging post-1945 world.

Unfortunately for Latin America, Washington was more concerned about rebuilding war-ravaged West European countries through the Marshall Plan and various other economic initiatives. This decisive shift to Western Europe, coupled with the onset of the Cold War and strong currents of anti-communism in U.S. society, left Latin Americans wondering if they would ever find a sympathetic hearing in the White House. More disconcerting for Latin Americans, though, was the apparent shift away from regionalism (i.e., Pan-Americanism) toward universalism or globalism. The strong show of support for Western Europe and Washington's enthusiastic endorsement of the United Nations (UN) demonstrated to Latin Americans just how rapidly their stock could decline. Latin American governments could see that the United States—by looking eastward—would inevitably begin to ignore its impoverished hemispheric brethren to the south.[36]

THE INTER-AMERICAN TREATY OF RECIPROCAL ASSISTANCE

In light of this changing context, the forging of a collective security arrangement was not surprising. Given the exigencies of Cold War diplomacy and the real security concerns of Latin Americans, the idea generated considerable support. Building upon the Act of Chapultepec—a key resolution of the 1945 Inter-American Conference on Problems of War and Peace, which was held in Mexico City—the Inter-American Treaty of Reciprocal Assistance (otherwise known as the Rio Treaty) sought to address these concerns.

After receiving the requisite notices of ratification, the Rio Treaty formally came into effect in 1948 (it was eventually ratified by all the signatories).[37] Stemming from years of prior inter-American deliberations, the Rio pact represented, in effect, a system of collective responsibility for purposes of hemispheric security.[38] According to Thomas and Thomas, the security treaty

distinguishes the obligations to be undertaken and the procedures to be followed in the event of an armed attack and the obligations to be undertaken and the procedures to be followed in the event of other acts of aggression or potential threats to continental peace.[39]

Stated differently, what had heretofore been an association of like-minded republics was now suddenly transformed into a full-fledged regional security organization. Interestingly enough, this treaty provided the inter-American community with provisions for enforcement without first establishing a formal constitution or meaningful provisions for pacific settlement.[40] This transformation, then, marked a watershed in U.S.-Latin American relations, since security arrangements were now taking precedence over formalizing an inter-American constitution, an economic covenant, and an effective mechanism for resolving hemispheric disputes.

The treaty itself, for all intents and purposes, rests on a solid legal footing.[41] It is consistent with Article 51 of the United Nations (UN) Charter, which permits members of a regional grouping to take immediate action—under the right of individual and collective self-defence—against an armed attack. Furthermore, it is subject to the regional stipulations of Articles 52-54 (Chapter VIII) of the UN Charter, which precludes the use of enforcement action (except with the prior authorization of the Security Council), in the case of any other act or threat of aggression. But since Chapter VIII is not mentioned in the legal text, Article 51 represents the judicial basis of the treaty. This is significant because it enables members of the inter-American system[42] to take action without first having to seek prior Security Council authorization.

The notion of taking action—and what precisely those actions would entail—is delineated more succinctly in Articles 6 and 8 of the treaty. Article 6 refers to the convening of the "Organ of Consultation" (Meeting of Foreign Ministers) if the

inviolability or the integrity of the territory or the sovereignty or political independence of any American State should be affected by an aggression which is not an armed attack or by an extra-continental or intra-continental conflict, or by any other fact or situation that might endanger the peace of America.[43]

Article 8, for its part, details the following menu of available measures:

recall of chiefs of diplomatic missions; breaking of diplomatic relations; breaking of consular relations; partial or complete interruption of economic relations or of rail, sea, air, postal, telegraphic, telephonic, and radio telephonic or radio telegraphic communications; and use of armed force.

In a clear case of an armed attack against an American republic — whether from an intra or extra-regional source—a number of obligations and procedures would be set in motion. Contracting parties to the treaty have a right as well as a duty to take measures, as requested by the victim, to help in meeting the attack. While this obligation to assist the injured country is clear, each state is free to decide for itself on the appropriate response. Once the Organ of Consultation has been enjoined to meet, however, a further obligation is placed upon the signatory states to arrive at a set of collective measures. After the Meeting of Foreign Ministers agrees upon collective measures, the parties are obliged to comply with their decision, which is made on the basis of a two-thirds vote. Although each country is bound by the decision to employ the specified measures, no state is required to use armed force without giving its consent.

Formalizing these procedures and obligations, particularly from a U.S. perspective, was an important accomplishment. Clearly, the Rio Treaty enabled the United States—the unabashed leader of the Western world—to strengthen further its hold on Latin America. The United States valued a stronger grip for ideological, economic, and politico-strategic reasons, and from the standpoint of superpower prestige (sphere of influence). To be sure, the security pact was an effective mechanism for insulating the hemisphere from extra-continental political, economic, and military influences. Further solidifying this hold was Washington's certainty that it could—given its enormous economic and military power—marshall the requisite number of American republics to support or block any hemispheric security-related petition. Moreover, since it would be the United States that would supply the military might to back up the treaty, it would invariably have a decisive and influential voice on Rio Treaty deliberations.

It also provided Washington with an effective instrument for preventing "indirect aggression," orchestrated mainly from Moscow, and thereby preserving hemispheric stability. This, in turn, presented ideologues in the White House, ever bent on maintaining the political *status quo,* with a pretext for protecting those military-dominated governments favourably disposed toward the United States. In effect, it allowed officialdom in Washington— overly concerned about Eastern Europe, the threat of international communism, and Soviet expansionism—to solidify U.S. hegemony in the region.[44]

Latin American governments, for their part, saw the Rio Treaty in an entirely different light. While they were cognizant of the ramifications of World War II, and what appeared to be U.S. observance of non-intervention commitments, they feared the possibility of Washington's manipulating the security pact in such a way as to impose its will on its weaker neighbours.[45] Nevertheless, they were determined to prevent any possible intervention, particularly of an extra-hemispheric nature, in the maintenance of regional peace and security.[46] There was also a deep-rooted feeling that the inter-American security system should be distinct from the UN, thus effectively avoiding the pitfalls of the world body. At that time, the UN was perceived to be suffering increasingly from a paralysing veto system, which was beginning to pit the U.S.-led West against the Soviet-led East. More important, though, the treaty provided a critical hedge against any threats—intra- or extra-hemispheric in nature—to the sovereignty of Latin American states. Since any threat, whether from the Soviet Union or an expansionist-minded Latin American state, would immediately activate the collective security measures and procedures of the pact, cherished Latin American sovereignty would be protected. The Rio Treaty, then, was consistent with long-standing Latin goals: namely, establishing legal frameworks; preventing extra-continental intervention; and maintaining political independence.[47]

THE CHARTER OF THE ORGANIZATION OF AMERICAN STATES

Although the Rio Treaty touched upon several key principles, it was the Charter of the Organization of American States (OAS), promulgated in 1948, that actually codified them.[48] Similar to the Rio Treaty, the OAS Charter was a product of the international milieu in which it was forged. Latin American concerns about Washington's apparent penchant for universalism, financial assistance (growing dependence on U.S. trade and investment), and constraining U.S. interference all factored into the OAS Charter equation. The United States, for its part, recognized another opportunity to further isolate the hemisphere from outside influences, especially from the Soviet Union.

As for the charter itself, it was the consolidation of decades of experience and deliberation on the principles and procedures of hemispheric relations. Put simply, the delineation of these principles in point form effectively "constitutionalized" the inter-American system. Before the charter was officially enunciated, the inter-American system functioned primarily in accordance with a multitude of conference resolutions. With a formal treaty, however, changes or modifications to the inter-American system would require more than simply passing resolutions. This, in effect, signalled the placing of hemispheric affairs on a far stronger legal and constitutional footing.

While the OAS Charter was the crowning legal achievement of the Ninth International Conference of American States, held in Bogotá in 1948, it was fashioned in a cautious environment. The Bogotá conference was not the realization of Bolívar's vision of a veritable hemispheric community, complete with a high degree of political, economic, and social content. According to Jerome Slater, the foreign ministers from each of the participating republics chose "the far less ambitious aim of building a security system with capabilities for political action limited to the minimum required for the keeping of the peace."[49]

Several factors help to explain why the United States and the other American republics were reluctant to accord the newly-emerging inter-American system greater politico-economic significance. First, U.S. officials were intent on avoiding any commitment that would inevitably require the transfer of huge sums of economic assistance to Latin American countries. Secondly, they believed that any notion of a truly hemispheric community would only serve to limit the formulation and implementation of American foreign policy.[50] The Latin Americans, on the other hand, were well aware of the strength of Latin American nationalism and thus were loath to advance any sovereignty-threatening political arrangement. Moreover, the wide chasm between the U.S. and Latin America and among the Latin American countries themselves, especially in terms of foreign policy objectives, economic and social models, military capabilities and political institutions, made forging an all-encompassing inter-American fraternity extremely difficult. The preponderance of U.S. economic, political, and military power weighed heavily on the minds of Latin American publicists and officials. Intra-regional border and boundary disputes, along with Argentina's designs on expansion, also made co-operation among Latin American governments problematic.

Notwithstanding these misgivings, the OAS Charter was (and continues to be under the 1985 Protocol of Cartagena) of significant hemispheric import. Indeed, it was the culmination of more than a hundred years of inter-American principles, aspirations, agreements, resolutions, and rules. At the same time, the document contains what the member countries agreed to be the framework and procedures of the organization. The various principles and structures of the body are dealt with in precise terms in the charter itself, which is divided into three main parts.[51]

The first part of the charter deals with the nature, purposes, principles, and membership of the OAS. It includes virtually every basic inter-American principle, which has received popular or official support, since the early nineteenth century. In addition, it addresses the fundamental rights and duties of states, pacific settlement of disputes, collective security, and economic, social, educational/scientific, and cultural standards.

The "purposes" of the hemispheric body, as set forth in the charter, are not completely foreign to inter-American political discourse. Indeed, there is a conspicuous emphasis on the strengthening of continental peace and security, the prevention and pacific settlement of disputes, the invocation of common action against aggression, the resolution of political, legal, and economic problems, and the promotion of co-operative action in the areas of economic, social, and cultural development. In terms of "principles," the charter discusses respect for international law, promotion of representative democracy, non-recognition of territorial conquest, recognizing an attack against one American state as an attack against them all, pacific settlement of disputes, respect for basic human rights, and regard for social justice and cultural values.[52]

Under the fundamental rights and duties of states heading, the charter echoes many of the advances made in 1933 at Montevideo, the site of the Seventh International Conference of American

States. For example, Article 18, in reflecting and reaffirming the long-standing Latin American preoccupation with non-intervention, states the following: "No State or group of States has the right to intervene, directly or indirectly, for any reason whatever, in the internal or external affairs of any other State." Furthermore, Article 19 notes: "No State may use or encourage the use of coercive measures of an economic or political character in order to force the sovereign will of another State and obtain from it advantages of any kind."[53]

The pacific settlement of disputes, according to the charter, "shall be submitted to the peaceful procedures" outlined in the document. Pursuant to Article 24, the peaceful procedures involve: "direct negotiation, good offices, mediation, investigation and conciliation, judicial settlement, arbitration, and those [means by] which the parties to the dispute may especially agree upon at any time." As for collective security, Article 27 is quite specific:

Every act of aggression by a State against the territorial integrity or the inviolability of the territory or against the sovereignty or political independence of an American State shall be considered an act of aggression against the other American States.

The second section of the charter, in contrast with the first, sets out the various "organs" through which the OAS achieves its purposes. The General Assembly, for instance, co-ordinates the work of inter-American agencies, strengthens co-operation with the United Nations, promotes collaboration in the economic, social, and cultural fields with other international organizations, approves the program and budget of the OAS, determines or fixes member state financial quotas, and sets standards to govern the operation of the General Secretariat. The Meeting of Consultation of Foreign Ministers, for its part, "shall be held in order to consider problems of an urgent nature and of common interest to the American States." (Any member may request a Meeting of Consultation, but it requires the support of an absolute majority before it is actually held.)

The Permanent Council,[54] as outlined in Article 81, "takes cognizance of any matter referred to it by the General Assembly or the

Meeting of Consultation of Foreign Ministers." It also has the important function of acting provisionally as Organ of Consultation under the Rio Treaty. Moreover, it has responsibility, *inter alia*, in the areas of pacific settlement, in electing members of certain agencies, in preparing the draft agenda for the General Assembly, and in convoking the Meetings of Consultation.

The Inter-American Judicial Committee, as the Charter indicates, "is to serve the Organization as an advisory body on judicial matters," and "to promote the progressive development and the codification of international law." It is also enjoined to "undertake the studies and preparatory work assigned to it by the General Assembly, the Meeting of Consultation of Foreign Ministers, or the Councils of the Organization." It may also, on its own initiative, devote itself to "such studies and preparatory work as it considers advisable, and suggest the holding of specialized judicial conferences." The Inter-American Commission on Human Rights,[55] on the other hand, seeks "to promote the observance and protection of human rights and to serve as a consultative organ of the Organization in these matters."

The General Secretariat, according to the charter, "is the central and permanent organ of the Organization of American States." As such, it is responsible for promoting "economic, social, juridical, educational, scientific, and cultural relations among all the Member States of the Organization." Furthermore, it advises other organs on the preparation of agendas, prepares the proposed program-budget of the organization, provides adequate secretariat services for the General Assembly and other organs, serves as a custodian of documents and archives, and submits to the General Assembly an annual report on the activities of the organization.

The Secretary-General, for his part, is elected by the General Assembly for a five-year term (and may not be re-elected more than once or succeeded by a person of the same nationality). The holder of this office "shall direct the General Secretariat, be the legal representative thereof" and "be responsible to the General Assembly for the proper fulfillment of the obligations and functions of the General Secretariat." The Secretary-General, however, "participates with voice but without vote in all meetings of the Organization." He can, however, "bring to the attention of the General Assembly or the Permanent Council any matter which in his opinion might threaten the peace and security of the Hemisphere or the development of the Member States."

Specialized Conferences, previously known as technical inter-American conferences, "are inter-governmental meetings to deal with special technical matters or to develop specific aspects of inter-American co-operation." While such conferences may be held at the request of the General Assembly, of the Meeting of Consultation of Foreign Ministers, or one of the councils, the agenda and rules of procedure "shall be prepared by the Councils or Specialized Organizations concerned."

As for these Specialized Organizations, they have had a long, and occasionally memorable, association with the inter-American system. Collectively, the six Specialized Organizations — the Pan American Institute of Geography and History (PAIGH), the Pan American Health Organization (PAHO), the Inter-American Institute of Agricultural Sciences (IAIAS), the Inter-American Children's Institute (IACI), the Inter-American Commission of Women (IACW), and the Inter-American Indian Institute (IAII)—represent an "organ" of the OAS.[56] According to Article 129 of the charter, Specialized Organizations "are the intergovernmental organizations established by multilateral agreements and having specific functions with respect to technical matters of common interest to the American States." In other words, these organizations are intended to promote co-operation in certain technical fields, mainly through studies, exchange of information, and recommendations to governments.[57] Although they enjoy "the fullest technical autonomy," they are required to submit to the General Assembly annual reports on the progress of their work and budget expenses. They are also urged to "establish cooperative relations with world agencies of the same character," all the while maintaining strenuously "their identity and their status as integral parts of the Organization of American States, even when they perform regional functions of international agencies."

The crafting of the OAS Charter, with its formal language on various organs and agencies, was very much a product of a Latin American obsession with legalism.[58] In fact, the formal-legalistic bent of the charter, as exemplified in the more than 150 articles of the organic pact,[59] reflects a Latin American penchant to install judicial safeguards primarily against the overwhelming power of the

United States. Consistent with this excessive preoccupation with "judicializing" hemispheric interchange is the third major legal document or pillar of the inter-American system, the American Treaty on Pacific Settlement.

THE AMERICAN TREATY ON PACIFIC SETTLEMENT

The basic aim of the American Treaty on Pacific Settlement, popularly known as the Pact of Bogotá, was to provide a comprehensive mechanism for settling inter-American disputes peacefully. This treaty, however, is regarded by many as far less significant than the Rio Treaty or the OAS Charter.[60] Like the charter, though, the Pact of Bogotá was a product of the 1948 International Conference of American States, which took place in Bogotá. Unlike the charter, it has not been ratified by a sufficient number of states. (As of this writing, fourteen countries have ratified the pact.)[61] In the main, the pact is not taken seriously by OAS members—as indicated by the fact that it has never been used and by the small number of states that have ratified the pact. According to L. Ronald Scheman and John W. Ford, as "one of the world's finest legal and worst political documents, it has a major flaw: It has been virtually ignored since it was signed."[62]

The compulsory nature of the treaty—especially in the areas of arbitration and jurisdiction of the International Court—makes for a strong legal document, but a poor political arrangement.[63] For this reason, the issue of revising the pact was placed on the agenda of the Tenth International Conference of American States, which was held in Caracas in 1954. While the United States and Brazil favoured modifying the document, Mexico argued that those states which have failed to ratify the treaty should simply be encouraged to do so. By 1957, the OAS Council, after recognizing that a majority of states were not in favour of revision, effectively closed the matter.[64]

Nevertheless, this notion of settling disputes peacefully was widely discussed at several "special" conferences and has appeared on the agenda of every International Conference of American States.[65] The Pact of Bogotá, despite its obvious failings, did represent an attempt on the part of delegates at the ninth conference to formalize, in treaty form, the pacific settlement of disputes. It sought to consolidate, in a single document, the various procedures for peaceful settlement that had appeared in earlier conciliation treaties and agreements. According to John C. Dreier, "it was the culmination of more than a century of effort by the Latin American states to make effective their desire to ban the use of force in their international controversies and to settle disputes by peaceful means."[66]

The settling of disputes by peaceful means—a long-standing principle of the inter-American system—was to be accomplished through an array of recognized procedures. These procedures, however, would only be activated in cases where normal diplomatic channels proved unproductive. In such circumstances, the disputants could avail themselves of the following procedures: good offices and mediation (usually by a third country), investigation and conciliation (normally by a commission), judicial procedure (through the International Court of Justice), and arbitration (by way of a tribunal). However, if these procedures failed to produce a peaceful settlement, the parties would have recourse to whichever procedure they deemed most appropriate.

SUMMARY

As one goes through this chapter, it becomes increasingly clear just how small a place Canada occupied in the world of Pan-Americanism. For the most part, Canada has watched the evolution of Pan-Americanism as a passive spectator. As subsequent chapters will demonstrate, officials in Ottawa tended to play down this evolutionary process. For a variety of reasons, not the least of which was a decidedly Canadian orientation toward Europe, these same officials preferred to remain on the sidelines of Pan-American developments.

At any rate, the gradual forging of an inter-American community, like the wrangling and collaboration that accompanied the development of such legal documents as the Pact of Bogotá, has been punctuated by periods of co-operation and intransigence. Through the 1889-1948 time-frame, U.S. and Latin American officials, while participating in inter-American conferences and various fora, managed to construct a solid constitutional basis for guiding inter-American affairs. There was also widespread agreement on finding appropriate mechanisms to settle hemispheric disputes peacefully, on expanding inter-American trade, and on facilitating economic development throughout the Americas.

More striking, however, was the fact that this same period was marked by confrontation and frustration, which fostered animosity and resentment. Indeed, continued Latin American frustration over its attempts to ensure the sanctity of non-intervention has served to harden attitudes and heighten inter-American tension.[67] Latin Americans in particular, after witnessing several instances of "Gringo" intervention and trying to cope with life under U.S. hegemony, have developed a deep-seated distrust of Washington. And successive U.S. governments—whether acting under the aegis of the Monroe Doctrine, the Roosevelt Corollary or the Truman Doctrine—have only exacerbated this fear.

While the concept of Pan-Americanism experienced difficulties and strains throughout the 1889-1948 period, it still remained a dominant theme. There was a realization among Latin American political and economic elites, irrespective of the fact that forging an inter-American community would make for an uneasy marriage, that Pan-Americanism offered the best possible option. Given the depressing nature of Latin America's economic and political standing throughout this period, the need to settle intra-regional border skirmishes and boundary disputes, and the desire to curb Argentinean expansionism, they had little choice but to take this avenue.

Greater inter-American co-operation also held out the possibility of increased benefits through closer ties with the United States. In addition to acquiring much-needed technology, Latin American elites saw Pan-Americanism as a means to secure large sums of money for economic, political, and military assistance. And as long as those carrots were dangled before the eyes of those elites, the idea of Pan-Americanism would be worth pursuing aggressively. The firmness of Pan-Americanism, then, was in some part a function of Washington's ability to provide those entitlements.

From a U.S. standpoint, Pan-Americanism was viewed through a different set of perceptual lenses. Economic considerations, particularly in areas of trade and investment, seemed paramount in the minds of American policy-makers. This is not to suggest, however, that geo-strategic concerns were unimportant. On the contrary, Washington was very much interested in preventing extra-continental intervention as well as protecting U.S. security interests. Politically speaking, the Monroe Doctrine continued to hold currency throughout this period, with unsparing emphasis on controlling a U.S. "sphere of interest" and maintaining hegemony in its own backyard. For these reasons, it was not surprising to see the United States play a major role in the creation of the inter-American system.

Within this context, the results of Pan-Americanism—at least over the course of the 1889-1948 period—can best be described as mixed. Administrations in Washington were successful in solidifying their hold on, and leadership of, the Western hemisphere. Latin Americans, while failing to receive their expected economic windfall, found themselves increasingly dependent upon the "Colossus to the North." But they did manage to establish the legal and institutional framework within which to advance their interests. Clearly, the Rio Treaty, the OAS Charter, and the Pact of Bogotá—each reflecting a culmination and codification of past accomplishments and experiences—offered them an opportunity to constrain U.S. foreign policy behaviour. On balance, then, Pan-Americanism has turned out to be what one might expect it to be: neither a notable success nor a complete failure. Perhaps one might argue that this was a portent for the future.

II

The OAS in Action: A Mixed Record

JUST AS THE RESULTS OF PAN-AMERICANISM WERE MIXED, SO, TOO, was the specific record of accomplishment of the Organization of American States (OAS). While the institution developed a shiny image in the late 1940s and 1950s, the sheen soon began to fade in the mid-1960s. By the 1980s the OAS seemed, at least in the eyes of many of its members and such non-members as Canada, to be suffering from a host of chronic ailments. Former Venezuelan President Jaime Lusinchi even went as far as to suggest in 1980 that "it is on the road to becoming a cadaver."[1] And the role of the institution before and after the U.S. invasions of Grenada (1983) and Panama (1989) has done little to dispel this perception.[2] With that said, this chapter outlines some, but by no means all, of the OAS's major successes and failures.[3] It also discusses whether or not these successes or failures shaped Canada's view of the hemispheric forum. The ensuing discussion is intended primarily to give the reader a general sense of why the hemispheric body has been successful in some cases and not in others. This is instructive because too often the OAS has been the subject of facile, one-dimensional treatments by panegyrists and critics alike. A more balanced interpretation, however, brings to the fore the "true colours" of the organization.

In terms of actual operational capability, the OAS has exhibited flashes, particularly early in its career, of competence and effectiveness, as illustrated by the case histories delineated below. It has also shown itself capable of utter ineffectiveness and ineptitude, especially in the post-1965 period. The purpose of this chapter, then, is threefold: first, to understand why the OAS adroitly handled border disputes, promoted constructive dialogue, negotiated temporary ceasefires, and prevented hostilities from breaking out; secondly, to grapple with why, in some cases, it was marginalized and fragmented, used as a blatant instrument of U.S. foreign policy, and virtually left as a spectator on the sidelines of inter-American affairs; and thirdly, and perhaps most important, to show how this "record of performance" influenced the Canadian government's attitude or position toward the organization.[4]

Accordingly, this chapter is useful in terms of understanding the precise nature of Canada's association with the inter-American community. For instance, it helps to illuminate why Canadian governments were reluctant to seek full membership in the hemispheric forum. Needless to say, the ability of the OAS to respond in an effective manner to crisis situations in the hemisphere, or to play a meaningful role in inter-American affairs in general, undoubtedly played some part in influencing decision-makers in Ottawa. Clearly, then, they were probably not about to opt for membership in an organization that was perceived as totally ineffective or, perhaps worse, irrelevant to events unfolding in the wider hemisphere.[5]

OAS SUCCESS STORIES

Only days after the Rio Treaty entered into force,[6] the hemispheric body was put to its first official test. On 10 December 1948 the Costa Rican government charged that an armed force, allegedly launched from neighbouring Nicaragua, had violated the territorial integrity of Costa Rica.[7] Pursuant to the provisions detailed in the OAS Charter, it demanded an immediate meeting of the council. One day later, the Costa Rican representative on the OAS Council requested the invocation of the Rio Treaty, specifically under the terms delineated in Article 6.[8]

On 12 December, with the OAS machinery fully activated, the council undertook a more detailed assessment of the Central American situation.[9] Apparently, each country was given roughly forty-eight hours to obtain relevant information in which to buttress their presentations before the council. Two days later, the council decided, on the strength of the briefings, to request a Meeting of Consultation—to be attended by the foreign ministers of those nations that had ratified the Rio Treaty—with the place and date to be announced later. After meeting the requirements of Article 6 of the security pact—namely, calling for a Meeting of Consultation of

Foreign Ministers—the council, at the suggestion of Washington, then took it upon itself to serve provisionally as Organ of Consultation. But this convocation, as Charles G. Fenwick explains, "was for the time being no more than a technical justification for the assumption by the council of the power to act as a provisional organ."[10] In effect, the council—and this is important to note—was empowered to confront this dispute at its discretion.

The decision of the council to act provisionally as the Organ of Consultation was made for several reasons. First, it provided the council with the necessary latitude to investigate the facts of the dispute and to work toward a peaceful settlement. Secondly, the Meeting of Foreign Ministers, with all its attendant powers under the Rio Treaty, was not particularly suited for conciliation purposes. It did, however, furnish the council with a potentially decisive trump card—specifically, the serious consequences that could follow from a convocation of a formal Meeting of Foreign Ministers, especially under the auspices of the security pact. Most important, though, was the fact that the techniques of good offices and mediation could be employed "in a less formal and less institutionalized framework."[11]

Following this decision, the council moved on 14 December to appoint a Committee of Information, which was charged with the responsibility of conducting an on-the-spot investigation.[12] The subsequent inquiry lasted six days, from December 18-23, and it took the members to San José and Managua. Once there, they interviewed government and military officials from both governments and spoke with exiled Costa Rican leaders in Nicaragua. Amid a growing sense that both sides were prepared to settle the controversy, the committee presented its final report to the provisional Organ of Consultation on 24 December.

Based on the findings of the report, which specifically censured Nicaragua for allowing its territory to be used by the invading force, the council responded promptly. It instructed both parties to refrain from further hostilities and strongly admonished each government to eliminate those "conditions" that had engendered the dispute in the first place. The council also requested each party to observe religiously the long-standing principle of non-intervention. Furthermore, it called for the creation of an Inter-American Commission of Military Experts to ensure the fulfilment of its recommendations.[13]

The Nicaraguan-Costa Rican dispute was effectively brought to a close in late February, 1949. After lengthy negotiations, under the stewardship of the council, an agreement between the two countries was finalized. On 21 February, during the course of a formal session of the full council, a Pact of Amity and Friendship was signed by representatives of the two governments. Common sense ultimately prevailed in this particular case, while the intermediary role of the OAS had been both apparent and laudable.[14]

This 1948 controversy clearly stands out as a case in which the OAS proved to be successful. According to John C. Dreier, "the OAS came through its first test with flying colors."[15] Indeed, it had responded to the challenge with swiftness, creativity, and vigour. In fact, the prompt response of the council may well have prevented the dispute from taking on a more ominous character, since hostilities had already resulted in the deaths of several people, and the possibility of a full-blown war involving forces from both sides was always present. In addition, the council exhibited a willingness to apportion responsibility, as well as to seek the basis for a negotiated settlement. Simply put, it played a leading role in the dispute by discharging its responsibilities effectively and by facilitating a peaceful resolution of the conflict.

As the Nicaraguan-Costa Rican dispute faded from the scene, another controversy involving Haiti and the Dominican Republic soon developed. In February 1949 the Haitian government accused the Dominican Republic of harbouring aggressive forces on its territory.[16] More specifically, it argued that Santo Domingo had given asylum to, and was supporting the activities of, Astrel Roland, a former colonel in the Haitian army who was charged with plotting the overthrow of the Haitian government. As in the previous Nicaraguan-Costa Rican episode, the Haitian government admonished the OAS Council—while acting as provisional Organ of Consultation—to intervene on its behalf.[17]

After listening to statements from both sides, the council decided that the dispute, since it did not actually involve the violation of Haiti's territorial integrity or political independence, did not warrant the convocation of the Organ of Consultation. On 3 January 1950 the Haitian government, once again fearing a possible attempt to remove it from power, invoked the Rio Treaty against the Dominican Republic.[18] Evidently, it claimed "that officials of the Dominican Republic had been involved in the plot and that now the territorial integrity, sovereignty, and political independence of Haiti were threatened and the peace of the Americas was endangered."[19] Three days later, the council met to consider the veracity and seriousness of the Haitian complaint.

Accordingly, the council, as it had done previously, decided to constitute itself as provisional Organ of Consultation.[20] It called for a Meeting of Foreign Ministers, but did not set a specific date or location. It then authorized the chair of the council to appoint an investigative committee, entrusted with the task of determining—in a reliable and accurate fashion—the nature of the Haitian-Dominican Republic situation. The Investigating Committee, composed of representatives from Bolivia, Colombia, Ecuador, Uruguay, and the United States, was thus instructed to conduct on-site investigations in Haiti, the Dominican Republic, Cuba, and Guatemala.[21]

The committee officially began its inquiry on 22 January, and concluded its investigation on 15 February. In its 13 March final report to the provisional Organ of Consultation, the Dominican Republic was singled out in the report for encouraging an attempted overthrow of Haiti's constitutional government. At the same time, it found that the Cuban and Guatemalan governments had been supportive of activities aimed at the destabilization of the Dominican government.

In April of 1950, the council delivered a firm, though carefully-worded, decision.[22] It recommended that the Dominican Republic take effective and immediate steps to prevent government officials from assisting seditious movements.[23] Additionally, the council established a special provisional committee or "watchdog" to ensure that its recommendations were fully complied with. When all parties agreed to co-operate with the council resolutions, the dispute was, for all intents and purposes, defused.

Once again, the OAS was highly successful in its efforts to resolve the Haitian-Dominican incident peacefully. As in the prior Nicaraguan-Costa Rican dispute, it reacted quickly and prudently. Similarly, it was not afraid to ascribe blame or to set out the terms of a possible settlement. In many respects, the council was beginning to emerge as an important instrument for the peaceful settlement of inter-American disputes. The OAS, in the eyes of a sceptical international community, was starting to generate a reputation as an effective multilateral entity.[24]

That image of respectability was further fortified, strangely enough, by the resurfacing of the Nicaraguan-Costa Rican controversy. On 11 January 1955, Costa Rican authorities claimed once again that their country had been attacked by hostile forces emanating from neighbouring Nicaragua. Subsequently, the Costa Rican representative in Washington requested a meeting of the OAS Council and once again invoked the Rio Treaty.[25] During the course of the Council session, agreement was reached on the question of convening a Meeting of Foreign Ministers, but without actually fixing the date or the venue. Not surprisingly, the Council proceeded, in accordance with the OAS Charter, to serve provisionally as the Organ of Consultation.

Almost immediately, an Investigating Committee was established, with the full consent of both Costa Rican and Nicaraguan authorities.[26] In addition, both governments promised to refrain from any actions that might further aggravate or intensify an already tenuous situation. The committee, for its part, was charged with conducting an on-site investigation, ascertaining the pertinent facts, and submitting a final report.[27] More specifically, it was responsible for establishing the location and nature of the alleged invading forces, the origins of those forces, and the actual supplier of military aircraft and sundry materiel.

In its report, the committee backed the Costa Rican allegation that the aggressor forces had indeed come south across the Nicaraguan-Costa Rican border. Consequently, the council met on 16 January to consider an appeal from the Costa Rican government for military assistance. Consistent with past OAS efforts at conflict resolution, there was a great reluctance on the part of a number of member governments to provide military support. However, heavy pressure from the Investigating Committee,[28] and the White House, resulted in an OAS consensus to assist Costa Rica. On the basis of a council resolution, the United States sold Costa Rica four combat planes (at the cost of $1 apiece), a development that was decisive in altering the military balance of forces in the dispute.[29]

By 25 January a ceasefire was in place and most of the rebels had crossed the border back into Nicaragua, where they were summarily interned. The OAS, in turn, watched over the negotiations between the two nations. The council also established a military presence on the scene to maintain the ceasefire, while the negotiations continued under OAS supervision. In fact, regular border patrols by an OAS force under the guidance of the Investigating Committee were subsequently implemented.[30]

After several months, the two governments arrived at a mutually satisfactory settlement. On 9 January 1956, Costa Rica and Nicaragua signed two bilateral agreements: one reaffirming their commitment to the 1949 Costa Rican-Nicaraguan Pact of Amity, and a second agreeing to the competence of the Committee of Investigation and Conciliation. The formal signing of the two accords effectively terminated the dispute.[31]

Clearly, the OAS had functioned commendably and had risen to the occasion. The role of the institution, writes Jerome Slater, "represented the most far-reaching intervention of the inter-American system in a hemispheric conflict until that point."[32] It sent a signal to the rest of the world that the regional body would be a force to contend with in inter-American affairs. As Dreier observes: "It brought the prestige of the OAS to a high point not only in the hemisphere but in the world at large."[33]

It was perhaps a textbook example of a case in which the machinery of the OAS was quickly activated and highly responsive. The OAS Council, through the creation of the Investigating Committee, was able to contain the dispute and restore a sense of normality. Its willingness to sanction military support, in conjunction with threatening additional punitive measures, was instrumental in bringing the two protagonists to the negotiating table. And its resolve in overseeing the ceasefire and employing the border patrols compelled the two countries to reach a peaceful settlement. It is understandable, then, why Gordon Connell-Smith noted in the mid-1960s that it was "perhaps the most successful action taken by the OAS to date."[34]

Not long after Nicaragua resolved its difficulties with Costa Rica, it became embroiled in a border dispute with Honduras. The long-standing boundary controversy was revived when the Honduran authorities established a new province, which included some of the territory claimed by Nicaragua.[35] On 1 May 1957, the

Honduran representative in the OAS invoked the Rio Treaty, alleging that Nicaraguan forces had invaded Honduran territory.[36] The very next day, the Nicaraguan government also invoked the Rio Treaty and counter-charged that it was Honduran aggression that was actually increasing tensions in the area.

The council held a special session on 2 May, after Nicaraguan authorities charged that Honduran troops had killed an unspecified number of Nicaraguan soldiers.[37] The council, as it had done in the past, decided to call a Meeting of Foreign Ministers, the seat and date of the meeting to be fixed later. Then it took the responsibility of acting provisionally as the Organ of Consultation. By 3 May an Investigating Committee had been established, with a mandate to determine the facts of the dispute. Two days later, the Committee, after some frantic shuttle diplomacy, was able to secure a temporary ceasefire between the two sides.[38]

Following the ceasefire agreement, both governments agreed to withdraw their troops. On 16 May the Investigating Committee submitted its report to the council. It was the committee's view that to assign responsibility for the alleged aggression was next to impossible. It did, however, recommend the creation of an Ad Hoc Committee to help supervise negotiations aimed at fashioning a peaceful settlement.[39] Once again, the collective contribution of the organization, buttressed by the moral support of the inter-American community, had succeeded in averting a potentially explosive confrontation.

As a first step, both sides agreed to place the territorial dispute before the International Court of Justice in La Hague, and to abide by its ruling. In November 1960 the court handed down its judgment confirming the validity of the King of Spain's 1906 award.[40] In response, Nicaragua requested the good offices of the Inter-American Peace Committee in resolving questions arising from the court's decision. The committee, after visiting Honduras, Nicaragua, and the disputed territory, decided to set up a Honduran-Nicaraguan Mixed Commission. By early 1962, the Peace Committee reported that the boundary dispute was, for the most part, settled.[41]

While this controversy ended in—in effect—an agreement to disagree, both sides refrained from further acts of aggression. The OAS played a central role in putting out the brush fire and normalizing relations between the two countries. By placing the OAS machinery in high gear, by activating the committee mechanism, and by acting as a catalyst for negotiations, it laid the groundwork for a diplomatic solution. Indeed, by responding in a swift and effective manner, it was able to arrange a ceasefire and generally to have a calming effect on the disputants.

The early 1960s also saw the OAS front and centre in a ground-breaking inter-American dispute involving Venezuela and the Dominican Republic. In mid-February 1960 the Venezuelan government complained to the OAS Council that the flagrant violation of human rights in the Dominican Republic was heightening international tensions in the Caribbean.[42] The council promptly referred the investigation of this serious charge to the Inter-American Peace Committee. On 6 June the committee's report concluded that the Dominican government had, in fact, been guilty of widespread violations of basic human rights.[43]

In early July Venezuela requested an immediate convocation of the Organ of Consultation, under Article 6 of the Rio Treaty, to consider acts of aggression perpetrated by the Dominican regime of General Rafael Trujillo.[44] The OAS Council once again called for a Meeting of Foreign Ministers (without setting the date or location) and declared itself provisional Organ of Consultation. At the same time, it appointed an Investigating Committee to look into the Venezuelan charges.[45] Subsequently, the committee found evidence which supported the claim that the Trujillo regime plotted to overthrow the Venezuelan government.[46]

By mid-August the first-ever Meeting of Foreign Ministers—acting as the Organ of Consultation under the Rio Treaty—was convened in San José, Costa Rica. The meeting focused, *inter alia,* on the interventionist activities of the Dominican Republic, including its involvement in the attempted 24 June assassination of Venezuelan Chief of State, Rómulo Betancourt. Venezuela, for its part, pushed for the full application of sanctions available under the terms of the Rio Treaty.[47] The majority of Latin American members, however, preferred the imposition of only moderate punitive measures (such as the breaking of diplomatic relations).[48] Accordingly, the Organ of Consultation recommended the employment of punitive sanctions, for the first time in inter-American history, against an American state.[49] Pursuant to Articles 6 and 8 of the security pact, the Organ of Consultation severed diplomatic relations with the Dominican Republic and suspended trade in arms and implements of war.[50] In January 1961 the OAS Council recommended extending the suspension of trade with the Dominican Republic to include oil, petroleum products, trucks, and spare parts.[51] According to Dreier, these sanctions were intended "either to punish the Dominican government for its past crime; or to bring about a fundamental change in the government."[52] General Trujillo subsequently resigned in November of 1961 and was later assassinated. Shortly thereafter, an OAS Special Committee recommended the lifting of sanctions on the grounds that the Dominican Republic no longer posed a threat to hemispheric peace and security.[53] That recommendation was approved, and the punitive measures were discontinued, in January of 1962.

The OAS response in this particular case is important for a number of reasons. First, it was willing to move dramatically and with considerable resolve. Secondly, it was not afraid to confront the thorny issue of punishing one of its own members. According to Ronald St. John Macdonald, it "marked one of the few occasions in the recent history of international organizations generally that a member state has been punished in peace-time by its own organization for actions against another member state."[54] Perhaps more important, it exhibited a firm interest—largely through the imposition of sanctions—in intervening uncharacteristically in the internal affairs of a member state. Despite its unstinting commitment to the principle of non-intervention, the OAS felt that intervention was key to resolving the controversy peacefully. It justified its qualification of the doctrine of absolute non-intervention by pointing to the fact that the Dominican Republic, through its own actions, had itself violated the sanctity of non-intervention. Put another way, the OAS would practice non-intervention only toward those member states which firmly adhered to the principle of non-intervention themselves.

In its formative years, as these cases clearly illustrate, the OAS was able to live up to its expectations. It was able not only to fulfil its obligations and responsibilities as outlined in the OAS Charter, but also to promote the principles and objectives of that document as well. From an institutional standpoint, it showed that it had in place the requisite machinery to deal with one of the hemisphere's most explosive type of situation—namely, the outbreak of hostilities. Indeed, it was quick to engage itself in the various disputes, and in a meaningful and decisive fashion.

The OAS, at least on the basis of the cases outlined above, functioned as a key institutional entity in the peaceful resolution of inter-American conflicts. It was politically relevant, exhibiting an ability to respond actively to a variety of pressing hemispheric disputes. It showed that it could—if it had the necessary political will—act as a useful intermediary, arbiter, and bridge-builder.[55] This record of securing successful outcomes should, however, be weighed against instances of the OAS's failure to do so.

OAS FAILURES

While the OAS has performed effectively on several occasions, it has been unable to do so on a number of others.[56] For instance, in 1954 the popularly elected Guatemalan government of Jacobo Arbenz was under siege from CIA-backed rebels who invaded the country from Honduras (and possibly even Nicaragua).[57] The anti-communist Guatemalan exile group was led by former Guatemalan army officer Lieutenant-Colonel Carlos Castillo Armas. By June 1954 the Arbenz government, unable to fend off the invading forces or defend itself against an international propaganda war stage-managed from Washington, had collapsed.[58]

Clearly, the Guatemalan controversy served to tarnish the shining image of the OAS.[59] First, there was no constituting of any Investigative Committee—as was the practice on previous occasions—to discover the facts of the case or to arrange any temporary ceasefire. Secondly, the OAS Council did not place in motion its previously successful consultative machinery.[60] In fact, it only called for a Meeting of Foreign Ministers to be held on 7 July 1954 in Rio de Janeiro—incidentally, "to consider the situation created by the intervention of international communism in Guatemala"—when the collapse of the Guatemalan government looked imminent. To be sure, the toppling of the government in June ensured that the meeting never even took place. Similarly, the Inter-American Peace Committee, after initial confusion on the part of Guatemala, waited some time before deciding to go to Guatemala, Honduras, and Nicaragua.[61]

But by the time that it had started its investigation, Arbenz had already been removed from power and a new government in Guatemala had already been installed.

Initially, the Arbenz government sought to avoid the OAS altogether, thinking that the hemispheric body was dominated by Washington, and thus would generally be unsympathetic to its plight. It hoped, however, to bring the invasion of Guatemala to the attention of the UN Security Council, and to request that the Security Council dispatch immediately a fact-finding mission to Guatemala.[62] The United States, in arguing vigorously against this course of action, pushed for the matter to be first referred to the OAS.[63] By bringing the case before the OAS, at least according to Inis L. Claude, "the United States was recommending what it hoped would prove a suicidal act."[64]

It was considered suicidal in the sense that the OAS would do little or nothing to prevent the demise of the Arbenz government. In fact, the OAS treated Guatemala as if it were the "defendant" rather than the "plaintiff."[65] Instead of condemning the CIA-backed invasion or offering assistance, as it had done in similar instances when non-communist states were invaded, it remained strangely inactive. In an over-critical comment, Arthur P. Whitaker noted that "the situation in Guatemala and the neighbouring countries unfolded in the traditional Central American way, almost as if neither the OAS nor the United Nations had ever come into existence."[66] In other words, the OAS in particular, and the UN to a lesser extent, did little or nothing to respond to what was clearly a flagrant violation of the organization's key principles and tenets.

The Guatemalan "affair"—or the failure of the OAS to respond effectively to the situation—marked a low point for the hemispheric body. In dragging its feet, the OAS Council allowed the situation to mushroom into a full-blown crisis. On an issue which involved illegal activities on the part of the United States and Honduras against another American state, the OAS simply remained on the sidelines as if nothing untoward had happened to a member state.[67] In the face of serious violations of inter-American norms and principles, the OAS not only played a peripheral role, but was also clearly unwilling to provide protection to an American state under attack. According

to Thomas and Thomas, whose interpretation typified the assessment of most informed observers, "the OAS did present a sorry spec-
tacle in coping with this case."[68] Even Dreier, a supporter of U.S.
policy, pointed out that the case of Guatemala "had somewhat
stained the shining armor of the OAS."[69]

While the events surrounding the Guatemalan affair produced
little in the way of an "official" Canadian response, it did not go
totally unnoticed. In the House of Commons, for instance, parliamentarians raised the issue with the government of Louis St.
Laurent. In June 1954 Stanley Knowles, member for Winnipeg
North Centre, asked the then Secretary of State for External Affairs
if he had "any comments to make on the situation in Guatemala."[70]
Mr. Lester Pearson, who was seemingly not in command of all the
facts, simply responded with a curt: "No, Mr. Speaker."[71] Four days
later, Pearson rose in the House to respond to a second Knowles
question on the subject by stating the following: "The political situation in regards to developments in Guatemala is certainly not clear,
although the military position would appear on the information at
our disposal, to be reaching a climax."[72]

Although it is difficult to discern precisely how the Guatemalan
controversy influenced Canada's position on membership in the OAS,
it seems clear from what evidence exists that its effect was not
favourable. In other words, the Guatemalan imbroglio did little to
sway decision-makers in Ottawa that now was a good time to join
the hemispheric body. The developments preceding the crisis
seemed to set the precise tone of the Canadian response. In an April
1954 letter from Jules Léger, then Canada's Ambassador to Mexico
to the Secretary of State for External Affairs, he explained: "The
Caracas Conference as seen from here has not strengthened hemispheric solidarity nor has it made United States' leadership more
attractive to the rest of the American community."[73] He went on to
say that there

is no great cause for rejoicing in the victory of Mr. Dulles on his anti-
communist resolution although it may have brought the peril of communist infiltration closer to home in this part of the world.[74]

It seems clear from Ambassador Léger's correspondence that he was unimpressed with the results of the Tenth Inter-American Conference and with the OAS itself. As he was at pains to point out in his letter:

Latin Americans are getting more and more restless. The regional organization, on the other hand, does not show any marked progress towards acquiring more strength. This could very well result in the slow disintegration of the OAS as a serious regional organization.[75]

Similarly, in an April 1954 letter to the Canadian Embassy in Mexico (and circulated throughout the region) from R.A. MacKay, Acting Under-Secretary of State, he recognized the troubles plaguing the body. He indicated that,

The problems of the O.A.S. and the Tenth Inter-American Conference are still fresh in the minds of many Latin American officials, and this is, therefore, an excellent time to obtain information on the Organization which would be valuable to the Department.[76]

From MacKay's letter, it seems as though DEA was not particularly upbeat about the OAS. The very fact that he was looking for information on the body would tend to confirm the fact that Canada was far from making any decision on joining the organization. In fact, the response from Canada's Ambassador to Venezuela, H.G. Noonan, was decidedly negative on this issue. In a letter written around the time of the Guatemalan crisis, he suggested that "the Organization was rather futile, potentially embarrassing and far-too-costly (in time and money) considering its achievements."[77]

But perhaps the most damning statement—written by C.F.W. Hoops at the time of the crisis—about Canada's position on OAS membership came from a DEA memorandum. In the words of Hoops: "On examining the record of the O.A.S. up to date, I have been unable to find anything that this Organization has done, or is likely to do which would be deemed an advantage to Canada."[78]

On the question of Canadian membership, he was even more blunt. As he explained:

My conclusion, for what it is worth, is that in joining the O.A.S., Canada would be attaching itself to a body which has accomplished little for its present members and would do nothing but create useless work and expense for us for many years in the future.[79]

Although the OAS was roundly criticized for being dilatory and ineffective in the case of Guatemala, it was severely excoriated for its role in the Dominican Republic crisis of 1965.[80] In April of that year revolutionary elements within the Dominican military establishment began an effort to overthrow the government of Donald Reid Cabral.[81] On 27 April the Inter-American Peace Committee, at the behest of the United States, convened to consider the Dominican situation. The next day, U.S. Ambassador to the Dominican Republic, W. Tapley Bennett, informed President Johnson that the lives of U.S. and other foreign nationals were in danger. (Apparently, it was Bennett who requested the landing of U.S. forces on the beaches of the tiny Caribbean country.) Shortly thereafter, U.S. marines, numbering close to 20,000, landed on the shores of the Dominican Republic, with the avowed objective of protecting U.S. lives.[82]

On 29 April, in the aftermath of the U.S. invasion, the OAS Council met and urged the establishment of a ceasefire and stated its desire to be kept informed of developments in the country.[83] That same evening, the council met again to consider a request by the Chilean representative that a Meeting of Consultation—under Article 39 of the OAS Charter—be convened on May 1 to discuss the crisis.[84] At the same time, there was agreement on a proposal to declare a "neutral zone" in the embassy area of Santo Domingo wherein foreign nationals would be given safe haven.

Following a report from the Papal Nuncio in Santo Domingo, the council decided on 30 April to send the Secretary General, José A. Mora, to the island country to establish an OAS presence at the scene.[85] In addition, he was instructed to assist the Nuncio in his efforts at securing a ceasefire and to provide immediate on-the-spot reports to the Meeting of Consultation. When the Meeting of Consultation was convened on 1 May, it had before it a number of draft resolutions. For instance, a Mexican proposal called upon the United States to withdraw its forces from the country immediately. In any event, it concluded with the adoption of a resolution creating a Special Committee, which was charged with investigating the Dominican situation, seeking a possible ceasefire, and helping to evacuate scores of refugees.[86]

By late May the Meeting of Consultation had moved to address the Dominican crisis on a number of fronts. There was agreement reached on the establishment of an Inter-American Peace Force (IAPF)—composed mainly of U.S. forces—for the Dominican Republic, which was responsible for restoring normal conditions in the country.[87] On June 2, the Meeting of Consultation established a new committee (the Ad Hoc Committee) to continue the work of the Special Committee and the Secretary General.[88] Through this committee, and its work in finding some common ground between the rightists and the constitutionalists (led by Antonio Imbert), a Provisional Government was installed on September 3, under the leadership of Hector García Godoy. And with the coming to power of a new government, the Inter-American Peace Force began to leave the country on September 21.

Clearly, the OAS was involved in the Dominican crisis, but the nature of that involvement was less than exemplary.[89] Not only did the body not condemn the intervention on the part of the United States, but it did absolutely nothing to prevent it from happening.[90] It played a minimal role in setting the agenda or in shaping the evolution of U.S. policy toward the Dominican Republic. And when Washington took control of events in the country, the OAS did remarkably little to constrain the United States, let alone hold it accountable for its actions. In short, the hemispheric body, as compared to officialdom in Washington, was at best peripheral, and at worst a willing agent of U.S. hegemonic designs.[91]

The image of a hapless OAS was further weakened by its inability or unwillingness to oversee the actions of Dominican as well as IAPF forces. It failed to condemn repeated violations of the ceasefire by troops loyal to the Imbert faction, "including a major drive that resulted in the killing of hundreds of constitutionalists or innocent bystanders and the jailing of thousands of others."[92] Nor did it do much to prevent a summer of murder and repression by Imbert's police and soldiers. Similarly, nothing was done to stop the IAPF from a series of alleged overreactions, which resulted in the loss of more than sixty Dominicans in one June incident.[93]

In many respects, then, the Dominican crisis marked a low-water mark in OAS affairs. Serious image difficulties, widespread anti-OAS sentiment, and general disillusionment with the body flourished in the aftermath of the emergency.[94] This development alone was a pointed illustration of just how badly the OAS fared in the Dominican crisis. According to Slater, "many did not expect the Organization to be able to play a significant role in hemispheric political affairs in the near future."[95]

Moreover, its questionable performance did little to enhance the institution's self-proclaimed contentions of independence and impartiality. Not only was its legitimacy challenged, but it became the target of intense hatred and ridicule. Some Latin Americans even went as far as to refer to it as "Otro Engaño Americano" (Another American Fraud). The OAS became increasingly perceived in Latin America as a front or cloak for promoting U.S. hegemony in the region. Stated differently, its implacable support for U.S. anti-communist policies left the OAS in a tide of rising Latin American scepticism and outright hostility.

Like the 1954 crisis in Guatemala, the U.S. invasion of the Dominican Republic exacted a minor response from Canadian authorities. Unlike in the Guatemalan affair, though, what discussion there was tended to focus specifically on the issue of OAS membership. Indeed, in early May 1965 the MP from Red Deer, R.N. Thompson, asked Prime Minister Pearson the following question:

Does he not think it would be advantageous at this time if Canada were a member of the Organization of American States, and does he not think that the reservoir of goodwill and the good offices of Canada could be used to better effect at this particular time if Canada were within the organization instead of without?[96]

But rather than take this opportunity to speak directly to the question of membership, the Prime Minister chose not to express his views on the subject. He simply responded by saying that "I am very interested to receive the hon. gentleman's opinion on this matter."[97]

Shortly thereafter, the MP from Oxford, W.B. Nesbitt, once again brought the question of membership before the House. Given the facts of the Dominican crisis, he expressed his relief that

Canada had not opted for full-fledged membership in the hemi-spheric body. As he indicated in his comments:

Had something been done I think Canada's position under the present circumstances in relation to the Dominican Republic would have been a difficult one indeed. No matter what we might then do we would make enemies. If we sided with the United States, as I think we should, we would unquestionably alienate a number of our Latin American friends. If our image is not very good in the United States at this time, it certainly would be far worse under these circumstances. I think it is advantageous that nothing has been done in this regard.[98]

There was a sense that the Liberal government—in the midst of the Dominican crisis—was shying away from the membership issue. In response to another question in the House, this time from John Diefenbaker (Leader of the Opposition), on the notion of an inter-American peace force, Pearson was clear and succinct. He stated that "we would prefer peace keeping forces of this kind to be under the United Nations rather than under any regional organization."[99] Later, Diefenbaker himself, in recognizing Pearson's (as well as Paul Martin's) lukewarm response toward the OAS, opined:

That is a long step backward from the views expressed by the hon. gentleman in 1959, 1960, 1961 and 1962, when he and the Prime Minister of the day stood so firmly for Canada joining the Organization of American States. Have they forgotten about that?[100]

The reverberations from the Dominican crisis also filtered through the Department of External Affairs. For the most part, the fallout from the crisis tended to work against the idea of Canada opting to join the OAS as a full-fledged member.[101] In a letter to DEA from Canada's Embassy in the Dominican Republic, the feeling was decidedly anti-OAS. According to the note,

recent developments in the Dominican Republic would hardly indicate that some minor Caribbean countries and Canada together, could have much influence in the OAS framework when the United Nations and major countries of the Western world, apart from the U.S., were quite hard-pressed to ameliorate aspects of the IAPF policies here, which to say the least, seemed rather unusual for this day and age.[102]

This general feeling of dissatisfaction with the OAS was even present within the ranks of the foreign service some twelve months later. In a May 1966 letter to the department from Canada's Ambassador to Peru, F.X. Houde, this negative sentiment was palpable. Ambassador Houde, among other things, noted: "I, for one, am far from convinced that Canada should join the OAS as it is now, nor are the prospects of substantial changes in the latter organization very bright at the moment."[103] Similarly, in a June 1966 DEA memorandum, the events surrounding the Dominican Republic were singled out for particular attention. It suggested that the U.S. invasion "registered heavily and unfavourably with some Commonwealth Caribbean nations as evidence of U.S. domination of the OAS, particularly in Caribbean affairs, and of the weakness of the OAS."[104]

While the implications of the Dominican crisis were felt in Canada, the political fallout that accompanied the Dominican crisis was long-lasting in Latin America and, in some ways, resurrected by the Falklands/Malvinas dispute in 1982. To be sure, both crises represented major turning points in the evolution of the hemispheric body in particular and Pan-Americanism in general. As with the crisis in 1965, many Latin American countries—in the wake of the Falklands/Malvinas dispute—felt that the OAS was manipulated by the United States and thus not the proper forum for advancing their interests. In other words, both crises did a great deal to dissuade Latin American governments from taking the body seriously. In fact, the Falklands/Malvinas conflict delivered a serious blow to the image of the institution in the eyes of many Latin Americans. Besides engendering a conspicuous polarization within the organization— pitting the English-speaking Caribbean countries against the Spanish-speaking member states—it convinced the Latins to look increasingly toward "made in Latin America" initiatives and prescriptions.

In any event, on 13 April 1982 the OAS Permanent Council, in its first formal action, offered to assist in getting peacekeeping efforts under way.[105] By 20 April Argentina called for, and succeeded in arranging, a meeting under the procedures of the Rio Treaty.[106]

From 26-28 April the Meeting of Consultation of Foreign Ministers was convened to discuss the looming crisis. Much to the dismay of the Argentinean contingent, it was unable to muster the necessary two-thirds majority to invoke punitive sanctions under the Rio Treaty.[107]

The Meeting of Foreign Ministers did, however, produce a mild resolution urging the cessation of hostilities, but without mentioning the use of sanctions.[108] But when it was convened again in late May, with British forces ashore on the island, it seemed to be more receptive to Argentina's plight.[109] While it was still unable to agree upon formal Rio Treaty sanctions—under Article 8—the sharp anti-U.S. rhetoric heard in that forum was unprecedented.[110] In the end, though, Argentina had to settle for a general resolution condemning the British and calling for each member to support Argentina "in the manner each considers appropriate."[111] With little or no Latin American support forthcoming, and British forces rattling their sabres, Argentina's resistance collapsed on 14 June. As Britain regained control of the islands, the dispute was replaced by more pressing Latin American issues (e.g., debt, the Central American quagmire, and the drug trade).

The 1982 Falklands/Malvinas dispute, followed by the 1983 U.S. invasion of Grenada, has become almost synonymous with an ineffective OAS. For Connell-Smith, "another chapter was written in the story of its decline."[112] Not only were Anglo-Latin tensions within the OAS heightened, but the OAS peace and security components were shown to be largely ineffectual. Its failure to embrace a larger role, to engage its peacemaking procedures, or to act more decisively—particularly in regard to the Rio Treaty—was duly recorded by Latin American officials. As the President of Venezuela, Carlos Andrés Pérez, recently commented:

The obvious preference of the United States for the interests of NATO destroyed the credibility and legitimacy of the Rio Treaty, to the point that few would today be inclined to invoke it even were the situation identical to others that in the past mobilized mechanisms of conflict resolution.[113]

In fact, there was a growing sense that perhaps Latin America as a whole should think seriously about developing a more distinctive role or identity in world affairs. More specifically, a role in which Latin American countries could align themselves with other Third World or developing states, where they could attempt to wean themselves from U.S. hegemonic influences, and where they could shy away from the OAS in favour of the UN.

The impact from the Falklands/Malvinas War also registered on policy-makers and opinion-makers in Canada.[114] And it did have implications for Canada's position toward membership in the OAS. At the political level, there was a sense of relief that Canada, at the time of the crisis, was not a member of the organization.[115] Generally speaking, Cabinet sentiment—as the imposition of economic sanctions against Argentina would attest—was solidly on the side of Britain.[116] In other words, the government appeared, at least on the face of it, to favour its North Atlantic links as opposed to its ties with the inter-American community. The crisis itself certainly did nothing to convince the political leadership that joining the OAS was an idea whose time had come.[117] If anything, it seemed to reinforce the prevailing view that non-membership in the OAS was far more of an attractive option for Canada.

From a bureaucratic standpoint, the effects of the crisis seemed to be more obvious. Officials in the Latin America and Caribbean bureau viewed the emergency as another example of the general ineffectiveness and decline of the body.[118] Certainly, it tended to strengthen the resolve of those in the bureau who were against the idea of Canadian membership in the OAS.[119] Simply put, it was seen as a disturbing development in inter-American affairs and thus a potent reminder of the potential "risks" that full membership for Canada would entail.[120]

While not a decisive factor, the crisis did serve to put the OAS membership question in a different light. Foreign policy officials were more cognizant of the fact that the OAS was becoming increasingly polarized, with some Latin American countries (Venezuela and Peru) musing out loud about creating a truly "Latin American" organization. In the words of one official:

While this extreme position has not won any significant support nor been actively pursued, the fact remains that there has been tension and difficulties within the organization between the Latin members on the one hand and the United States and the English-speaking Caribbean members on the other hand which could have a serious, although, yet undetermined effect on the Organization.[121]

This same official went on to state that the Falklands/Malvinas crisis did "present us currently with a greater potential political hazard so far as OAS membership is concerned than our customary fears about a falling-out with the USA on Cuba would suggest."[122]

Within the department, then, there was a general sense that Canada's non-membership in the OAS was a blessing of sorts. As one departmental paper explained:

It was fortunate that we were not members of the OAS in April, 1982 and were not seated at the meeting of Consultation of Foreign Ministers as the only Member State to have imposed sanctions on Argentina (i.e. at the first session, before the USA did the same.)[123]

In a similar vein, it went on to state the following: "As an Observer State, we were never named specifically as the perpetrators of 'economic aggression' against Argentina but as a Member, we could scarcely have avoided marked attention."[124] The paper seemed to be concerned about the possible negative impact that Canada's stance during the crisis would have had on its chances for eventual membership. It suggested that a wide variety of Latin American opinions should be canvassed so as to "be absolutely certain before we take any steps formally to seek membership."[125] In short, there would not be a recommendation coming forward in the coming months advocating full membership in the forum.

The above-mentioned polarization and irrelevancy of the OAS—which was particularly acute in the minds of the political leadership in Latin America—helped to spawn an upsurge of Pan-Latinism.[126] There was a tendency to look inward, toward greater regional cooperation, in solving Latin America's panoply of problems. For instance, debilitating wars in Nicaragua and El Salvador were virtually ignored by the hemispheric forum. It was as if the organization believed that the conflicts would miraculously go away by themselves. In light of this situation, the Contadora and Esquipulas vehicles for peace, in working outside the auspices of the OAS, were instrumental in bringing some semblance of stability to war-torn Central America.

At the same time, certain sub-regional Latin American bodies, including the Latin American Economic System (SELA), were imbued with more political and diplomatic significance. Bolstered by the leadership of such influential Latin American countries as Mexico, Brazil, Argentina, and Venezuela, economic issues were brought to the front burner. There were discussions and consultations on various proposals for increasing regional trade, reducing barriers to goods and capital, and moving toward greater economic integration.

On the crippling issue of external debt, about which the OAS did remarkably little, a number of Latin American countries joined forces in the mid-1980s. Debtor countries, in forming the Cartagena Group, sought to publicize their plight and to seek relief from their creditors. More important, these countries hoped that their grouping would not only politicize the debt problem, but would also lead to the formulation of a panoply of solutions.

By 1986 the Rio Group—which is composed of the major states in Latin America—was firmly established. This grouping of key countries sought to confront the region's long list of critical economic and social difficulties. In addition to economic and political questions, it set out to resolve the increasingly violent Central American crisis. In short, this group—in conjunction with the other sub-groupings—started to supplant the OAS as the principal voice of Latin American concerns and aspirations.

The further decline of the OAS, and the growth in Latin American dissatisfaction with it, was evidenced by its role in the 1989 U.S. invasion of Panama (as it was in the 1983 U.S. invasion of Grenada).[127] While not all the details on how the OAS responded to the invasion are yet in the public domain, some things are clear. On 20 December, one day after "Operation Just Cause" had been launched, the OAS Permanent Council met to consider events in Panama.[128] Nicaragua introduced a resolution calling on all OAS members to condemn the use of force against a member state and demand the immediate withdrawal of U.S. forces. Reportedly, the 21 December session was abruptly halted only five minutes after it convened. Representatives were apparently divided over the precise wording of a proposed resolution condemning the intervention.[129] By 22 December the OAS passed a resolution which deeply regretted the invasion of Panama and urged "the immediate cessation of hostilities and bloodshed."[130] In other words, despite a clear violation of the OAS Charter, the best that it could do was to muster a mild rebuke of Washington's intervention. Although the situation and circumstances are obviously different, the response of the OAS was very reminiscent of its lacklustre performance in both the 1954 Guatemalan and 1965 Dominican crises.

Besides issuing a tempered criticism of U.S. actions, the OAS was essentially a bit player in the invasion of Panama. Washington did not even bother to inform the hemispheric body beforehand of its invasion plans.[131] There was no talk of convoking a Meeting of Consultation, sending an Investigating Committee to monitor events in Panama, or even demanding the withdrawal of U.S. forces. Put simply, the OAS, when it was faced with a situation wherein a member state violated the sacred principle of non-intervention, remained practically invisible.

Although military strongman Manuel Antonio Noriega was thoroughly disliked throughout Latin America, most leaders in the region would have clearly preferred a diplomatic solution to the crisis.[132] Yet the OAS made only a half-hearted attempt to have Noriega move aside and allow for a peaceful transition of government. The reality was that the OAS, ever reluctant to interfere in the internal affairs of member states, was loath to go much further. As Carlos Andrés Pérez, the President of Venezuela, explained:

Nonintervention, by omission, became a passive intervention against democracy and in favor of a dictator, since no account was given to the fact that instead of protecting the people of Panama, whose sovereignty had been trampled by the denial of its will expressed in elections, nonintervention protected the dictator Noriega who intervened in the electoral process.

As a result, it effectively brought on what most people had hoped to avoid—namely, unilateral intervention on the part of the United States.[133]

SUMMARY

It seems quite obvious from the preceding discussion that those cases where the OAS was unsuccessful had the most impact on Canada's position/attitude toward that body. In such cases as the Falklands/Malvinas and Panama where the OAS was conspicuously ineffective, several forces combined to produce this result. For example, there did not appear to be a keen interest on the part of the governments involved to avail themselves of the OAS. In fact, Guatemala had no intention of approaching the hemispheric body in 1954. Furthermore, the OAS Council showed no particular interest in taking an active role in the Dominican crisis of 1965, the Falklands/Malvinas dispute in 1982, or the U.S. invasion of Panama in 1989. In point of fact, they were all cases in which the OAS seemed content simply to sit on the sidelines, watching stoically as events unfolded.

It is important to recognize that all of these cases, different as they were, placed the idea of Canadian membership in the OAS in a negative light. In the case of Guatemala in 1954, the documents examined clearly indicated that the OAS had not been held in high regard by Canadian authorities. In a general sense, it was viewed as ineffective and detrimental to Canadian interests in the region. And it seems from the sharp tone of some of the letters that the Guatemalan affair did little to dispel this sentiment. If anything, it tended to reinforce the notion that joining the OAS would not be an appropriate move to undertake. Indeed, there was a real sense that Canada might be better off remaining outside of the organization.

Similarly, the 1965 Dominican crisis appeared to work against the likelihood of Canada seeking full membership in the body. It tended to highlight a number of negative implications—such as the fact that the organization was heavily dominated by Washington, the possibility that Canada would inevitably find itself caught between the U.S. and Latin American governments, and the general ineffectiveness of the hemispheric forum—of the OAS itself and Canadian membership in particular. Simply put, it was a pointed reminder to officialdom in Ottawa that the OAS was incompatible with Canadian interests.

If the Dominican crisis muddied the waters, then the 1982 Falklands/Malvinas debacle knocked the wind out of the Canada-OAS sails. Its impact was not lost on the minds of policy-makers— clearly strengthening the hand of those who were opposed to the idea of Canadian membership in the OAS. To be sure, if there had been some doubts about the potential costs of Canadian admission, they were suddenly removed by the Falklands/Malvinas crisis. It was another visible symptom of a growing problem—namely, the increasing ineffectiveness and irrelevancy of the OAS. Within this context, Canadian officials were convinced that the benefits of membership did not outweigh the perceived costs of joining.

Interestingly enough, cases such as the Falklands/Malvinas dispute, where the OAS was unsuccessful, warrant further comparison. These disputes all impinged upon the larger foreign policy interests of the hemisphere's reigning superpower. In the Guatemalan and Dominican Republic crises, removing the alleged threat from "international communism"—as perceived from Washington—took precedence over allowing the OAS to play a meaningful role. In the Falklands/Malvinas controversy, the White House chose the North Atlantic link over Pan-Americanism. And as for Panama, Noriega suddenly became a liability when he started to talk openly about his support for the U.S.-backed contras and the existence of plans for a possible U.S. invasion of Nicaragua. In cases, then, which impinged or affected larger questions of U.S. foreign and security policies, the OAS has been effectively marginalized.

Clearly, the role of the United States in all of these disputes has been a common thread. In all of the OAS failures, administrations in Washington have been the dominant or driving force, thereby leaving the OAS with little room in which to manoeuvre. This fact alone goes a long way toward explaining why the OAS was largely ineffectual in these cases. In other words, when the United States has been committed to advancing its own agenda or securing its own narrowly-conceived interests, the OAS has failed woefully.

In recognizing the strengths and weaknesses of the organization, one gets a better understanding of Canada's attitude toward the hemispheric forum. Clearly, the effectiveness or ineffectiveness of the OAS was a factor—almost invariably looming in the background—

in influencing the Canadian position on the issue of full membership. Accordingly, it makes sense to follow this chapter with an examination of Canada's position on OAS membership.

III

Canada and the Inter-American System, 1890-1968

C̲ANADA'S INVOLVEMENT IN INTER-AMERICAN AFFAIRS, PARTICU-
larly for the years 1910-1968, can best be characterized as irregular
or inconsistent. Successive Canadian governments have blown hot
and cold over the question of drawing closer to the hemisphere's
principal political institutions—namely, the Organization of
American States (OAS) and its predecessor, the Pan-American Union
(PAU). Their seemingly "on-again, off-again" disposition toward
greater involvement in the inter-American system has engendered
a panoply of confusing and contradictory signals—domestically
as well as internationally. This chapter will elucidate the reasons
behind such peculiar behaviour, which in turn will explain why Canada
has adopted such an ambivalent attitude toward inter-American
institutional life.

This chapter outlines the evolution of Canada's position on
greater hemispheric involvement without attempting a detailed
account of Canada's multifaceted association—economic, strategic,
cultural or religious—with the inter-American system.[1] Rather the
focus will be, for the most part, on Canada's stance toward the hemisphere's major political institutions. It is hoped that a better understanding may result not only of the key actors involved in shaping
Canadian thinking on inter-American affairs, but also of where
hemispheric relations are situated on Canada's foreign policy agenda.
The principal purpose of this chapter is to outline the factors which,
prior to 1968, influenced Canada's attitude toward hemispheric
institutional life.

HISTORICAL BACKGROUND: CANADA AND THE
PAN-AMERICAN UNION

In a January 1888 U.S. Congressional bill, which instructed the president to petition representatives from the countries of the Americas to attend a conference in Washington, Canada's participation was mentioned. However, when the amended legislation became law in May, no provision for inviting Canada was included at that time.[2] Undoubtedly, Canada's close ties with Britain, and the fact that its foreign policy was directed exclusively by the British Foreign Office until about the mid-1920s disqualified it, at least initially, from participation in the burgeoning Pan-American movement. (It is worth noting in passing, however, that Canada was not precluded from attending the conference because it was a constitutional monarchy—while the countries of the Americas were under presidential systems of government). At that time, though, it was unlikely that the Canadian government would have accepted an invitation, even if one had been forthcoming.[3]

In many ways, the events of the late 1800s prefigured Canada's association with inter-American political life for the next two decades. According to R. Craig Brown, "Canadian interest in Latin America and awareness of the problems and aspirations of Latin America was notable for its non-existence."[4] Indeed, its commercial interest in the hemisphere was at best minor, its attendance at special Pan-American conferences was sporadic, and it steadfastly avoided membership in any of the newly-created inter-American institutions. While it did take part in the work of the Pan-American Sanitary Bureau (the forerunner of the Pan-American Health Organization) and was a member of the Postal Union of the Americas and Spain in the early 1900s, it remained largely outside the parameters of Pan-Americanism.[5]

Notwithstanding its predilection to remain on the sidelines of inter-American affairs, Canada could not—even if it wished—distance itself from hemispheric developments altogether. However, as early as 1909, John Barrett, the then-Director General of the Union of American Republics, paid a courtesy visit to Prime Minister Sir Wilfrid Laurier in Ottawa. Apparently the two men discussed, among other things, the possibility of Canada's entry into the inter-

American family.[6] From Laurier, and from a later visit to Sir Robert Borden, Barrett received little in the way of encouragement. While both Laurier and Borden expressed guarded interest, they shied away from going any further.

Interestingly enough, in 1910 the U.S. Secretary of State Elihu Root indicated, at least symbolically, his interest in having Canada become a full hemispheric partner. He instructed his officials to place the Canadian coat of arms on the cornices of the inner court—with those of the other twenty-one republics—of the newly-built headquarters of the Pan-American Union (PAU).[7] In addition, the boardroom was to have a Canadian panel mounted and a chair with "Canada" inscribed on the back for use at the Council table. This chair has, over the years, come to be ignominiously referred to as the so-called "empty chair."

Despite the placing of a chair for Canada in the PAU headquarters, the Canadian government still preferred to remain aloof from the hemispheric body. Official Ottawa was more interested in channelling its energies and resources into developing its West and Northern territories, achieving full independence (especially in a foreign policy sense) from Britain, and protecting its sovereignty from its powerful neighbour to the South.[8] The Canadian public, for its part, was largely uninformed and uninterested in Pan-Americanism and maintained a general attitude of indifference.[9] Similarly, the Canadian business community had very little commercial/trade or investment interest in Latin America and the Caribbean.[10] Businesspeople in Canada, according to P.E. Corbett, believed that "the peoples south of the Rio Grande were of such a different sort that the less we had to do with them the better."[11] Simply put, Canadian interest or involvement in hemispheric affairs was, for all intents and purposes, limited.

There were other reasons why Canada preferred to view the PAU safely from outside its corridors. In the wake of World War I, Canada looked increasingly toward the emerging British Commonwealth and the fledgling League of Nations. Participation in these multilateral fora, as opposed to inter-American institutions, was viewed by Canadian officials as more important. There was a sense that Canada's overall interests could best be safeguarded in a "global" rather than a "regional" institutional environment. At the same time, official government interest in Latin America was minuscule; Canada felt no ambitions of an imperialistic nature, and economic interchange with the region was insignificant.[12]

Similarly, public opinion in Canada—particularly in the post-war period—was generally uninterested in inter-American developments. Although French-speaking Canadians, largely for cultural and religious reasons, expressed a greater interest in Latin America, the general populace was decidedly unenthusiastic about the region.[13] Some Canadians felt that increased involvement in inter-American political life would have the undesirable effect of weakening Canada's traditional ties with the British Commonwealth.[14] Others were simply suspicious of Pan Americanism and feared that the United States might be contemplating the eventual absorption of Canada. As John P. Humphrey noted: "In the opinion of most Canadians, Pan Americanism was little more than a cloak for Yankee hegemony and imperialism."[15] As a result, it was virtually ignored in government, commercial, and media circles.

Canada's disposition toward things Pan-American was not altered by the coming to power of Mackenzie King in 1921. There still existed an acute lack of interest, on the part of many Canadians, in closer relations between Canada and the inter-American system. This state of indifference was also unaffected by the results of the 1926 Imperial Conference. The resulting Balfour Declaration—which formally acknowledged that the Dominions were no longer subordinate to Britain—was not followed by any great outpouring of public or official support for Canada to play a larger role in inter-American institutional life. A wide body of opinion continued to evince a preference for maintaining traditional links with both Europe and the United States. From an official standpoint, moreover, the King government was more interested in fostering Canada's own political development and in coping with the ramifications of living next door to a major power.[16]

To assist Canada in coping, Ottawa established direct diplomatic relations with the United States in 1927. And for the first time, Canada's membership in the PAU became a matter worthy of serious discussion. Much of the discussion, though, revolved around Washington's reservations about Canada's constitutional status and its British-influenced foreign policy. The U.S. State Department, in particular, disliked the idea of Britain, through possible manipulation of Canadian membership in the PAU, interfering in what was perceived as a U.S. sphere of influence.[17]

Despite U.S. misgivings, the 1928 International Conference in Havana did broach the topic of Canadian membership. In fact, both the Mexican and Chilean delegations indicated, albeit unofficially, their support for Canada's entry.[18] Furthermore, the U.S. delegation, while unwilling to initiate such a motion, was apparently prepared to accept Canadian membership.[19] In the end, no formal resolution on the issue was introduced at the conference. In any event, the Canadian government was unenthusiastic about the prospect of obtaining admission at that time.[20]

Not even the proclamation of the Statute of Westminster in 1931, legally affirming Canada's independence, altered Canada's position toward inter-American affairs. Indeed, complete control over the direction of Canadian foreign policy did not translate immediately into any heightened awareness on the part of officialdom in Ottawa of Pan-Americanism.[21] Additionally, the Canadian Parliament and public, along with the business community, still evinced no interest in forging closer links with their hemispheric brethren.[22] In this context, questions about Canada's membership in the PAU were simply brushed aside with the curt response that no official invitation had been received.[23]

However, by the time of Roosevelt's enunciation of the "Good Neighbor policy" and the 1933 International Conference in Montevideo, such a response was no longer valid. At the conference itself, Ecuador introduced a resolution inviting Canada to take its logical place within the Pan-American movement.[24] While Mexico and Chile were more enthusiastic about Canadian membership in the PAU, Peru was reluctant to formalize the official invitation, largely for procedural reasons.[25] The United States, for its part, actually took steps to ensure that the question of admission did not come before the conference. Instead, the discussion of Canada's entry—at the behest of the U.S. delegation—was merely mentioned in a report and not formulated in terms of any official recommendation.[26] Washington was less concerned about the "technical difficulty" of

Canada's being a constitutional monarchy (as opposed to a republic) and more apprehensive about the possibility of having the British meddling in its own "backyard."[27]

Still, the Canadian government expressed no serious interest in the idea of joining the PAU as a full-fledged member. Nor, it seems, were a handful of Latin American governments entirely comfortable with the notion of Canadian membership. There were some doubts about the possible benefits that would be derived from the admission of another predominantly English-speaking country. Interestingly enough, Brazil's mild opposition appeared to stem largely from its fear that any invitation to the Canadian government would be promptly rejected.[28]

By 1939, Prime Minister King—in his classic cautious and go-slow approach—stated what several Latin American governments had sensed all along: namely, that Canadian membership in the PAU "should be given consideration in the future."[29] He hinted, however, at the fact that public opinion in Canada had not sufficiently galvanized around the issue to warrant a change in Canada's position.[30] With the exception of some Québec nationalists, a bevy of Canadian isolationists, and a few newspapers in Canada, the general populace was not enamoured of the notion of Canadian participation in inter-American affairs.[31] Moreover, the outbreak of World War II effectively placed the whole question of Canadian membership in a political deep freeze.

Nonetheless, Canadian indifference toward Pan-Americanism, especially from a political and economic standpoint, seemed to be showing some signs of change. Officials in Ottawa, gravely concerned about the German conquest of Europe, started to look seriously at cultivating allies on this side of the Atlantic, as a possible hedge against such an eventuality. The government also began to reexamine its strategic position and Canada's geographical proximity to the American republics.[32] Consequently, Canadian officials exhibited more interest in the inter-American system than they had at any other previous time.

Closer ties with Latin America also made sense from an economic standpoint. The realization that Canadian markets would disappear in continental Europe because of the war necessitated a shift to the emerging Latin American marketplace. (Given Canada's poor trade balance with the United States, government officials thought that earning "hard currency" from these countries would help ease Canada's foreign exchange difficulties.)[33] As a result, Canada's trade relations with both Brazil and Argentina showed signs of improvement in 1940, with exports growing from $8.5 million to more than $11 million.[34] According to P.E. Corbett, "a year of war did more than fifteen years of illustrious trade commissioners."[35]

In addition to commercial and financial considerations, there were growing pressures from both the United States and Latin American countries for Canada to increase its involvement in hemispheric affairs. Washington felt that a small power such as Canada—with no hegemonic designs—would be given a better hearing in Latin American capitals.[36] It also saw Canada as a friend that would be useful in bringing the neutral republics on the side of the Allied war effort.[37] Lastly, it wanted allies, largely for reasons of hemispheric security, to support the forces of democratic pluralism against the perceived threat of creeping totalitarianism.

Latin American governments, in contrast, were eager to establish diplomatic relations with Canada.[38] The process of establishing diplomatic contacts began in 1940, with the exchange of envoys with both Argentina and Brazil. Shortly thereafter, negotiations began in earnest for the establishment of Canadian missions in Chile and Mexico.[39] Not wanting to be left out, a number of countries in the region petitioned Ottawa about the possibility of exchanging diplomatic representatives.

The Department of External Affairs (DEA), while somewhat reluctant to support the exchange of emissaries with Latin American countries, was unenthusiastic about Canada joining the PAU.[40] But with momentum apparently building, the Canadian government informed Brazilian authorities of its desire to participate in the 1942 Meeting of Foreign Ministers in Rio. And in a startling turn of events, Ottawa made known its intentions in December of 1941 that it would be willing, if formally invited, to enter the PAU.[41]

The King government was evidently prepared to accept the responsibilities, commitments, and ramifications of PAU membership. The report of a trade mission, which had toured Latin America in 1941, recommended that Canada should "immediately" join the Pan-American Union.[42] Support for membership was also forthcoming because of the government's desire to attend the 1942 Rio meeting, which was to discuss a number of pressing hemispheric security issues.[43] (Canada was very interested in participating in the deliberations on the production and control of strategic materials.)

There were other reasons why December of 1941 was a turning point for Canada on the issue of PAU membership. Clearly, the Japanese surprise attack on Pearl Harbor, effectively forcing the United States into the war, brought closer to home the importance of hemispheric security.[44] A sudden enthusiasm within DEA favouring admission was also a crucial factor, with people like Jean Désy (an embassy minister in Brazil), Hugh Keenleyside and Escott Reid (respected foreign policy officials) all pushing for Canadian entry.[45] In short, then, international events, heightened security concerns, and bureaucratic factors, when taken together, help to explain why Canada was finally willing to enter the PAU in late 1941.[46]

This tangible commitment on the part of Canada, along with its interest in inter-American affairs in general, was received warmly by the majority of Latin American governments.[47] However, when Washington realized the full nature and extent of Canada's growing commitment to the hemisphere, it reacted unfavourably. Needless to say, Canada's decision to seek full membership in the PAU raised the ire of White House officials.[48] They were particularly upset over the fact that Ottawa had approached the Brazilians before discussing the matter with them first. President Roosevelt himself was strongly opposed to the idea of Canada even participating in the meeting of foreign ministers in Rio, let alone joining the PAU—primarily because of Canada's Commonwealth connection.[49]

On the question of Canadian membership in the PAU, the Roosevelt Administration (especially a clutch of State Department officials) was particularly adamant. The upcoming meeting in Rio, as far as Washington was concerned, was strictly for American republics.[50] It was also intent on preventing the issue of Canadian membership from diverting the foreign ministers' attention away from other key wartime questions. More important, the White House was still very concerned about the possibility of Britain— through Canada—insinuating itself into hemispheric affairs.[51] It was obvious that Canada's decision to follow Britain's lead into the war (albeit two and one-half years earlier) did little to mollify or assuage

U.S. reservations. In the words of Douglas G. Anglin, "the thoughts and actions of Canadians seemed altogether too British for United States liking."[52]

Clearly, in the face of strident U.S. opposition, Prime Minister King was not about to challenge Washington on the issue of PAU membership. (There has been some suggestion that King was not too keen on the PAU and, therefore, not particularly upset with U.S. resistance to Canadian participation at the Rio meeting of foreign ministers or, for that matter, to Canada's admission to the body.[53]) While Canada refrained from attending the 1942 Rio meeting, it did not pull back entirely from the hemisphere. Canada did take part in the 1942 Pan-American Sanitary Conference in Rio and the Inter-American Conference on Social Security in Santiago. In 1943, Ottawa also decided to become a member of the Inter-American Statistical Institute, a specialized agency of the PAU. The issue of Canadian membership would, however, have to wait until after the war.

Following the conclusion of the war, though, Prime Minister King seemed to shy away from the notion of drawing closer to the inter-American system.[54] Curiously enough, King's change of heart coincided with the U.S. State Department's warming to the idea of Canada's admission to the PAU.[55] Its past concerns and reservations about Canadian membership seemed to suddenly fade in the aftermath of the war and now, after more than thirty-five years of opposition, favoured entry.

Notwithstanding Washington's change of heart, the reasons for Canada's reluctance to become part of the inter-American family remained intact.[56] One of the reasons stemmed from King's belief, despite assurances to the contrary by Latin American governments, that Latin America was essentially unimportant to Canada and to Canadians.[57] In 1944 a public opinion survey was released that reinforced King's coolness toward the region in general and the PAU in particular. Roughly 70 per cent of those Canadians surveyed knew absolutely nothing about the PAU.[58]

Indifference toward things Pan-American also began to recur among Parliamentarians as well as the media. Within the DEA, an erstwhile proponent of Canadian membership in the PAU, there was growing opposition to the idea. Some officials pointed to the "caucus tactics" of Latin American delegations, which disturbed Canadian foreign policy-makers, at the UN and other international gatherings.[59] These same policy-makers also saw more benefits in supporting, and bolstering, the globally-orientated UN as opposed to a regional organization like the PAU.[60] Not surprisingly, then, the Canadian government chose to concentrate its energies and resources on ensuring international peace and security through the UN.

In 1947 U.S. Senator Arthur Vandenberg, the powerful Chairman of the Senate Foreign Relations Committee, provided the clearest expression of the U.S. position on Canadian membership in the PAU. He injected new energy into the membership debate in Canada when, in a Pan-American Day speech, he noted:

By every rule of reason we should wish her here. I would welcome the final and total New World unity which will be nobly dramatized when the twenty-second chair is filled and our continental brotherhood is complete from the Arctic Circle to Cape Horn.[61]

Lester B. Pearson, the then Under Secretary of State for External Affairs, expressed the government's position with regard to the PAU in a March 1947 address to a U.S. audience.[62] He stated that Canada's decision not to join the PAU was based on its membership in the Commonwealth and the UN, as well as its belief that Canada's relations with the Americas could proceed in a positive fashion outside of the hemisphere's principal institution. Decision-makers in Ottawa were also intent on participating in more lofty international institutions, and not just those dominated solely by the United States (read the PAU).[63] In the end, it was King who actually told U.S. President Truman not to press Canada on the issue of joining the hemispheric body.[64]

Notwithstanding King's request, Washington did not lose interest in having Canada join the PAU. U.S. officials, in concert with other Latin American diplomats, even took the step of removing from both the 1947 Rio Treaty and the 1948 Charter of the Organization of American States (OAS) the term "American Republics" and replacing it with "American States." This change in phraseology, however, had little impact on the Canadian public, which still remained largely uninterested in events south of the U.S.-Mexican border. In fact, many Canadians were more keen on the UN and did not want Canada, through increased hemispheric involvement and commitments, to grow any closer to the United States.[65]

CANADA AND THE ORGANIZATION OF AMERICAN STATES (OAS)

By 1949 Canada had begun to turn its attention away from inter-American concerns and toward a recovering Western Europe. With the Cold War heating up, Canada played a leading role in the creation of the North Atlantic Treaty Organization (NATO).[66] Prime Minister Louis St. Laurent, not unlike King, began to emphasize the significance of North Atlanticism as opposed to Pan-Americanism. At a press conference in the chancery of the Canadian Embassy in Washington, he made this orientation perfectly clear: "At the present time we consider it much more urgent to bring about this North Atlantic Union than to extend one that might be regarded as exclusive for the Western Hemisphere."[67] He went on to mention

Canada's potential domestic political difficulties concerning Canada's membership in the O.A.S. These difficulties stem mainly from indifference of the Canadian public to the O.A.S. due possibly to lack of knowledge. It was not likely, under present circumstances, that the Government would wish to join the O.A.S. outright.[68]

Regarding Canada's position toward the OAS, St. Laurent appeared to share the dilatory sentiments of Mackenzie King.[69] Indeed, it was not until March 1953 that the government's position on Canada's participation in the hemispheric forum was articulated officially in the House of Commons. St. Laurent informed the House that the "position of the government of Canada in this respect has not changed since I last referred to this subject on February 12, 1949, when I spoke at a press conference in Washington."[70] He noted that in his opinion: "'So far it has not appeared to us that there would be any decided advantage in a formal membership in the Pan-American Union'."[71] One year later, Lester Pearson, the then Secretary of State for External Affairs (SSEA), responded to a question in the House about possible Canadian membership in the OAS by saying: "In reply to that question I can only say that the necessity for making such a decision has not arisen because we have not received such an invitation."[72]

The general feeling in External Affairs also seemed to be leaning against the idea of membership.[73] In an October 1952 memorandum from L. Dana Wilgress to the SSEA, Wilgress was concerned about sending out any signals that would illustrate any sort of Canadian interest in seeking a closer association with the OAS. In his words: "I am not convinced that membership in the O.A.S. would benefit Canada or improve our situation to a degree corresponding to the effort involved."[74] He concluded by saying that "I do not feel I can recommend that we become more closely associated with the O.A.S. at this time."[75] A March 1953 DEA memorandum also captured this negative attitude toward the membership question when it pointed out: "It should not be overlooked that one reason which has impelled Latin American countries to think seriously about our membership in the O.A.S. is the desire to have a counterweight to the United States."[76] Similarly, a February 1955 DEA brief from the Latin American section suggested that

the great majority of resolutions passed are words and little else. I think that the main argument against joining the O.A.S. is one which cannot be advanced too openly and that is that the Organization is ineffectual and for the time and money spent on it achieves very little.[77]

By early 1957 the department's position on possible Canadian entry into the hemispheric forum was fairly solid: "Canada would prefer, for the time being, not to receive an invitation to join the Organization."[78]

By the end of St. Laurent's term in office, it was clear that the government was content to remain aloof from the OAS.[79] Hence, it was really not until the Conservatives came to power in June 1957, under the leadership of John Diefenbaker, that the whole membership debate was revived. Diefenbaker seemed attracted to the idea of charting a new and different course for Canadian foreign policy, particularly with respect to Latin America.

Sidney Smith, Diefenbaker's newly-appointed Secretary of State for External Affairs, expressed an interest himself in acquiring a greater knowledge of Latin America. In 1958 he visited Brazil, Peru, and Mexico, where he detected a great deal of eagerness on the part of Latin American officials for Canada to join the OAS.[80] After returning from the region, he was apparently prepared to push the idea of Canada joining the hemispheric body.[81] However, Smith's sudden death in March of 1959 effectively placed the issue, at least temporarily, on the political back burner.

When Howard Green succeeded Smith in the portfolio, he also exhibited a keen interest in expanding diplomatic contact between Canada and Latin America. Officials in External Affairs, for their part, began recognizing the potential ramifications of the large bloc of Latin votes at the UN.[82] Green believed that Canadian diplomats worked well with their Latin American counterparts and also noticed that these same Latin delegations tended to support Canadian initiatives at the UN.[83]

At the same time, there was talk of a Central American free trade area and the possibility of a second trade bloc involving all of South America and Mexico. (Out of these discussions emerged the Latin American Free Trade Association, LAFTA.) Ottawa, in light of these developments, was concerned about protecting Canada's existing economic interests and exploring any potential for new trade opportunities.[84] The coming to power of Juan Perón in Argentina and Fidel Castro in Cuba—along with the accompanying security implications—also played heavily on the minds of policy-makers in Ottawa. Additionally, many Latin American governments, which were growing increasingly disenchanted with Canada's continued aloofness toward the region, pressed the Canadian government to become more involved in the hemisphere.[85] For these reasons, debate over whether Canada should join the OAS took on added significance.

In fact, there appeared to be a growing consensus in 1960, particularly in government circles, for Canada to seek entry into the hemispheric body.[86] Appearing before the House of Commons External Affairs Committee, Howard Green—a supporter of Canada's admission—raised the issue of Canadian membership. Although the United Church of Canada was opposed to entry, opposition parties, the Canadian Labour Congress (CLC), and the National Federation of Canadian University Students (NFCUS) all urged full membership in the OAS.[87] Prime Minister Diefenbaker himself, while no doubt watching the debate closely, remained strangely silent.[88]

In April of 1960 Diefenbaker paid a visit to Mexico, the first Canadian prime minister to do so.[89] When questioned by a journalist about the possibility of Canadian membership in the OAS, he responded by suggesting that Canada might be interested in sending an observer to the quinquennial OAS conference in Ecuador, which was scheduled for May of 1961.[90] Besides Mexico, Canadian officials, led by Howard Green, also visited several Latin American countries in May, including Argentina and Chile. After returning to Ottawa, Green announced the creation of a new Latin American Division within the Department of External Affairs.[91] (Prior to this move, the entirety of Latin American affairs was handled by a single officer in the American Division.)

With momentum for joining the hemispheric body seemingly mounting, the debate suddenly shifted ground. Diefenbaker was reported to have said, during a news conference in Jamaica, that Canada was not interested in joining the OAS. While the report on his comments was later dismissed as inaccurate, it did generate some interesting editorial comment.[92] Three months later, Howard Green asked the public to express their views on the subject of Canadian membership. In response to his appeal, Canadians sent a number of letters to External Affairs—clearly indicating their preference on the membership issue. And according to a December 1961 memorandum, the majority of letters, some 205 in total, opposed the idea of joining.[93]

But perhaps the most telling blow to the OAS question came from the President of the United States. In May of 1961, John F. Kennedy—in a speech before Parliament—encouraged Canada to participate more fully in hemispheric affairs (read joining the OAS).[94] The Diefenbaker government, clearly taken aback by Kennedy's comments, quickly declined to accept Kennedy's opaquely-delivered invitation.[95] Four months later, Secretary of State for External Affairs Howard Green, responding to a question by Lester Pearson, stated that

One of the least effective ways of persuading Canada to adopt a policy
is for the president or the head of state of another country to come here
and tell us what we should do, no matter if it is done with the best
intentions. Even when it is done in that way it is not the best way to
get results.[96]

According to Ogelsby, "the surest way to dampen Canadian enthusiasm for any project involving the United States is to appear eager
for Canadian participation."[97] To be sure, it would have been pure
political folly for the Diefenbaker government to have been seen as
kowtowing to U.S. entreaties or caving in to pressure from
Washington.

It was becoming clear that the Diefenbaker Cabinet, along with
the Canadian public, had little interest in the membership issue.[98]
Economic problems in Brazil, in conjunction with political unrest in
Argentina and Venezuela, did little to spur interest in seeking admission. At the same time, turmoil in many of the Central American
countries tended to caution Canada against joining. And the 1962
suspension of Cuba—largely at the behest of the United States—at
the OAS Meeting of Foreign Ministers in Uruguay, and the subsequent imposition of sanctions against Havana, only served to illustrate the value of remaining outside the hemispheric body.[99]

Not surprisingly, the Cuban missile crisis in October of 1962
once again sparked debate about Canadian membership in the OAS.
Lester B. Pearson, the then leader of the opposition Liberals,
inquired about the possibility of Canada participating in OAS deliberations on Cuba without actually becoming a full member.[100]
Diefenbaker promptly dismissed Pearson's suggestion as unnecessary
and chose to remain largely neutral on the Cuba question.[101] In
other words, the fallout from the missile crisis had no substantive
impact on the Canadian government's coolness on the membership
question. If anything, it reinforced Ottawa's predilection for aloofness toward the OAS.[102]

While Canada's steadfast reluctance to join the inter-American
community remained unchanged, attitudes in Latin America were
beginning to shift. In fact, a certain Latin coolness toward Canada's
admission into the OAS appeared to be developing.[103] Some Latin
American governments were disturbed by Ottawa's unwillingness to

break diplomatic relations with revolutionary Cuba.[104] Others were simply frustrated with Canada's desire to establish wholesale diplomatic contacts throughout the region and, at the same time, dither over the issue of joining the OAS. Put simply, Latin American officials had grown tired of waiting around for Canada to undertake a substantive move to indicate its firm commitment to the region.[105]

It was in the face of public apathy toward inter-American affairs, and growing Latin American dissatisfaction with Canada, that Lester Pearson took over the reigns of power in Ottawa. Although he had previously supported the idea of Canadian membership in the OAS as opposition leader, he was less sanguine as prime minister.[106] In fact, when he went to Washington in May of 1963, President Kennedy once again broached the topic of OAS membership—but Pearson reacted coolly to the idea and the matter was simply left unsettled.[107] And when the topic was raised by Diefenbaker in the House of Commons in May 1963, Pearson's reluctance to embrace the OAS was clearly evident. He responded with the following statement:

The right hon. gentleman asked me this afternoon to declare myself once and for all, finally and irrevocably for or against membership in the organization of American states. The right hon. gentleman having avoided making any such declaration himself for six years has now, with the new freedom given to him by opposition—and I understand and appreciate his position—come out boldly against Canada's entry into the organization of American states. If I understand what he said this afternoon, as far as he and his party are concerned the doubt is resolved. There would be no membership in that organization. We on this side will, in due course, declare the policy of the government in this matter. It has taken hon. members opposite six years; they might give us a few more weeks.[108]

While this clarification never really materialized, Pearson's Secretary of State for External Affairs, Paul Martin, did announce in early May 1963 that Canada would send observers to an OAS-sponsored conference in Bogotá.[109]

While the Martin announcement to send observers to the Inter-American Conference of Ministers of Labour (on the Alliance for

Progress)[110] was done primarily to placate the Latins, the Pearson government did exhibit an interest in broadening Canadian-Latin American relations.[111] For instance, in December of 1964 Ottawa announced that it would make available up to $10 million to the Inter-American Development Bank (IDB).[112] The IDB, in return, would administer the assistance—for economic, technical, and educational projects in Latin America—on behalf of Canada. It is worth noting that this was the first time that a non-member of the OAS had actually entered into such an arrangement.

Nonetheless, when the United States invaded the Dominican Republic in May of 1965, landing some 20,000 marines on the beaches in and around Santo Domingo, the possibility of Canadian membership in the OAS became less likely. To be sure, it did nothing to bolster the arguments of those who were in favour of Canada joining.[113] In fact, it gave ammunition to those who were critical of the OAS itself and opposed to Canadian membership. In 1966 the Canadian government informed the White House and Latin American leaders that it had no intention of joining the hemispheric body.[114] Even after Trinidad and Tobago joined in March of 1967, the Canadian government was unmoved from its position of non-membership.

SUMMARY

The study of Canada's "on-again, off-again" approach to the PAU and the OAS for the years 1910-1968 gives rise to a number of interesting points and observations. In addition to indicating the major players—such as key political executives and foreign policy officials—involved in the debate over Canadian membership in the principal inter-American institutions, this chapter has highlighted some of the central factors explaining why Canada chose to remain aloof from these bodies. It has also emphasized the low priority of inter-American issues in the conduct of Canadian foreign policy.

Indeed, inter-American developments have rarely, if ever, been a major foreign policy concern for Canada. When the British Foreign Office was directing Canada's foreign relations, it only paid lip-service to what was happening in Latin America. Even after the passage of the Statute of Westminster in 1931, Canadian foreign policy tended to focus almost exclusively on relations with Britain and the United States. In later years foreign policy mandarins in Ottawa often refused postings in Latin America, realizing just how low a priority Latin America was.[115] And it was not until 1960 that a Latin American Division was actually established within the Department of External Affairs. While there were periods when Canada's foreign policy accorded more attention to relations with the Americas, that interest was never really sustained. By the end of the Pearson government, inter-American affairs—especially from a domestic political and foreign policy standpoint—was simply not a major concern.

Canada's decision to remain outside the confines of the PAU and the OAS, while based on a reasoned and thoughtful evaluation, also reflected this lack of foreign policy salience. It also stemmed, in part, from the changing nature of the wider international system itself. The two World Wars dramatically affected how Canada viewed these two hemispheric bodies. World War II, in particular, seemed to jolt Canada from its complacency—if only temporarily—and underscored the potential benefits of greater inter-American involvement.

However, when the international community, in the postwar period, turned its energies toward constructing a global body, Canada seemed to back away from involvement in the regionally-oriented PAU. Besides being actively involved in the founding of the UN and still maintaining its Commonwealth linkages, Canadian officials tended to espouse a more North Atlantic orientation or vision. Undoubtedly influenced by the onset of the Cold War, Ottawa looked increasingly toward rebuilding ties with Western Europe and creating the NATO alliance.[116]

When the Cold War started to heat up in the hemisphere in the early 1960s, largely revolving around U.S.-Cuban relations, Canada's opposition to OAS membership was reinforced. Clearly, the government did not approve of the OAS's suspension of Cuba in 1962 or its imposition of punitive sanctions against the tiny island country. Nor did the Canadian government support the 1965 U.S. invasion of the Dominican Republic.[117] In many ways, the Cuban and Dominican crises were potent reminders of why Canada should not join the OAS. In this sense, then, changes in the international environment—whether structural or hegemonic in nature—have tended to persuade governments in Canada not to seek membership in inter-American political institutions.

In addition to developments in the international system, domestic factors played a major role in Canada's opting for non-membership. Without a doubt, Canada's political leadership has, over the years, had a tremendous impact on the membership question. Indeed, when Prime Minister King was supportive in 1941, the Canadian government was prepared, for the first time, to accept admission. But when leaders such as Diefenbaker and Pearson expressed certain reservations, the issue tended to remain dormant.

Like the political leadership in Canada, the bureaucracy was also intimately involved in the membership debate. Even though External Affairs ministers such as Howard Green and Paul Martin supported Canadian entry, officials in DEA were, for the most part, unconvinced of the merits of joining. The one clear instance in 1941 when DEA officials were pushing for membership, the government indicated its intention to join. In the main, though, foreign policy mandarins in Ottawa have steadfastly opposed Canadian admission to the PAU and the OAS.

Domestic sources of opinion also had some impact, in a limited fashion, on the membership question. Public opinion in Canada, generally speaking, had been essentially uninterested in either the PAU or the OAS.[118] While not vocal about either organization, the general public had tended—throughout the period in question—to oppose membership. Business groups and a handful of non-governmental organizations, for their part, seemed to view Canadian membership in a favourable light, but not with a great deal of enthusiasm or vigour. Notwithstanding a minority of advocates, the media and the "attentive public" in Canada tended to oppose Canadian membership in inter-American institutions. In short, no societal constituency in Canada, from 1910-1968, was actually pushing for greater Canadian involvement in the PAU or the OAS.

There has, however, existed a constituency outside of the country carefully watching the membership debate in Canada. The United States, for instance, has figured prominently in Canadian thinking toward inter-American institutions. Up until 1945, Washington—fearing British interference in its sphere of influence—

was opposed strenuously to Canadian membership in the PAU. In the postwar period, however, the United States, in looking for a reliable ally and another country to share the financial burden, pressed Ottawa to join the OAS. Although prodding from Washington was unsuccessful (and at times counterproductive), it did serve to spark debate on the issue in Canada. By 1967, though, it would be fair to say that U.S. support for Canadian membership was not foremost in the minds of decision-makers in Ottawa.

Latin American governments also comprised a constituency backing Canadian membership in inter-American institutions.[119] For many years, they encouraged Ottawa to demonstrate its commitment to the region by joining the PAU and then the OAS. Latin American officials looked upon Canada as not just another source of development assistance, but as a voice of moderation, a shining example of a model democracy, and a potential bridge-builder between the Latins and the United States.[120] By the 1960, however, many countries in the region had grown increasingly frustrated with, and tired of, Canada's prolonged discussion—as opposed to decisive action—on the issue of membership. But as far as Canadian governments were concerned, their decision on membership would be based on its perceived interests and not on the platitudes and entreaties of Latin American officials.

By early 1968 the membership issue was, for all intents and purposes, a non-issue in Canada. With no domestic or external forces driving the debate, the *status quo* became the preferred option. In June 1968, however, this acceptance of the *status quo* was called into question by the electoral victory of Pierre Elliot Trudeau. Almost immediately, he expressed an interest in shifting Canada's foreign policy focus away from middlepowerism and NATO Europe toward other regions of the world—including Latin America and the Caribbean. Trudeau's early formulation of a hemispheric policy in general and a new approach toward the OAS in particular is the subject of the next chapter.

IV

Canada-OAS Relations: The Trudeau Years

WITH THE ARRIVAL IN OTTAWA OF PIERRE TRUDEAU AS CANADA'S fifteenth prime minister, the nature of Canadian-Latin American relations experienced a subtle metamorphosis. No longer would the Canadian government view our hemispheric cousins as an afterthought or, more important, as peripheral to Canada's external relations. Indeed, Latin America would be given a higher priority within government circles and singled out as a region deserving of greater Canadian foreign policy attention. Accordingly, the seemingly dormant issue of OAS membership was once again brought to the forefront of Canada's hemispheric relations.

This chapter examines the dynamics of the membership question during the Trudeau era—largely because this period represented a new phase in Canada-OAS relations. It is not, however, designed to show that Canada's relations with Latin America were conducted more on a bilateral as opposed to a multilateral basis.[1] Nor is it a study of how Canada's relations with Latin America—especially during the Trudeau years—expanded politically and economically as well as in the areas of development assistance and cultural exchanges. That discussion has taken place elsewhere, conducted by a number of informed specialists.[2] Rather, it is intended to outline how exactly the Trudeau government sought to draw closer to hemispheric institutions, particularly the OAS.

In order to accomplish this task in a cogent fashion, a two-fold framework of analysis will be employed. First, this chapter begins by detailing the nature and extent of the Trudeau government's incremental approach toward inter-American political institutions. To make this section more manageable, it is divided into three timeframes—1968 to 1972; 1973 to 1977; and 1978 to 1984. Secondly, it discusses the various reasons why the Trudeau government's view of these institutions was less than favourable. It concludes with a number of general observations on the OAS membership issue during the Trudeau era.

OAS MEMBERSHIP REVISITED, 1968 TO 1972

Trudeau himself, before becoming prime minister, seemed genuinely interested in increasing contacts between Canada and Latin America. In part, this stemmed from his own personal interests: he had travelled throughout the region, was fairly knowledgeable about it, and spoke Spanish fluently. Naturally, his interest eventually precipitated questions about his own position on Canadian membership in the OAS. During the Liberal leadership race in April 1968—in the course of one of the policy workshop sessions—he was asked pointedly by a delegate about the membership question. He responded by saying that Canada should indeed enter the OAS at some point in the future—but not at that moment. He qualified his answer, however, by stating that Canada should do so only after it had developed a coherent policy toward Latin America and one that enabled Canada, if the need arose, to function independently of the United States.[3] This qualified support would continue to be the common denominator of Trudeau's position on this topic for many years to come.

Just prior to his 25 June election victory, Trudeau indicated his desire to examine not just Canada's policy toward Latin America, but "the fundamentals of Canadian foreign policy to see whether there are ways in which we can serve more effectively Canada's current interests, objectives and priorities."[4] He went on to say that Canada has

to explore new avenues of increasing our political and economic relations with Latin America where more than four hundred million people will live by the turn of the century and where we have substantial interests.[5]

Hence, part of the subsequent foreign policy review—which took place from May 1968 to June 1970—would focus on Canada's overall relations, or lack thereof, with Latin America. Undoubtedly, Trudeau felt that increased contacts with the OAS, within the context of a Latin American policy framework, would contribute to advancing Canadian interests.[6]

External Affairs Minister Mitchell Sharp's "voyage of discovery" in the fall of 1968 was meant to signal Canada's interest in strengthening ties with Latin America. It was the largest Canadian mission ever sent to the region and Sharp, along with a handful of other Cabinet ministers, a number of cultural representatives, and a coterie of government officials, came back from the trip quite impressed with what they had seen.[7] According to J.C.M. Ogelsby, they were moved by

the modern and elegant cities like São Paulo, Mexico, and Buenos Aires. They received full coverage in the media of the countries they visited. They had the honour guards, the gala social occasions, and the normal round of discussions with government officials, business leaders, and—for the first time—university and cultural figures.[8]

Interestingly enough, there was little or no discussion of the OAS membership question with Latin American leaders or in the ministerial mission's final report. Their report did, however, serve as a useful primer and valuable source of information for the more comprehensive review of Canada's relations with Latin America.[9]

When *Foreign Policy for Canadians* was published in the summer of 1970, it generated a sizeable amount of interest within the academic community. Yet the 32-page booklet entitled *Latin America,* engendered little more than a yawn from interested observers and area specialists. While it was well-written and touched upon most of the high-points of Canadian-Latin American relations, it did not map out any long-term strategy or set of policy objectives to guide Canada's policy toward the region. It did, however, confront the perennial issue of Canadian membership in the OAS head-on, and with unusual clarity.

Although it comprised barely five pages, the section on membership, which was entitled "A Choice For Canada," was instructive. It began by stating the obvious: "The Government has already made known its intention to strengthen relations with Latin America."[10] From there, it went on to list three possible ways in which this strengthening could be achieved. First, the government could simply continue on much like before, "expanding trade and investment and modestly increasing development assistance but letting political, cultural and scientific relations evolve on an *ad hoc* basis."[11]

Secondly, it could deliberately set out "to broaden and deepen relations with Latin America not only economically but also politically and in the fields of cultural, educational, technological and scientific exchanges."[12] Within this option, the government, while also seeking to maintain "bilateral relations with individual countries," could also "apply to join the OAS as a full member." The third option, and perhaps the least contentious, was to pursue systematically a policy designed

to strengthen links of all kinds with the countries of Latin America, embarking upon nation-to-nation programmes in the economic, cultural and political spheres, while at the same time drawing closer to the Inter-American System and some of its organizations without actually becoming a member of the OAS.[13]

The final paragraph in the section on OAS membership clearly indicated a preference for the third option.[14] "The Government's purpose," according to the booklet, "is to develop closer relations with Latin America to the mutual advantage of Canada and the Latin American countries."[15] The government concluded, though, that membership in the OAS, at this time, was not an appropriate course of action. Instead, it suggested that

Canada should draw closer to individual Latin American countries and to selected inter-American institutions, thus preparing for whatever role it may in the future be called upon to play in the western hemisphere.[16]

In opting for the "middle course," the Trudeau government felt that it would

permit Canada's relations with the countries of Latin America to develop rapidly and, by improving Canadian knowledge and understanding of those countries and their regional institutions, prepare for a better-informed and more useful Canadian participation as a full member of the OAS.[17]

While the government did not endorse OAS membership at the present time, it did not rule it out for the future. Meanwhile, the Canadian government would seek "a formal link between Canada and the OAS countries ... at a suitable level." When established, Canada's representative to the body "would arrange for Canadian attendance at meetings of inter-American bodies in which Canada has an interest and at which Canadian attendance would be appropriate."[18]

In late June 1970 Canada first broached the idea of a "formal link" before the OAS General Assembly. Mitchell Sharp's parliamentary secretary, Jean-Pierre Goyer, proposed the notion of creating the position of permanent observer. He hoped that Canada's overture would be recognized as part of the government's intention "to move as quickly and as constructively as possible in the direction of full cooperation in the hemisphere."[19] Goyer went on to say that "today's session may fairly be regarded as marking a new departure in relations between Canada and its fellow members in the new world."[20]

On the membership issue, though, there would be no dramatic shift in policy. Indeed, Goyer made it clear that the government, after careful consideration, felt that "the best present course for Canada is to draw closer to individual Latin American countries and to selected institutions of the OAS and other inter-American institutions."[21] He also announced that Canada, as part of this policy, would seek full membership in the Pan-American Health Organization, the Inter-American Institute of Agricultural Sciences, the Inter-American Indian Institute, the Inter-American Conference on Social Security, and the Inter-American Export Promotion Center.

In the spring of 1971 a Canadian observer delegation attended an OAS General Assembly meeting in San José, Costa Rica. At this gathering, a resolution was passed creating the status of permanent observer.[22] (In July Canada's application for membership in the Pan-American Health Organization (PAHO) was approved.) But it was not until early 1972 that Canada formally petitioned the OAS Permanent Council for status as a permanent observer. And on 2 February External Affairs Minister Mitchell Sharp announced that Canada's application for observer status (along with Israel, Spain, and Guyana) had been approved unanimously.[23]

With this "window" on the OAS, Canada was expected to gain valuable knowledge and experience concerning the actual functioning of the inter-American system. This move into regionally-based multilateral fora would not, however, be at the expense of Canada's bilateral relations with Latin America. Jean-Luc Pépin, Minister of Industry, Trade, and Commerce, made this clear in an October 1970 speech before a conference on inter-American development and integration. He stated that

the government had decided to move ahead on a sound, practical basis, to learn more about the OAS as we participate in more of its activities, and to strengthen our bilateral relationships with individual members of the organization.[24]

Pépin's address was important because it reinforced the impression that official Ottawa was committed to expanding its hemispheric contacts.

In any event, permanent observer status, which Canada was at the forefront of instituting, represented another half-measure on the part of the Trudeau government.[25] In effect, opting for observer status was a means of avoiding any harmful political ramifications, while still gaining an entry to the OAS. Canada would not have to take sides—either with the United States or against it—on any inter-American issue coming before the Permanent Council. At the same time, it served to placate Latin American governments by signalling Canada's genuine interest in broadening its ties with its hemispheric friends and not merely doing so to enhance its relations with the United States. As a permanent observer, Canada was unable to vote in the Permanent Council or at the General Assembly. It was, however, permitted to participate in some OAS deliberations, such as the informal Foreign Ministers' meetings and in the sessions of the Inter-American Economic and Social Council and the Inter-American Council for Education, Science, and Culture.

Nevertheless, the Canadian mission to the OAS, according to a DEA statement, was viewed as integral to "strengthening Canada's relations with Latin America and with inter-American institutions."[26] The press release went on to note:

It should facilitate the rapid development of Canada's relations with countries of the Americas and serve to improve our knowledge and understanding of the Organization of American States and of Latin American institutions.[27]

This new status was viewed by the government as basically a means of increasing Canadian political and commercial relations with Latin America, consistent with the lexicon of the "Third Option" to reduce Canada's reliance or dependence on the United States.

In its capacity as permanent observer, Canada attended the 11-20 April OAS General Assembly in 1972.[28] Furthermore, Paul St. Pierre, parliamentary secretary to Mitchell Sharp, announced Canada's intention—despite what was stated in the booklet on Latin America—to seek full membership in the Inter-American Development Bank (IDB).[29] He said that Canada was willing to do so because "the Bank is a significant instrument in improving the quality of life in this region in assisting nations to develop their resources, their economies and their societies."[30] On 3 May 1972 Canada officially became the twenty-fourth member of the IDB.[31] According to Sharp, this step represented "a significant milestone in the broadening of Canada's relations with the Americas."[32]

Clearly, membership in the IDB was a key move in terms of strengthening Canada's commercial ties with the region. A DEA release observed:

Our closer association through the Bank with the countries of the Hemisphere should serve to increase the knowledge and understanding of the Canadian business community of the needs of the region and their ability to participate in meeting those needs.[33]

It also followed the middling course articulated by *Foreign Policy for Canadians* of drawing closer to the inter-American system.[34] Indeed, Senator Paul Martin, speaking before the May meeting of the IDB's Board of Governors, stated the following: "We consider Canada's accession to full membership as the culmination of our search for a more practical and effective form of involvement in the problems of the hemisphere."[35]

By the end of 1972, then, the Trudeau government had moved, albeit slowly, to strengthen its institutional linkages with the inter-American system. The key initiative was a modest half-measure of opting for permanent observer status within the OAS. Additional steps such as joining two specialized organizations of the OAS, and seeking full membership in the IDB, implied a shift in Canada's cautious approach toward hemispheric institutional involvement. The

next five years, however, particularly with respect to OAS membership, would exhibit few signs of meaningful policy change.

CANADA REMAINS ALOOF FROM THE OAS, 1973 TO 1978

In early 1973 noises about reforming the OAS were once again being
heard in the corridors of the old Pan-American Union building.
This, of course, did little to embolden officialdom in Ottawa to
draw even closer to the inter-American system, since the government clearly believed in preserving the *status quo* with respect to
membership in the hemispheric forum. Canada did, however, support those efforts intended to inject a new sense of relevancy into the
hemispheric body. Speaking before the OAS General Assembly in
April 1973, Pierre de Bané, parliamentary secretary to Mitchell
Sharp, expressed the Canadian government's endorsement of the
OAS's review of its activities and structures. In his remarks, he mentioned the fact that Canada's future "association with the OAS would
depend to some extent on the results of this review and revision of
institutional structures and objectives."[36]

In the end, the review had little or no impact on either the OAS
or on Canada's policy toward it. In fact, there were few references to
the membership issue—over the course of the next three years—by
any member of the government or public official. For the most part,
the membership question, while never completely dormant,
remained in a virtual holding-pattern. It was really not until
Trudeau's high-profile visit to the region in early 1976 that it experienced somewhat of a resurgence.[37]

Trudeau's official visit to Cuba, Mexico, and Venezuela was, by
most accounts, modestly successful.[38] Perhaps the most important
result of the visit was the reservoir of goodwill it engendered for
Canada in the region, in no small measure thanks to the actions of
the Prime Minister himself.[39] As for the issue of Canadian membership in the OAS, Trudeau discussed the issue with all three Latin
American leaders. Not unexpectedly, he maintained that the
Canadian government, while aware of the issue, was in no hurry to
alter its previous position.

With the OAS reevaluating its role in the hemisphere, Trudeau
suggested that now was not the time for Canada to contemplate

admission. He went on to say at a press conference in Havana that Canada was satisfied being a permanent observer and, "pour le moment, nous n'avons pas l'intention de changer cette position, ni pour le plus, ni pour le moins."[40] At a later press conference in Caracas, he told Venezuelan President Carlos Andrés Pérez—in a more opaque fashion—that his government "had no closed mind on the subject" and "would look at the question again."[41] But he cautioned that to speak of any decision to seek membership in the OAS was "still a bit premature." He did say, however, that Canada would, without providing any specifics, "review the question."

The membership issue resurfaced once again when Trudeau visited Washington in September 1977, where he witnessed the signing of two new Panama Canal treaties. Partaking in the ceremonies, Trudeau suggested, was consistent with Canada's determination to deepen its involvement in hemispheric affairs. As for the OAS, he told U.S. President Carter, who raised the issue, that Canada's permanent observer status was as close to the OAS as "we can get without being actually in it."[42] In addition, he indicated that any decision on full membership would have to be put on hold while the OAS continued to reassess itself.[43] By the end of 1977, then, the Trudeau government was still intent on remaining aloof from the hemispheric body.

THE OAS FILE REMAINS CLOSED, 1978 TO 1984

Through 1978 and into 1979 there was virtually no serious movement on the membership question. It was almost as if the issue had been placed in a political deep freeze for a year or more.[44] And after Trudeau was returned to power in late 1980, his government continued its cautious approach toward the OAS. It really was not until the summer of 1981, through the sessions of the sub-committee on Canada's relations with Latin America and the Caribbean, that one could discern the government's position on the membership question.[45]

Appearing before the sub-committee, Secretary of State for External Affairs, Mark MacGuigan indicated no desire to change Canada's position vis-à-vis the body.[46] With MacGuigan was Assistant Under-Secretary, Bureau of Latin America and Caribbean Affairs, Richard Gorham, who simply stated that "for the time being it would be preferable to concentrate our efforts on expanding our bilateral relations with the individual countries and maintaining the same level of active interest in the OAS that we do have."[47] In addition to saying that the *status quo* was not adversely affecting Canada's bilateral relations with various countries in the region, he indicated that any departure on the membership issue

needs a broader consensus in the Canadian public to understand why we are doing it, what are the advantages, what are the disadvantages, what kind of commitments we are getting into, and I do not think that there is that type of feeling in Canada.[48]

The Director of the Latin American Division, Martin Collacott, was also cool to the idea of Canada seeking admission. If Canada were to become a full member, he argued, "I do not think it would have the clear-cut value that it might have had, say, 20 years ago."[49]

Curiously enough, the sub-committee, while criticizing the effectiveness of the OAS in various areas, took a decidedly different view. There were those who believed that Canada, if it were a full-fledged member, could work to strengthen the organization, would be more able to obtain its foreign policy objectives in the areas of technical assistance, trade and investment, and human rights, and could help to normalize relations between the United States and Cuba.[50] Accordingly, they recommended to the government that Canada should seek full membership in the hemispheric body, while refraining from signing the Rio Treaty. For the majority of the sub-committee, it was "time to recognize that Canada is a nation of the Americas" and "accept the opportunities, responsibilities and risks which that entails."[51]

Notwithstanding this recommendation,[52] the Trudeau government showed no signs of altering its long-standing approach toward the OAS. In fact, it seemed to be quite content with simply following the same line as before and indicating its support for maintaining the *status quo*. In April 1983 a senior official from DEA pointed out that no consensus existed in Canada on the membership issue and that "many people believe that we found exactly the balance that Canadians so dearly love."[53] Thus, by the end of the Trudeau reign in 1984, Canada had little interest in seeking full membership in the OAS, while it did draw closer to the inter-American system as a whole.[54]

CANADA AND THE OAS: EXPLAINING THE
TRUDEAU GOVERNMENT'S ALOOFNESS

Clearly, the Trudeau government, for almost fifteen years, made a
conscious decision not to seek full membership in the OAS. The key
issue, though, is not that it was extremely reluctant to join the hemispheric body. Rather, it is why the Liberal government chose not to
do so, and the reasons that underpin that choice. This section of the
chapter, then, is intended to explain the Trudeau government's decision to remain outside of the formal structures of the OAS.

Before embarking on this undertaking, it is important to acknowledge the prevailing domestic as well as international climate in
the 1970s and early 1980s. Acquiring a sense or feel for the internal
and external environments—and the pressures emanating from
them—helps to produce a better understanding of Canada's aloofness from the OAS. Indeed, if one is to develop a clearer picture of
the Trudeau government's firm reluctance to join the body, it should
be understood in relation to both the domestic and the international
milieu. For it was the dynamics of these environments that inevitably affected agenda-formation and the decision-making process
during the Trudeau years. Obviously, if the government was preoccupied with a host of other pressing internal issues, it would have
precious little time to focus on lesser matters—such as the OAS.[55] At
the same time, the nature of the external environment—whether
positive or negative—also coloured the government's thinking on
this particular foreign policy question. Simply put, the climate in the
domestic and international arena had a direct impact upon whether
the Trudeau government chose, or refused, to arrive at a certain foreign policy decision on the membership issue.

Domestically, the general climate in Canada—throughout the
1970s and early 1980s—was, in a word, unsettled. Economic issues,
in conjunction with constitutional questions, posed major and
recurring problems for the government. As such, they engendered
considerable media attention and consumed enormous government
energies and resources. High inflation, rising unemployment, astro-
nomical interest rates, ballooning government deficits, and a crushing
recession were all integral "buzz words" of the period in question.
No government, regardless of its political stripe, could afford to give
merely lip-service to these matters. Thus, they would have the atten-

tion not only of the political leadership in Canada, but also of a number of line departments in the government. Economic questions, then, would figure prominently in the Trudeau government's deliberations and decision-making focus.

Similarly, questions of a constitutional nature topped the Liberal government's issue-agenda during this period. Almost invariably, national unity matters would colour, and often distort, the Canadian political landscape. Whether it was aboriginal issues, wrangling with the provinces over resource ownership and revenue-sharing, or the rise of the Parti Québécois in the mid-1970s, constitutional questions were an inescapable millstone around the government's neck. And like economic matters, they required a large amount of government attention and resources. In fact, many policies—some even of a foreign policy nature (viz., relations with France and francophone African countries)—were framed in such a way as to strengthen the Canadian federation economically and politically, often at the expense of the provinces. Within this context, it was difficult to conceive of any government concerning itself with external matters, when the forces of internal dissolution appeared to be gathering momentum.[56]

From an international standpoint, the milieu was almost as challenging. The oil crises in 1973 and 1979 further complicated economic and constitutional issues in Canada. As a trading country thrust into an increasingly competitive international economic climate, Canada was compelled to find new ways of expanding and promoting trade. As a result, the Trudeau government was committed to diversifying and strengthening its relations—as espoused by the "counterweight" terminology of the so-called "Third Option"—with Western Europe, francophone Africa, and the Pacific Rim.[57]

In addition to a foreign policy agenda already crowded with issues stemming from Canadian linkages with NATO, the UN, and the Commonwealth, was the ever-present Canada-U.S. relationship. Beginning with the Nixon Administration's 10 per cent import "surcharge" in the early 1970s and ending with the Reagan administration's utter contempt for Canada's Foreign Investment Review Agency (FIRA) and the National Energy Program (NEP) in the early 1980s, it was clear that bilateral relations during this period were not always harmonious. Some commentators have even speculated that the

Canada-U.S. relationship—especially during the early part of the 1980s—was in the midst of a serious "crisis."[58] As Canada's principal foreign policy "problem," it has—over the years—evoked a considerable amount of political energy and diplomatic resources, leaving questions about possible OAS membership marginalized. It would not be a gross inaccuracy to state that all the other issues on Canada's foreign policy agenda, including the OAS, are subordinate to, and often overshadowed by, the exigencies of the Canada-U.S. relationship.

The climate throughout most, if not all, of Latin America also seemed to be one of crisis. During the 1970s and early 1980s, economic conditions in the region were horrendous. Besides long-standing problems such as chronic unemployment and underemployment, negative growth rates, exorbitant inflation rates, and widespread impoverishment, many Latin American economies were highly inefficient—stemming from numerous trade barriers—as well as plagued by heavy public-sector involvement. Not surprisingly, many of these economies were, by the early 1980s, teetering on the verge of collapse. Politically speaking, non-democratic and authoritarian regimes—such as those in Chile, Argentina, Uruguay, Brazil, and Paraguay—seemed to dominate the Latin American political landscape.[59] And during the early 1980s political strife in Central America, particularly in El Salvador and Sandinista Nicaragua, was becoming increasingly more prevalent.[60] By late 1983 it was clear that conditions in the region were worsening rather than showing any signs of improvement or recovery. Within this regional context, the Trudeau government was loath to join an organization that was supposed to address these pressing issues and was clearly unable to do so effectively. Simply put, there was remarkably little for Canada to gain at this time by joining this ponderous and impotent gathering of countries—hence Ottawa's penchant for downplaying the membership issue.

While the internal and external environments undoubtedly affected the Trudeau government's view of Latin America in general and the OAS in particular, they were certainly not the only forces at play. Needless to say, the political leadership in Canada, along with the bureaucracy, influenced the debate over OAS membership. Domestic sources of opinion, including the public, Parliament, pressure groups, the business community, and the media, also played a sizeable role. Lastly, actors from outside the country—namely, from Latin America—helped to shape the Trudeau government's decision to maintain its firm preference for permanent observer status.

It is instructive to note that Prime Minister Trudeau went on record, as early as 1964, as supporting Canadian membership in the OAS. An October 1964 *Cité Libre* editorial, for instance, viewed membership in the body positively "because Canada was an American nation."[61] But it also cautioned that the country should join only if Canada were to retain the freedom to formulate its own policies and the ability to disagree with the other members of the body. Trudeau was probably less interested in the political ramifications of the OAS and more concerned about the trade side of the Latin American equation.[62] Rather than focus almost exclusively on the OAS as an institution, he tended to view the region in terms of trade promotion and commercial advantage. Although it is difficult to pinpoint Trudeau's precise view of the OAS, it does seem clear that he did not want to proceed too rapidly toward closer association with that body.[63] What was equally certain was that he was unwilling to champion the membership issue in Cabinet.[64]

The Trudeau Cabinet, generally speaking, was largely against Canada joining the OAS as a full-fledged member. Influential members such as Gérard Pelletier and Mitchell Sharp, for example, were either lukewarm or opposed to membership.[65] It was evident that no minister was prepared to push the question of membership within the Cabinet. It was also clear that Allan J. MacEachen, a Cabinet heavyweight throughout the Trudeau years, was strongly opposed to Canada's joining the hemispheric body.[66] And as long as MacEachen had the ear of the Prime Minister, and remained firmly against membership, the issue was unlikely to go any further.

It was also doubtful that the bureaucracy, mindful of the fact that Cabinet was not on-side, would have pressed for OAS membership.[67] In any event, over the years 1968-1983 the Department of External Affairs (DEA) exhibited no sustained interest in the membership question.[68] If anything, the department was unconvinced of the actual merits of joining the body.[69] Some returning diplomats from Latin America did, however, favour Canadian membership in the OAS. But those from the old school preferred to focus Canada's limited foreign policy resources on the UN, NATO, and the Commonwealth.[70] These same officials were probably not at all impressed with the prospect of having to work alongside their loquacious Latin counterparts.[71] In short, the bureaucracy was neither fully committed to, nor seriously interested in pushing for, Canadian admission to the OAS.

Similarly, public opinion in Canada was, for the most part, remarkably uninterested in the OAS. Repeatedly, government officials would, over the years, skirt the membership question by pointing out that no public consensus existed for such an initiative. Indeed, in a 1969 survey, which was conducted at a Liberal party annual meeting, only 26 per cent of the delegates supported the idea of Canada's seeking admission to the OAS.[72] And in a 1977 study for DEA, the report noted the following about Canadian opinion: "Interest in OAS has declined, due to disapproval of OAS decisions regarding Cuba and in view of indications of waning interest in the organization in Latin America."[73] According to Ogelsby, "it is probably fair to say that most Canadians have a negative 'gut' feeling about the organization."[74]

Other domestic sources of foreign policy, such as Parliament, pressure groups, the business community, and the media, did not come out strongly in favour of membership either. Throughout the Trudeau era, the Canadian Parliament remained relatively silent on the membership question, with the exception of the 1982 sub-committee report on Canada's relations with Latin America and the Caribbean—which recommended joining the OAS. But even the sub-committee had harsh words for the hemispheric body, and four of its members opposed the recommendation to join. In the main, there was no sizeable group of MPs pushing for admission, no groundswell of support in Parliament, and no sustained interest in the issue by parliamentarians in general. Pressure groups in Canada, particularly throughout the 1970s, seemed to express little interest in the membership issue. And by the early 1980s, they were focusing their attention mainly on the conflicts raging in Central America.[75]

In contrast to these groups mentioned above, the business community—or at least the Canadian Association for Latin America (CALA)—was initially in favour of Canada joining the organization.

By 1979 it was urging the government to take its "full and rightful place in the Americas."[76] Yet, before the parliamentary sub-committee, a CALA spokesperson, E. Hugh Roach, responded to a query on the OAS by saying that he had "never seen much purpose in pushing for the full status because I believe Canada does enjoy the best of both worlds."[77] The media, like the unenthusiastic business lobby, was generally opposed to the idea of OAS membership. Indeed, editorial comment from Canada's largest newspapers appeared to remain consistently against admission during the Trudeau years. For example, a December 1982 editorial in the *Toronto Star* noted: "Since 1972, Canada has been content to be a permanent observer at the organization. And we should stay that way."[78] Similarly, a *Globe and Mail* editorial stated: "There is much to be said for keeping one's options open—a policy best achieved in this case by our remaining interested but unentangled."[79] While there were undoubtedly some Canadian businesses and newspapers favourably disposed toward membership, no solid consensus supported admission.

Granted, the extent to which domestic factors influenced the making of Canadian foreign policy at this time is debatable.[80] It is important to remember, however, that if a preponderance of opinion from these varied sources favoured membership, the Liberal government might have instituted such a move. However, since there existed no firm "constituency" in Canada pushing hard for admission, the government could simply adhere to its modest and cautious approach toward the OAS. A 1977 study prepared for DEA, which seemed to capture the lack of pressure on the government to move on this issue, suggested that it was "unlikely that a decision to enter OAS would excite much interest, pro or con."[81]

Just as there were no internal forces pushing for membership in the OAS, so, too, there was no sustained external pressure. Occasionally, during the Trudeau era, various Latin American officials raised the issue of Canadian membership.[82] But there seemed to be no concerted effort on the part of major Latin American countries to petition Canada to join.[83] In the last Trudeau government, there were few signs that the Latins were still interested in Canada as a full-fledged member. The Director of the Latin American Division at DEA, Martin Collacott, stated—in testimony before the sub-committee on Latin America and the Caribbean—that "we have not received any representations from major countries now for some years."[84] In the absence of any pressure from the major hemispheric players, then, the government was unlikely to deviate from Canada's permanent observer status.

SUMMARY

During the Trudeau years, the question of Canadian membership in the OAS was, in the main, a minor foreign policy issue. It certainly was not at the forefront of the Liberal government's agenda or high on DEA's list of policy priorities. It was rather an issue that raised its head occasionally, only to be dismissed by the unenthusiastic comments of Trudeau or some other senior government official. Indeed, once Ottawa had proposed and received observer status in 1972, it was felt in government circles that the question of full membership would be put to rest temporarily.[85] From that point onward, there really was no serious discussion of Canada's actually opting for admission.[86]

This reluctance on the part of the Trudeau government was partly a function of the prevailing domestic and international environment. First, more pressing domestic political and economic issues—whether on the economy or constitutional matters—made consideration of the OAS membership issue exceedingly difficult. With both economic and national unity questions at the top of the government's agenda, political will and prime ministerial attention were necessarily diverted from the membership issue. Secondly, in the absence of prime ministerial direction and sufficient bureaucratic resources, the question was unlikely to infiltrate an already over-burdened policy agenda. Lastly, the general international climate throughout the Trudeau period tended to counsel against drawing too close to Latin America, especially from a multilateral standpoint. In fact, the energy crisis of the 1970s actually encouraged the establishment of stronger Canadian bilateral relations with such countries as Mexico and Venezuela.[87] Put simply, domestic and international pressures, when taken together, seemed to work against the possibility of the Trudeau government opting for membership in the OAS.

When domestic sources of Canadian foreign policy are taken together, a similar conclusion suggests itself. First, there was no real constituency—within the country or without—pushing for full Canadian membership in the OAS. The move to acquire permanent observer status seemed to satisfy just about everyone, including many of Canada's friends in Latin America. Secondly, in acquiring observer status, the government incurred no negative side-effects or retaliation from countries in the region. In fact, Canada was able to establish friendly bilateral relations with a number of Latin American countries and show a steady, if unspectacular, growth in terms of trade. Lastly, there was no compelling set of reasons why Canada should join the OAS, and no sense of how it would benefit from doing so.

Perhaps the single, most important "brake" on the membership issue was the political leadership in Canada. Neither Trudeau, nor his Cabinet, were prepared to move beyond observer status to full membership. Had the Prime Minister been willing to discard Canada's image as a hemispheric dilettante, the country would have entered into a full partnership with the Americas. But as long as he, and the Cabinet, remained lukewarm to the idea of admission, it was simply not going to come about.

By the end of the Trudeau years in 1984, the issue of OAS membership was, for all intents and purposes, a non-issue. With no pressure from Latin American governments forthcoming, and an apathetic Canadian public, the OAS file would once again be collecting dust. And with MacEachen as External Affairs Minister—a long-time opponent of membership—the issue was not only dropped, but indeed was effectively dead. In June 1983 MacEachen made this clear in more diplomatic terms, when he stated that "a decision to join the OAS would have to be based on a firm conclusion that it would have decisive advantages for our political relations with Latin American states and for the promotion of Canadian interests in the region."[88] His response very much typified the approach espoused throughout the Trudeau years—namely, that the benefits of remaining outside the OAS seemed to outweigh the costs of joining it. Once again, then, after much deliberation, Canada opted to maintain its traditional fence-sitting role in its relationship with the hemispheric body. A general accounting of the reasons underscoring this aloofness toward the OAS, as well as the various actors who provided them, is the focus of the next chapter.

V

OAS Membership: The Actors and the Debates

Dᴇʟɪʙᴇʀᴀᴛɪᴏɴꜱ ᴏɴ ᴛʜᴇ ɪꜱꜱᴜᴇ ᴏꜰ ᴍᴇᴍʙᴇʀꜱʜɪᴘ ɪɴ ᴛʜᴇ ᴏᴀꜱ ʜᴀᴠᴇ dominated Canadian-Latin American relations for decades. According to R. Craig Brown:

When Canadians have debated Canada's relations with the Latin American nations they have most often done so within the context of joining the Organization of American States, thereby assuming that that was the only way in which to pursue a more active policy in Latin America.[1]

Successive Canadian governments, as indicated in previous chapters, have frequently grappled with the question of joining the hemispheric body. Until recently, those same governments—almost invariably after some period of discussion and debate—have refrained from opting for full membership.

Notwithstanding the fact that it was difficult to predict or foresee with any certainty the possible implications of OAS membership for Canada, this did not prevent critics and supporters of membership from expressing their views. To be sure, proponents and opponents of admission—representing various segments of the Canadian political system—have engaged in a series of provocative debates. Each group has, in turn, sought to buttress its position with a bevy of arguments and likely "Canada-in-the-OAS" scenarios. Neither "camp," however, was successful in galvanizing public opinion in favour of, or against, joining.[2]

The purpose of this chapter, then, is to delineate the actors who have figured prominently in the Canada-OAS membership issue. In addition, it discusses the panoply of arguments both for and against admission—as articulated by these actors. Moreover, it examines the reasons why these same actors put forth their respective positions on the membership question. Finally, it concludes with a number of general observations about the debates themselves and the key issues which they brought to the fore.

CANADA'S POLITICAL LEADERSHIP AND THE ISSUE OF OAS MEMBERSHIP

By the early 1960s the question of membership in the oas was catapulted to the top of the Diefenbaker government's issue-agenda. As Ogelsby contends: "1961 was the heyday of Canadian enthusiasm for the OAS."[3] Senior government ministers, including the like of Howard Green, were favourably disposed toward Canadian admission to the hemispheric body. Newspapers in Canada, reporting on Diefenbaker's visit to Jamaica in early 1961, began to expound on the efficacy of joining the forum.[4] And the debate was fuelled even further by U.S. President Kennedy's ill-advised speech to the Canadian Parliament in May of that same year. Among other things, he opined:

I believe that all free members of the Organization of American States would be both heartened and strengthened by any increase in your hemispheric role. Your skills, your responses, your judicious perception at the council table—even when it differs from our own views—are all needed throughout the inter-American community.[5]

His comments, however well-intentioned, were not only disparaged by the Diefenbaker government, but were also interpreted as completely ignoring Canadian sensibilities.

Canadian interest in the membership issue was subsequently sparked by the heightened tension in U.S.-Cuban relations in the 1960s. In 1962 Castro's Cuba was unceremoniously suspended from the OAS, primarily at the urging of Washington.[6] At the same time, the hemispheric body employed punitive sanctions against Cuba, including the suspension of all diplomatic and trade relations with the tiny Caribbean country. Clearly, OAS member states—with the conspicuous absence of Mexico—stood firmly against the perceived onset and consolidation of so-called "communist influences" in the region. These actions, it is instructive to note, seemed to leave an indelible mark on Canadians in general and Ottawa decision-makers in particular. They recognized, in a pointed fashion, that Canada would—if it became a full-fledged member—be under tremendous pressure to adopt OAS positions which it might find objectionable.

Similarly, the 1965 crisis in the Dominican Republic created a flurry of Canadian interest in the activities of the OAS. Most of that interest, though, was negative in tone—doing little to improve the organization's poor image in Canada.[7] For many, it was merely another case of Washington using the hemispheric forum to legitimize what was clearly a unilateral U.S. foreign policy expedition. For others, it was a sharp reminder that Canada, when it came to the OAS, should proceed prudently and cautiously.

Throughout the 1960s, then, these—and undoubtedly other factors—served to foster debate in Canada over the membership issue. Canadians from various segments of the polity entered the fray, cogently expressing their positions on the question. Even actors from outside of the country weighed in with their views on the possibility of Canada filling the so-called "empty chair." Regardless of the group, it was an issue in which political actors felt strongly about, whether in favour or against admission. As a result, the two "camps"— in seeking to influence the political leadership in Canada—marshalled and proffered a welter of arguments to bolster their respective positions.

Nonetheless, in the 1960s, as in the 1970s and 1980s, there was a noticeable absence of any public consensus on the membership issue. As John W. Holmes noted: "There is, I would estimate, no popular majority either for joining or not joining."[8] For the most part, the Canadian public remained largely uninformed and disinterested not only in the membership question, but also in the OAS itself. Still, spirited discussion on the issue took place both within and without government circles in Canada.

The political leadership in Canada was, for all intents and purposes, opposed to the idea of membership.[9] John Diefenbaker, not one to espouse a continentalist view, was wary of involving Canada in a region and a hemispheric organization that did not figure prominently in Canada's foreign policy interests. And after Kennedy's ill-fated address to the House of Commons, Diefenbaker wrote in his memoirs: "I was not about to have Canada bullied into any course of action."[10] (Even as leader of the official opposition, he expressed concerns about the possibility of Canada, if it opted for membership, being used by the Latin American countries as merely a conduit for their dealings with the United States).[11] Donald Fleming, a senior minister in the Diefenbaker Cabinet, was more concerned about how OAS membership would affect Canada's development assistance programme. More specifically, he was worried about the possibility of Canadian membership's drawing away scarce funds from the Colombo Plan and other Commonwealth-related aid initiatives.[12]

It is less clear, though, precisely where Lester Pearson stood on the issue of OAS membership. It is probably safe to assume—since he made few references to the topic—that Pearson was unenthusiastic about the body.[13] Given his vast experience in matters of Canadian foreign policy, it is likely that he was uncomfortable with the potential negative ramifications that admission would have on Canada-U.S. relations. Stated differently, he may well have feared that Canada's voting in the OAS, particularly if it differed from Washington's view, would spill over and somehow sour or damage bilateral relations, which were considerably more important from Ottawa's vantage point. Conversely, Paul Martin, Pearson's External Affairs Minister, was on record as supporting membership. He believed that joining the hemispheric body was "part of the ultimate destiny of Canada as a country of the Western Hemisphere."[14] As a country of the Americas, to take Martin's point one step further, it was important for Canada to participate actively and responsibly in inter-American affairs.

In the late 1960s Pierre Trudeau was also supportive—at least conditionally—of Canada's joining the OAS. But he was uneasy about the prospect of Canada's having to subordinate any semblance of independent thinking on hemispheric matters to the whims of officialdom in Washington. Gérard Pelletier, a key figure among Trudeau's inner circle, was not in favour of full membership.[15] He tended to believe that it would be better for Canada to strengthen its relations with the region bilaterally, as opposed to multilaterally.

Throughout the 1960s, then, the weight of "official" opinion seemed to go against full membership. In the main, there were serious concerns about how membership might distort Canada's foreign aid programme, hurt Canada's Commonwealth linkages, and place Canada in the unenviable position of fighting Latin America's battles in Washington. There was also a sense that Canada's contribution to the region would be more effective if it stemmed from the establishment of solid bilateral relations with many of the countries in Latin America. Perhaps more important, there was a realization within the political leadership that membership in the OAS would only further complicate Canada's relations with the United States.

For most of the 1970s the political leadership in Canada seemed reluctant to embrace the idea of Canada as a full-fledged member of the OAS. Trudeau himself, while initially supportive, always seemed to be looking for reasons not to join. He had concerns about the apparent domination of the organization by the United States, the fact that Cuba was still outside the hemispheric family in 1976, and the unending sense that the OAS was constantly in a state of reviewing and reforming its structures and activities. Others in his Cabinet, such as Mitchell Sharp and Allan MacEachen, were simply unconvinced of the merits of joining the body. MacEachen, in particular, seemed to believe that the costs of membership—especially in terms of Canada-U.S. relations—clearly outweighed the perceived benefits. Sharp, for his part, was uneasy about Cuba's continued suspension from the body and the organization's tendency to divide the hemisphere between the United States and Latin America.[16] From his discussions with thoughtful and sophisticated Latin Americans, he felt that Canada could play a more constructive role in the region by remaining outside of the OAS.[17]

The return to power of Pierre Trudeau in 1980 was not accompanied by any resurgence—at least in governmental circles—of the membership question. With economic and constitutional matters dominating the Liberal government's political agenda, the question of joining the OAS was unlikely to penetrate Trudeau's list of priorities. Furthermore, domestic squabbles with the provinces—in conjunction with problems in the Canada-U.S. relationship (viz., the National Energy Program, acid rain, and the Foreign Investment Review Agency) effectively kept the issue, particularly from an official standpoint, in a virtual holding pattern. It was really not until the House of Commons sub-committee on Canada's relations with Latin America and the Caribbean began its hearings in the spring of 1981 that the issue was revived.

After sixteen months of listening to expert testimony, examining briefs from interest groups and associations, and travelling in Latin

America, the sub-committee produced a final report in late November 1982. To the surprise of many, the sub-committee—by a narrow margin—came out in favour of Canada seeking admission to the OAS. According to the report, "the Sub-committee recommends that Canada seek full membership in the Organization of American States and sign the Bogotá Charter. We would recommend that Canada not sign the Inter-American Treaty of Reciprocal Assistance until a full review of its security obligations and implications is completed by the government."[18] With this recommendation, once again the debate on the membership issue was renewed, if only briefly.

During most of the 1980s, though, the political leadership in Ottawa remained sceptical about the merits of joining the OAS. Trudeau was preoccupied with north-south issues and, by 1983, with arms control and disarmament questions.[19] Presumably, the 1982 Falklands/Malvinas conflict and the 1983 U.S. invasion of Grenada did little to endear the virtues of the hemispheric body to Trudeau. Many of the past arguments against membership began to look increasingly valid—namely, that the OAS was proving itself to be largely ineffectual, that it was desperately in need of reform, and that it was looking more and more like an appendage of the U.S. State Department. Cabinet leaders, such as Allan MacEachen, were still firmly against the idea of OAS membership.[20] While travelling in Colombia in 1984, he indicated that it was "not self-evident whether Canada could make a difference in the OAS or whether it would be in the interest of Canada itself."[21]

Throughout most of the remainder of the decade, the issue was essentially dormant.[22] In the first term of the Mulroney government, from 1984 to 1988, it remained so. Clearly, hemispheric affairs—let alone the question of OAS membership—were not a top priority for the Conservative government. Even DEA's 1985 green (or grey) paper, *Competitiveness and Security: Directions for Canada's International Relations,* devoted only a few scant lines to the OAS. For the most part, it merely repeated oft-heard bromides about the lengthy debate around the idea of Canadian membership in this organization. It concluded by asking: "Where do Canadians stand on this issue?"[23] Basically, Prime Minister Mulroney and his government seemed more preoccupied—at least from a foreign policy standpoint—with securing closer relations with the United States.[24] For this reason, greater hemispheric involvement—and the membership issue in particular—was unlikely to figure prominently in the government's external thinking.

OAS MEMBERSHIP: A SCEPTICAL BUREAUCRACY

Like the political leadership in Canada, from the early 1960s to the late 1980s the Department of External Affairs (DEA) was generally opposed to Canadian admission to the OAS, and for some of the same reasons.[25] Chief among them, during the 1960s, was the diffi- culties that membership would likely pose for Canada-U.S. relations. Mandarins in the department did not want to see any good will, diplomatic credit, or "privileged" status with the United States jeop- ardized by the positions Canada might have adopted in the OAS. For them, there were already enough areas of bilateral contention with- out needlessly complicating matters with the added dimension of inter-American affairs. It made little sense to DEA bureaucrats to risk sacrificing harmonious relations with its most important neighbour, especially in a forum which was of marginal foreign policy import for Canada.

Those from the "old school" tended to view the OAS in relation to the Commonwealth or to Western Europe. Since Canada was a member of the Commonwealth and NATO, so the argument went, it should focus its foreign policy energies on strengthening ties with these institutional structures. For them, Canada had more interests at stake in Europe than in Latin America. And they felt that mem- bership in the OAS could have the undesired effect of moving Canadian foreign policy in an "isolationist," or at least hemispheric, direction, which was contrary to Canada's long tradition of interna- tionalism and commitment to the Atlantic community.

It is worth noting here that there was no outright competition between the Latin Americanists and Europeanists in the depart- ment.[26] Indeed, those who were espousing closer relations with the inter-American community were not ostracized by other officials within the department or prevented from having their views reach the minister's office. The issue at stake was more a matter of Canadian foreign policy priorities and narrowly defined interests.[27] It was not, then, a case of External Affairs officials' not recommending membership in the OAS because the department was heavily oriented toward the European side of Canadian foreign policy. Still, for a variety of economic, political, security, and historical reasons, DEA concentrated its resources more on its European—as opposed to Latin American—contacts and linkages. Simply put, Latin America, unlike Western Europe, was not perceived as one of Canada's foreign policy priorities.[28]

In any event, officials in DEA were also opposed to admission for a variety of other reasons. Department bureaucrats, for instance, felt that the cost of membership, from annual dues to contributions to any voluntary funds, would be too high. They believed that scarce resources could be used more effectively in other areas of Canada's foreign relations. In addition, these same officials were concerned about the security implications that would follow from OAS membership. More specifically, they were worried about the obligations and commitments that the Rio Treaty would place on Canada.[29]

Furthermore, foreign policy officials were unimpressed with the voting structure of the OAS (in comparison with that of the UN), where two-thirds majority vote requires full compliance by all members.[30] They believed that Canada could find itself having to fall into line on issues where it differed strongly with other member states. Moreover, it could, particularly in the wake of the Dominican crisis in 1965, end up merely rubber-stamping U.S. foreign policy forays in the region. Simply put, it was not in Canada's interests to join an organization in which the voting process was vulnerable to U.S. pressure and where the institution itself appeared to be dominated by Washington.

Obviously, bureaucrats in External Affairs, like their political masters, were not favourably disposed toward the idea of membership. Interestingly, many of the arguments against joining that had held sway during the 1960s were still very popular among foreign policy officials in the 1970s. There were concerns about how membership would affect Canada-U.S. relations, about the actual functioning of the OAS itself, and the ever-present worry about the financial costs of admission. Even in the security domain, DEA officials were uneasy about the possible implications of Canada's having to ratify the Rio Treaty. According to the 1970 foreign policy review,

The potential obligation to apply political and economic sanctions against another country by virtue of an affirmative vote of two-thirds of the members is a difficult feature of the OAS from the Canadian point of view.[31]

There were, however, some new variations on this general theme of non-membership during the 1970s. For instance, officials expressed reservations about the impact that admission would have on Canada's aid programme for the region. In the words of the booklet on Latin America,

OAS membership might tend, at least initially, to restrict Canadian freedom of action in development assistance matters... and other OAS development assistance programmes could absorb most available resources for a period of many years.[32]

There was also a feeling that joining the OAS—and thus opting for the multilateral route—could lead to a deterioration in bilateral relations with the major countries in the region. Put another way, if Canada focused its energies and resources on the OAS, it would almost certainly result in the neglect of the bilateral side of Canadian-Latin American relations. This development, officials felt, would not be conducive to Canada's stated objective of drawing closer to the inter-American system. There was a sense, then, that Canada could best contribute to improving the region's well-being through cosy bilateral, as opposed to multilateral, relations.

During the early part of the 1980s officials in External Affairs were still basically against membership.[33] Like the political leadership in Canada, they were uneasy about the potential costs—and the paucity of practical benefits—of joining. While many of the arguments articulated in the past still held currency, there were a number of new points brought forward. For example, there was a general sense in the department that the very credibility of the hemispheric body was increasingly being brought into question.[34] Foreign policy mandarins saw the irrelevancy of the forum—despite attempts at reform and years of reviewing its activities—as a solid reason against joining. They also believed that OAS member states themselves, by conducting a large part of inter-American business outside of the organization, did not take the institution seriously. So with the reputation of the OAS in serious decline, particularly after the fallout from the Falklands/Malvinas war, officials felt that the timing for membership was clearly inauspicious.

There was also a sense in DEA that the OAS was becoming increasingly marginalized in inter-American affairs.[35] They could not help wondering why it would be in Canada's interests to join an organization that was, for the most part, virtually invisible or silent on the major issues facing the hemisphere.[36] On the question of foreign debt, economic development, and conflicts raging in Central America, the OAS was essentially relegated to the sidelines. In its place, countries in the region banded together—in one case forming Contadora and its successor, Esquipulas—to confront and, if possible, resolve many of the difficult issues facing them.[37] Thus, with the major Latin American countries seemingly abandoning the OAS in favour of regional and more focused initiatives (largely because of the cumbersome and ponderous nature of the hemispheric body), it made little sense for Canada suddenly to seek admission.

CANADA AND THE OAS: VIEWPOINTS FROM THE SIDELINES

Unlike the bureaucracy, Canadian MPs expressed little interest in the debate over OAS membership. During the early 1960s Lester Pearson, then-leader of the Liberal opposition and obviously intent on scoring some political points, urged the ruling Conservatives to seek membership in the hemispheric forum. He argued that admission would enable Canada to play a moderating role in discussions on ridding the hemisphere of the so-called "communist menace."[38] Paul Martin, opposition foreign affairs critic, felt that membership would better enable Canada to play a leading role in the hemisphere.[39] For the most part, though, Canadian parliamentarians contributed little to the debate over OAS membership.

The Canadian Parliament was generally quiet on the membership issue throughout the 1980s, although some parliamentarians did make their views known. Senator Peter Stollery, in a letter to the *Globe and Mail*, objected to the argument that Canada should not join the OAS for fear of upsetting the Latins or Washington. According to Stollery, the same argument "could be used to oppose Canada's membership both in the United Nations and NATO. I simply do not understand these obscure and dated arguments against what should be full Canadian participation in the affairs of our hemisphere."[40]

Writing in 1984, Maurice Dupras, a Liberal Member of Parliament and former Chair of the sub-committee on Latin America and the Caribbean, argued that "the potential benefits of full Canadian membership now far outweigh the drawbacks."[41] He argued that Canada had much to offer the OAS, and not just by adding its voice to hemispheric concerns or engaging in creative diplomacy. For instance, Canada could, by seeking admission, work to strengthen the OAS in the area of human rights. Through its membership on the Inter-American Commission on Human Rights (IACHR), Canada "would give the Commission added vitality, would increase its visibility, and would improve its overall effectiveness."[42]

He went on to suggest that Canada should alter its preference for aloofness from the OAS, replacing it with full membership. It was a mystery to Dupras why Canada should not be involved directly in those issues that affected Canadians. He also pointed to the example of Canada's relations with Cuba as proof that Ottawa had little to risk in opting for admission. As he observed:

If the open and cordial relationship Canada enjoys with the United States has been able to withstand such a profound irritant as trade and diplomacy with Cuba, then relations between Ottawa and Washington are unlikely to be seriously affected as a result of differing points of view over issues raised within the context of the OAS.[43]

Like the Canadian Parliament, the business lobby in Canada, was not particularly interested—during much of the 1960s and 1970s—in seeking out commercial opportunities in Latin America. Whether for reasons of a cultural, political, or geographical nature, it was unenthusiastic about the potential for expanding trade and investment links with the region. While there are few if any references to what precisely the business community's position was on admission to the OAS, it would be fair to say that it was largely indifferent throughout the 1960s and 1970s. Generally speaking, it was cautious about the idea of Canada joining the OAS—feeling somewhat sceptical about deriving any possible trade advantages.[44] (This scepticism may, in part, be a function of the region's minor trade importance to Canada and the business community's preference for focusing its attention and resources on the United States.)

In general, the business community in Canada—which was represented primarily by the Canadian Chamber of Commerce and the Canadian Association for Latin America (CALA)—played a peripheral role. Although CALA was on record as supporting admission in the early part of the 1980s, it was not prepared to lobby the government in a vigorous fashion. By the mid- to late 1980s, however, the business community had rarely if ever raised the issue with the government of the day.[45] Interestingly, there is some evidence that a few Canadian multinationals—with operations in Latin America—were less than enthusiastic about OAS membership. They were concerned mainly with the possibility that the OAS might alter the Charter language on "collective economic security" so as to encourage wide-scale nationalization as a means of redistributing wealth among the poor.[46] Some businesses were also concerned that Canadian involvement in inter-American affairs might lead to officialdom in Ottawa scrutinizing the actions and operations of Canadian businesses in the region.[47]

As for outside forces, Kenneth McNaught touched upon the role of foreign entities in the membership debate throughout the 1960s. The United States, he argued, wanted Canada to join and thus be in a position to carry Washington's message to Latin America. Of course, the United States—since about the mid-1940s—has viewed positively the prospect of having Canada, a wealthy middle power and staunch ally, on its side of the OAS Council table. Other Latin American countries expressed a similar desire, albeit for different reasons. Many of them tended to think that Canada's membership would bring "a new element of understanding" and a healing brand of pragmatism and political maturity.[48] According to John Sokol, who reported on Latin American intentions, "they are not principally after our dollars."[49] Instead, they saw great opportunities for Canada to share with the Hispanic world its industrial development experiences, technical assistance, advanced technologies, and agricultural expertise. In short, they wanted Canada in the OAS for all the reasons for which Canadians are noted—namely, fairness and compassion, pragmatism and moderation, and economic progress and technological development.

The print media in Canada, however, tended to be more divided over the membership issue. Newspapers such as the *Edmonton Journal, La Presse,* and the *Globe and Mail,* to name only a few, opposed membership throughout the 1960s.[50] In a March 1960 editorial, the *Globe and Mail* was concerned about the possibility of Canada's international reputation being needlessly tarnished by its involvement in resolving hemispheric disputes. It went on to state: "These conflicts are of little direct concern to Canada and it is hard to see why we should make enemies gratuitously by taking part in them."[51] Editorial writers were also worried about the negative repercussions that Canada would have to contend with if it sided with the Latins against the United States. According to the editorial, "we would risk a dangerous quarrel with a powerful neighbor over issues remote from our own vital interests."[52]

In a May 1963 editorial, the *Globe and Mail* once again expressed its opposition to the notion of OAS membership. This time, it saw admission to the body as little more than Canada subordinating itself to Washington's desire to find someone else "to help pay the bills." Furthermore, it contended that Canada could play a more constructive role in resolving the "Cuba question" from outside the hemispheric forum. According to the editorial, "it would be the better part of statesmanship to keep ourselves free of disqualifying entanglements in the OAS."[53]

Conversely, the *Winnipeg Free Press,* the *Montreal Star,* and the *Ottawa Journal,* among others, all came out in favour of Canada joining the hemispheric forum. In some respects, an editorial in the *Calgary-Albertan* reflected the arguments of those editorialists across the country in favour of membership in the OAS. The editorial pointed out that Canada, by staying outside of the framework of the organization—and thus not participating fully in hemispheric affairs—was in effect "shirking" its responsibilities. It went on to state that Canada could jeopardize its good reputation in Latin America if it continued "to play such an unconstructive part in the affairs of the region."[54] In short, the editorial seemed to support the notion that admission to the OAS would enable Canada to play a leadership role in the Americas.

Newsmagazines in Canada, particularly *Maclean's,* tended to be cool toward the membership issue.[55] Ian Sclanders' June 1963 article against Canadian membership contained a number of interesting points. Indeed, he advocated non-membership because of "the utter mess Latin America is in and the selfish refusal of Latin America's ruling classes to lift a hand on behalf of their own countries."[56] He went on to support his case by arguing that Canada, as a "have" country, would inevitably find itself pressured to make loans or other fiscal arrangements available to impoverished Latin American countries. According to Sclanders, "Canada would have difficulty both in resisting appeals for assistance from the Latins and in resisting U.S. hints that Canada's taxpayers should be helping the U.S. help Latin America."[57] For him, membership would be totally counterproductive, since it would likely lead to a reduction in Canada's prestige and political effectiveness in the region.

Newspaper coverage of the issue, perhaps reflecting the lack of governmental attention accorded the issue in the 1970s, was generally sparse.[58] Besides the occasional reference, there was nothing that even approached the editorial comment of the 1960s. Since the Trudeau government was not contemplating any change in Canada's status *vis-à-vis* the OAS, there was really no need to editorialize. However, the late Senator Eugene Forsey, an avid letter-writer, did weigh in with his contribution to the debate. Writing after Trudeau's visit to the region in 1976, he stated that OAS membership

would be the perfect way to lose friends and influence people the wrong way. The Americans would expect us to back them. The Latin Americans would expect us to line up against the United States. We should end by being thoroughly disliked and distrusted by both sides.[59]

Canadian newspapers in the early 1980s, particularly the major ones, were still opposed to membership.[60] A December 1982 *Globe and Mail* editorial, which referred to past arguments against membership such as U.S. dominance of the body and the lingering question of Cuba, suggested that Canada should remain "unentangled" in the OAS. As the editorial writers explained: "Are we really ready to wade into a part of the world that has often proclaimed its presence by denials of human rights, nasty dictatorships, assassinations, torture and disappearances by the thousands?"[61] Similarly, an editorial in the *Toronto Star* questioned the efficacy of joining a hemispheric forum that included among its ranks the likes of Chile and El Salvador (countries with atrocious human rights records) as well as a body that chose to side with Argentina—instead of Britain—during the Falklands/Malvinas crisis. It went on to state further that "the 28-member Organization of American States has proved ineffective in promoting peace and security in the region" and that "its political bias lies far to the right of the Canadian government's."[62]

The academic community, unlike the media in Canada, was generally divided over the efficacy of Canadian membership in the OAS.[63] During the 1960s those in favour of admission proffered a number of arguments and reasons to underscore their case. Similarly, those opposing membership were quick to put forth their rationale for remaining outside of the forum.

Those urging membership felt that it was the *sine qua non* for greater Canadian participation in hemispheric affairs. Put another way, if Canada hoped to play a larger role in the region—as it should—it would have to join the principal political institutional entity in the hemisphere.[64] For them, there was no surer sign of Canada's interest and commitment to the region than sitting at the OAS Council table with the other member countries. By participating fully in OAS deliberations, they argued, Canada would be better able to shape and influence developments in the region.

W. Arthur Irwin, a former Canadian diplomat in Latin America, argued that Canada could not avoid or escape these developments, regardless of how isolationist the government professed to be.[65] For him, it would be both prudent and in Canada's interests to participate fully—with voice and vote—in the hemispheric decision-making process. As Irwin explained: "I do not share the view that an ostrich policy is the policy best calculated to serve our interest."[66]

He argues that Canada—whether inside or outside of the OAS—has little choice but to confront the major issues confronting the hemisphere. It makes better sense, then, for Canada to partake in influencing the collective decision-making process in the hemisphere so as to deal with these issues and to shape the course of events in the region. "Surely it would be the better part of wisdom to seek to influence a developing situation," writes Irwin, "rather than to stand in isolation and await an outcome over which we have no share of control and on which we will have to make a policy decision in any event."[67]

In addition to arguing that Canada's interests are best served through active participation in the OAS's decision-making process, Irwin hinted at the fact that Canada—as a full-fledged member— would benefit from a security-related standpoint.[68] He went on to note: "We stand to gain enormously from collective measures to maintain political stability in the hemisphere."[69] By sitting at the council table, he argued, Canada would be informed of hemispheric security problems and, more important, would be able to discuss these matters frankly and openly. While Irwin himself did not make the point, it seems implicit in his thinking that Canada's security was inextricably linked to the security of the Latin American republics. And if Canada hoped to advance and protect its own security interests, it would be in a position to do so through the activities and structures of the OAS.

Irwin also noted that Canadian membership would enhance both the stature of the OAS and Canada's prestige in Latin America. With a new middle power among its ranks—carrying a reputation unsullied by imperialist intrusions into the region—the organization would undoubtedly be strengthened. According to Irwin, Canada's admission

would confirm its geographical logic and we would bring to it the economic weight and political experience of a country which despite its relatively small population qualifies as one of the most important in the Americas.[70]

As for Canada, its prestige would be augmented through increased dialogue and mutual understanding as well as expanded regional contacts on the political, diplomatic, economic, and cultural levels. Canada's standing in the region could not but improve, at least in Irwin's eyes, since its membership in the club would enable it "to deal with other members on a basis not available to outsiders."[71]

Moreover, Irwin challenged the argument that Canadian membership in the OAS would adversely affect Canada-U.S. relations. In fact, he seemed to believe that admission would serve to place Canada's relations with the United States on a better footing. By not joining, he added, Canada risked the possibility of irritating the White House and thereby souring the tone of Canada-U.S. relations. He cautioned,

There are already signs that our continued aloofness is being construed in Washington as refusal on our part to accept a share of hemispheric responsibilities appropriate to our position and status in the hemisphere.[72]

As a corollary to this point, Irwin attempted to debunk the so-called "ham-in-the-sandwich" argument. That is, that Canada would inevitably find itself backing the Latin American governments against Washington and thus risk the ire of the White House. But if this were true, he pointed out, "there would be no case for membership in the United Nations or NATO, not to mention numerous other groupings."[73] He suggested, moreover, that the U.S. government would respect—and indeed insist upon—the independent judgment of a staunch ally. For this reason, he insisted that Canada should not be deterred from acquiring membership out of fear of antagonizing the United States.

In fact, full membership for Irwin would help Canada to manage its relations with the United States. As a multilateral body, it could serve as a useful counterweight or equalizer against the preponderance of U.S. power. By working in concert with other like-minded Latin American countries, Canada could be better situated to shape or modify U.S. behaviour. Strength in numbers, along with skilled Canadian diplomats and the legal requirements of the OAS, could actually increase Canada's negotiating strength and thereby help it to protect its interests. According to Irwin, "we should apply such political skills as we may possess to making realistic use of whatever available forces may be utilized to advantage in our continuing struggle for national survival."[74]

Irving Brecher and Richard A. Brecher, exponents of membership, echoed some of Irwin's arguments. They argued, for instance, that Canada's obligations under the Rio Treaty would not tie its hands completely. To be sure, if Canada—like Mexico—wanted to skirt the issue of imposing sanctions, it could do so without any serious repercussions.[75] In addition, they suggested that Canada's traditional linkages with the Commonwealth should not automatically disqualify it from seeking admission to the OAS. They went on to state:

Membership in the Organization of American States has in no way prevented twenty American republics from being 'members in good standing' of the United Nations. Nor has Trinidad and Tobago been at all disposed to treat its recent entry into the OAS as a negation of membership in the Commonwealth.[76]

To Irwin's collection of arguments, the two McGill University professors added the possibility of Canada contributing in a positive fashion to OAS reform. In the wake of the Cuban and Dominican crises, they admitted that the machinery of the organization was less than ideal. But the most effective way to revitalize and strengthen its structures was for Ottawa to opt for full membership—not to remain on the outside looking in. As they accurately pointed out, "major improvement can come only from within and not from the casual observer with hardly a foot in the door."[77]

In his small booklet, *Canada and the Organization of American States,* John Harbron outlined both the pros and cons of admission. While he attempted to do so in a balanced fashion, his analysis tended to lean toward support for membership. By joining, he indicated that Canada would benefit from "increased exposure to Latin American culture, to personal contacts with Latin Americans, and to Latin American experience with economic development techniques and policies having relevance for Canada."[78] He also added to the debate the argument that membership would open up new trade opportunities with the various countries of Latin America. According to Harbron, a Canadian mission at the OAS "might well help to supply Canadian businessmen going to the Latin American market with some useful commercial information, especially since Latin American officials appointed to the OAS are typically drawn into temporary service from the small commercial classes found in most Latin American republics."[79]

Although the arguments in favour of membership were articulated in an intelligent fashion throughout the 1960s, a number of academics espoused the opposite view. David Edward Smith, for example, challenged many of the assumptions and arguments put forth by W. Arthur Irwin. By becoming a full-fledged member, Smith argued, Canada could find itself in a rather awkward position, and needlessly so. He pointed to both the Cuban and Dominican crises as potent reasons why Canada should continue to remain aloof from the hemispheric body. Indeed, if Canada had been a member at this time, it would have been obliged to consider "the adoption of trade embargoes, the breaking of diplomatic relations and the establishment of an inter-American police force."[80]

In addition, he directly refuted Irwin's contention that Canada—by joining the OAS—would register an increase in prestige in the region. For Smith, a country does not join an international organization in hopes of accumulating prestige or national respect. Rather, it does so because it has certain interests—security, social, political, and economic—which it intends to protect and advance.[81] More important, Canada's prestige or reputation in the region could actually dissipate or worsen through its membership in the forum. He noted that Latin America's good will toward Canada would quickly fade if it sided with the United States against the Latins on more than one occasion.[82] Clearly, on the Cuban and Dominican crises, Canada would have been compelled to take a stand in some form or another. As Smith observed: "The result could only have been a reduction in Canadian prestige either in Washington or the capitals of some of the more progressive members of the OAS."[83] So instead of membership fortifying Canada's reputation in the region, he argued that it could jeopardize any good will or diplomatic credit that Canada had in Latin America.

He also challenged Irwin's point that membership would offer Canada the best means of influencing events in the hemisphere. In contrast, Smith argued that Canada may be more effective in shaping developments in the area from outside the confines of the OAS. In other words, cultivating cosy, bilateral relations with countries in Latin America—as opposed to an enhanced multilateral commitment—was a more prudent course for Canada to chart. For him, Canada would still be in a strong position to share its expertise, technology, democratic experience, and development assistance with countries in the region. He summed up his argument by stating the following: "Past neglect of Latin America will not be remedied by joining the OAS; actually, membership may diminish the effectiveness of any new role Canada might want to play in this area."[84]

Harbron's reasoning, like that of Irwin's, did not escape Smith's line of argument. For instance, he took issue with the notion that Canada needed to join the OAS in order to secure increased benefits from the hemisphere. As Smith noted: "There is no evidence that Canada must become a partner in the inter-American system before she and the Latin American republics may enjoy the benefits of closer relations."[85] At the same time, he questioned whether enhanced trade and investment opportunities would flow from Canada's membership in the organization. Indeed, he pointed out that "the general assertion that members of the OAS enjoy trade advantages as a result of being members has not been statistically demonstrated."[86] He felt that Canada's occupation of the long-standing "empty chair" would bring with it few, if any, benefits of a commercial/trade nature.

R. Craig Brown, like Smith, took aim at those who favoured Canadian membership in the OAS.[87] First, he questioned the wisdom of joining an organization which essentially served to maintain U.S. hegemony in the region.[88] Was it really in Canada's best interests, he wondered, for it to be part of a body that sanctioned U.S. intervention in a member country like the Dominican Republic? Secondly, he was unconvinced that Canada could best confront the myriad problems of the hemisphere—including those of a social, political, economic, and security nature—through admission to the OAS. In fact, he believed that Canadian membership was not, in and of itself, going to reduce the seriousness of the problems or somehow precipitate a number of practical solutions and meaningful responses. Finally, he warned that the OAS "is an American solution to an American problem. It is not a Canadian solution to a Canadian problem."[89]

Historian Kenneth McNaught also situated himself firmly in the camp of those opposing membership. He was concerned about the possibility of membership undermining any hopes of an independent Canadian policy toward the region.[90] He was worried that past instances of independent Canadian thinking—such as pushing for the expulsion of South Africa from the Commonwealth or Canada's refusal to endorse U.S. policy toward Cuba—would inevitably be diminished by admission to the OAS. According to McNaught, "joining OAS would tend very strongly to blur the Latin American impression of our independence of the United States."[91] In other words, Canada's *bona fide* reputation for independent-minded foreign policy actions, which sometimes differ from those of official Washington, could be compromised through accession to membership.

In addition, McNaught cautioned against membership precisely because the United States seemed to be encouraging such a move. He appeared to imply that a less-tainted Canada, if it became a full member, could be under tremendous pressure from the White House to become a mouthpiece for Washington in Latin America. By doing so, Canada would be placed in the unenviable position of working to purify "the picture of the United States in Latin America."[92] Put simply, McNaught feared the prospect of a Canada in the OAS being relegated to the role of a lackey, merely doing the "dirty work" for Washington throughout the Americas.

Not surprisingly, the academic community maintained a fairly consistent interest in the issue throughout the 1970s. Those opposed to membership drew upon many of the arguments used in the 1960s to support their case, such as the confusion and disarray that characterized the OAS and the fear of being used (especially in light of Canada's growing economic dependence on the United States) as little more than a stooge of the United States. Similarly, those in favour of membership reiterated a number of reasons that were popular in the 1960s to bolster their position, including potential economic gains and as a clear demonstration of Canada's commitment to Latin America. Both sides, though, were able to revamp—and in some cases add new twists to—their thinking on the subject.

Those in favour of non-membership pointed to the political situation in Latin America—where social injustice continued unabated, where despots still engaged in flagrant violations of basic human rights, and where unsavoury governments preferred corruption and exploitation to fairness and equality. As Dale C. Thompson and Roger F. Swanson explained: "By entering the OAS, [Canada] would also be accepting as associates some of the most flagrant dictatorships in the world."[93] David R. Murray, in a similar vein, argued that Canada has benefited more from remaining outside the formal structures of the OAS. He indicated that it has "been able to avoid all the cold war pressure imposed on Latin American members of the OAS by the United States to support American actions whether in Guatemala in the 1950s, or against Cuba and Santo Domingo in the 1960s and Chile in the 1970s."[94] In short, those opposing admission were more convinced that Canada could participate effectively in hemispheric affairs without the constraints of membership.

Proponents of membership, however, seemed to believe that the conditions in the 1970s were ripe for joining. With reforms of the OAS Charter coming into force in the early 1970s—particularly in those areas of an economic and social nature—the organization was thought to be better equipped to confront the many challenges of the hemisphere. It was important for Canada to join in order to register its full support for these and future changes. James J. Guy appeared to be suggesting that it was finally time for Canada to "consolidate" its linkages with Latin America by joining the OAS.[95]

John Harbron, among others, was under the impression that the Canada-U.S. relationship had matured to the point that it could withstand any tensions arising out of Canada's membership in the OAS. In fact, he went on to note: "This view has lost a good deal of its validity, not only because Canadian-American relations have entered rough waters without any intrusion of hemispheric differences but because Canada, under the OAS Charter, like other member states, could abstain from decisions on crises in other member states."[96] J.C.M. Ogelsby also discounted the argument that Canada's relations with the United States would suffer as a result of OAS membership. On at least two occasions, he argued, Canada took positions in the Inter-American Development Bank (IDB) that were completely at variance with those holding sway in the White House. In the case of Chile in 1973, the Canadian representative criticized the idea of using the IDB "as a lever and a whip to punish recipient countries involved in 'bilateral' disputes over expropriation and compensation."[97] And it is instructive to note that although Canada chose to differ with Washington in this case, there was no sign of any U.S. retaliation or that it strained the Canada-U.S. relationship.

As was the case in the 1960s and 1970s, the academic community continued to exhibit an intellectual interest in the question.

True to form, it still remained divided on the issue of membership. Not surprisingly, many of the arguments used by opponents and proponents in the earlier period were dusted off and repackaged. And with few academics focusing their research on the topic in the 1980s, even fewer new approaches to the matter were being developed.

Donat Pharand, however, took issue with many of the arguments espoused by those who opposed membership. He challenged the notion that opting for full membership would somehow compromise Canada's position as an independent actor in world politics. For him, joining the OAS, and working in concert with other like-minded Latin American countries, would actually enhance Canadian sovereignty and independence. As Pharand explained, "This would inevitably result in Canada developing a leading role, not only in the Organization itself, but in world affairs generally."[98]

At the same time, he dismissed the oft-heard view that Canada's membership in the OAS would inevitably disrupt Canada-U.S. relations. Not only did he argue that the Canada-U.S. relationship was strong enough to withstand differences of opinion on inter-American matters, but he also suggested that Washington would not be interested in using Canada as an "interpreter" or interlocutor in its dealings with Latin America. To buttress his point, he noted that

A review of the similarities and differences in the Canadian and U.S. objectives in the Latin American and Caribbean regions has demonstrated that the similarities were considerable indeed and the differences were basically a matter of emphasis and approach.[99]

In addition to discounting the so-called "U.S. problem," he refuted the argument that the OAS was little more than an ineffective "talk shop," hopelessly unable to confront pressing hemispheric problems. He pointed out that "it has to be admitted that criticisms of ineffectiveness focus more on cases where the OAS did not take any action rather than those where it did, even with a certain degree of success."[100] He rightly noted that the OAS had some early successes in the area of dispute settlement and conflict resolution. Additionally, he argued that the organization possessed the potential to do some excellent work in the areas of development and human rights.

Indeed, he referred, with some justification, to the solid work of the Inter-American Commission on Human Rights. In short, he believed that there was nothing drastically wrong with the OAS *per se,* maintaining that the difficulties were a function of the membership itself.

One of the reasons that Pharand cited for joining was the fact that, for a number of years, several member states encouraged Canada to do so.[101] These states, according to Pharand, firmly believed that Canada's participation would add considerably to the health of the OAS. He referred to the fact that

Canada is considered to be an integral part of the hemisphere, a dependable and stable country, and it is genuinely believed that it would make an appreciable contribution toward the improvement of the functioning of the Organization.[102]

And he warned that Canada's continued aloofness from the body could not only foster frustration and resentment in Latin America, but it could also lead to a sharp drop in Canada's influence in the region.

Robert Jackson, in a similar vein, suggested that "the arguments for joining have become stronger."[103] Like Pharand, he believed that the "symbolic" benefits of joining would further bolster Canada's already sizeable reservoir of diplomatic good will. This, in turn, could be important in terms of cultivating better relations with individual Latin American countries. If nothing else, joining would certainly signal the importance that Canada attached to relations with the Americas. He also indicated that the notion of the OAS as a ministry of the U.S. State Department no longer applied to the extent that it once did. "Much of the stigma of U.S. domination that used to color Canada's view of the organization," writes Jackson, "has abated as countries such as Mexico and Venezuela have become stronger."[104] These countries, he stated, were no longer afraid to mount vigorous opposition or to go against proposals which they felt were not in their best interests. In this context, he felt that Canada should not be deterred from membership by old-style thinking.

Those opposed to membership, for their part, reintroduced many of the arguments used by their colleagues in the 1960s and 1970s.[105] Reservations about the impact that joining would have on Canada's aid budget, the effectiveness of the hemispheric body, and the possibility of getting caught between the United States and Latin American countries were all put forth. David R. Murray, however, suggested that the most pressing issues in the hemisphere—namely, trade, development, and human rights—tended to lend themselves to bilateral solutions.[106] For this reason, it would be better for Canada, he argued, to deal with these issues bilaterally rather than through membership in the OAS.

Edgar J. Dosman also put forth his case against membership in the OAS.[107] Like Murray, he felt that Canada could best achieve its objectives in the region, especially those of an economic nature, through strong bilateral ties with countries such as Brazil, Venezuela, and Mexico. He also questioned the wisdom of joining a forum that was likely unreformable and certainly at the margin of inter-American political life. For him, the OAS had proven itself to be sin-gularly ineffective in the area of hemispheric peace and security, as the conflicts in Central America could attest. He suggested that per-haps the UN would be better suited to deal with the hemispheric issues of conflict resolution and development. Lastly, he noted that Canada, instead of allocating funds to the cost of admission, could use those resources more effectively. He suggested that the money would be better spent on "new political offices in the region or improved analytical capabilities in Ottawa."[108] The bottom line for Dosman was the fact that it was not necessary for Canada to join the OAS in order for it to strengthen its ties with the region.

SUMMARY

For most of the period in question, the debate over the membership issue was waged largely—though not exclusively—within academic circles. At various times, the question of joining the OAS received serious consideration at the political level in Canada. From a bureau-cratic standpoint, the question was monitored on a regular basis and reviewed, on occasion, in an in-depth fashion. Almost invariably, the response from the bureaucracy and the Cabinet was the same—namely, the time for joining the OAS had not yet arrived. While the book on the OAS was not completely closed, it was placed high on the shelf. Or, as one interested observer has noted: the issue of Canadian membership in the OAS—especially during the early 1980s—was placed in "semi-permanent sleep."[109]

Still, by examining the various arguments and reasons proffered by both proponents and opponents of OAS membership, one gets a good sense of the complexity of the issue. Clearly, it is not a question that lends itself to simple analysis and clear-cut answers. As the discussion in the preceding pages illustrates, many actors, forces, and opinions were in play. Perhaps the multiplicity of variables goes some way toward explaining why Canadian governments have, over the years, appeared so indecisive or uncertain about the issue.

What is certain is that although the actors changed, the roles of participants in the membership debates remained the same. Generally speaking, the political leadership, the bureaucracy, Parliament, the academic community, the media, and foreign governments—in some form or another—shaped the debate throughout the 1960s, 1970s, and 1980s. What is equally noticeable over the course of these years is the extent to which the political leadership (including the Cabinet) and the foreign policy-making bureaucracy in Canada remained key players in the discussion, although the individuals changed. Of course, if both the political leadership and the bureaucracy had been strongly in favour of admission, the debate would have ended in the early 1960s. As it was, the two groups, for a variety of reasons, were unconvinced of the merits of joining the hemispheric body. The resulting lack of political will made it highly unlikely that any affirmative decision on the membership issue would be forthcoming.

Just as the main players have remained relatively consistent over the years, so, too, have the principal reasons for and against joining the OAS. Those espousing membership tended to buttress their position by arguing the following: that admission was part of Canada's responsibilities as a hemispheric actor, that it would strengthen Canada's ties and influence in Latin America, that it should have a seat at the table in order to participate fully in the issues confronting the hemisphere, and that it would enable Canada to advance and protect its inter-American interests. Conversely, those opposing membership always seemed to come back to the same arguments— namely, that it would have a negative impact on Canada-U.S. relations, that the OAS was constantly in a state of disarray and paralysis, and that Canada could solidify its relations, and achieve its objectives, through stronger bilateral, as opposed to multilateral, contacts.

Throughout these years, each camp would repeat, with minor adjust-
ments, these same themes and arguments to underscore their respective positions.

But it is not simply the staying power of these arguments
throughout the decades that is striking. What is just as interesting is
the fact that while the domestic and international environments
changed considerably, analysis and debate on the membership issue
remained largely the same. The result was a noticeable tendency on
the part of both proponents and opponents to strengthen, or to justify, their arguments by drawing upon the changing nature of these
environments. For instance, proponents of admission would point
to the growing strength of the Latin American republics or the
maturity of Canada itself and the resiliency of the Canada-U.S. relationship to counter the other side's arguments. Similarly, opponents
of joining would almost invariably note disparagingly the crises in
Cuba, the Dominican Republic, or Chile to underpin their arguments against membership. In other words, both sides—rather than
adjusting their thinking and arguments to reflect the changes in the
domestic and external environments—simply incorporated them
into their pre-conceived positions. As a result, much of the analysis
was characterized less by critical and evolving thinking and more by
complacency and sterility.

In any event, neither the reasons for, nor those against, membership were particularly convincing. It is difficult to understand
why Canada should refrain from joining the principal hemispheric
institution for financial reasons, reservations about reforming the
body, or out of fear of antagonizing officialdom in Washington. At
the same time, it seems somewhat strange to seek membership in the
OAS on the basis of Canada's being "a nation of the Americas," of
joining as a prerequisite for stronger relations with Latin America, or
because Canada would deal better with the multitude of serious
problems facing the hemisphere. Clearly, many of the arguments
articulated by both sides in the debate were weak, unsubstantiated,
and—in many cases—not sufficiently thought out.

In some ways, then, the debate throughout the 1960s, 1970s, and
1980s has missed the mark. Both sides failed to develop their arguments from a single, key question—specifically, what are Canada's

principal policy objectives in the hemisphere? Only after this question has been answered and clarified should a discussion about the actual means for achieving those aims have taken place. In other words, the debate should not have revolved solely around the reasons for or against membership in the OAS. Rather, it should have focused on the most appropriate and effective means of enabling Canada to advance its interests and to secure its hemispheric policy objectives. Simply put, the central issue should not have been about joining or not joining *per se,* but whether Canada could best achieve its policy goals in Latin America with or without the OAS.

VI

Canada Joins the OAS

ALTHOUGH PAST GOVERNMENT STATEMENTS ON OAS MEMBERSHIP were often preceded by a period of public discussion and input, this was not to hold true in the final months of 1989.[1] Unlike previous Canadian governments, which would periodically express their views on the membership question, the Conservative government of Brian Mulroney had not clarified very precisely where it stood on the issue. Hence, when word that his government was on the verge of opting for full membership in the hemispheric forum reached the public domain in late August 1989, it came as a startling development to many.[2]

The Prime Minister's admittedly opaque reference to OAS membership amounted to a "bolt out of the blue," leaving seasoned pundits and area specialists in a state of disbelief.[3] Furthermore, no serious debate on the question had occurred in the months leading up to the announcement—contrasting sharply with past occasions of informed debate and analysis—within Parliament, the academic community, the media, NGOs, and the public in general. Lastly, word that Canada was contemplating joining the organization was broached in Kennebunkport, Maine, where the Prime Minister was vacationing with U.S. President George Bush. This fact alone served to create the public perception that the Prime Minister was merely kowtowing to the wishes of President Bush.[4]

Once the initial period of wonderment subsided, however, a token debate ensued in the Canadian print media. Not surprisingly, the discussion echoed past treatment of the issue—namely, a detailing of the pros and cons of full membership.[5] This time, though, the press engaged in discussion about the "mystery" of where the idea to join the organization had originated. One political commentator suggested that the initiative was first hatched in the Prime Minister's Office (PMO).[6] Others have argued that it could have been little more than an arbitrary decision on the part of the Prime Minister himself, who was apparently quite impressed with the ornate splendour of the OAS building in Washington.[7] All this has led Brian J.R. Stevenson to contend that the notion of Canada joining the OAS, at least on the surface, "occurred with little reason or necessity."[8]

This chapter attempts to solve this puzzle by shedding some much-needed light on the dynamics surrounding Canada's decision to join the OAS.[9] It outlines the various reasons or factors that account for the federal government's opting for full membership. In doing so, it also reveals the principal actors involved in the OAS membership decision. It concludes with some general observations about the decision-making process itself.

Although the Mulroney government's decision to join the OAS did not signify a "fundamental" shift in foreign policy, it did represent a notable departure from the course of past Canadian governments.[10] As the Prime Minister himself said at the San José hemispheric summit in October 1989: "Canada's presence here today signals a new departure in our relations with Latin America."[11] Indeed, successive Canadian governments have for decades been reluctant to join the organization as a full member. Even the Trudeau government's cautious move in 1972 to institutionalize permanent observer status was basically a variation on Canada's tradition of remaining aloof from the body.

Acknowledging this departure from past Canadian governments, however, says little about why the Mulroney government opted for membership in late 1989.[12] By employing a probing framework of analysis, the purported mystery surrounding the actual decision to join can be unravelled. With the help of key sources or "change-agents" (i.e., the political leadership, the bureaucracy, and external developments) of foreign policy, the decision to join can be better understood and explained.

It is worth noting that the decision to seek admission to the OAS amounts to more of a subtle change in the conduct of Canadian foreign policy. Stated differently, joining the hemispheric forum represented less of a fundamental reorientation or shift in policy and more of a new or different "means" for dealing with inter-American affairs or for implementing Canada's policy toward the region as a whole. It signified a new instrument of statecraft, through which

Canada's relations with the Commonwealth Caribbean and Latin America could be solidified and enhanced. Simply put, it entailed changes in "what" will be done and "how" relations with the hemisphere will be conducted, while leaving the principal goals of the Canadian government—such as regional stability, democratic development, and economic prosperity—largely intact.

THE POLITICAL LEADERSHIP

Political elites in Ottawa were very much a factor in the changing nature of Canada-OAS relations. Clearly, Prime Minister Mulroney, and his then-Secretary of State for External Affairs (SSEA) Joe Clark, played a crucial role in the decision to seek full membership.[13] According to Clark, after the return to power of the Conservatives in 1988 "the Prime Minister and I began to consider areas in which it would be sensible for Canada to take new initiatives."[14] Evidently, one of those areas was Latin America, which Canadian governments have traditionally viewed as a low priority region.[15] Both men, then, appeared to be willing to consider new departures in Canadian foreign policy, including the broadening of linkages with the wider hemisphere.

Obviously, the Prime Minister was a central figure in the decision to seek admission. According to Stevenson, "it appeared as though the decision to join came from the clear blue sky and was perhaps simply an arbitrary decision made by the Prime Minister himself."[16] Certainly, Prime Minister Mulroney played a leading role in setting the major themes and direction of Canadian foreign policy during his tenure.[17] For instance, when the United States invaded Panama in December of 1989, Mulroney articulated the Canadian government's position before officials in the Department of External Affairs had an opportunity to brief him. In addition, during the Persian Gulf crisis, he preferred to make key foreign policy decisions largely by himself, with the help of a handful of key ministers and advisers.[18] It is inconceivable, then, that Mulroney—always anxious to appear decisive—would not have played a pivotal part in the decision to join the OAS.

The accession to membership can also be viewed in conjunction with the Prime Minister's penchant for establishing closer, "super" relations with the United States. Put another way, the decision to seek admission could be seen as an outgrowth of Mulroney's desire to cultivate closer bilateral relations with our superpower neighbour to the south. Or, more specifically, it may be described as a natural progression or product of his continentalist vision, consistent with his government's negotiation of the 1988 Canada-U.S. Free Trade Agreement (FTA).[19] In this context, the decision to join can be viewed more in terms of Canada-U.S. relations rather than Canadian-Latin American relations.

In any event, the Prime Minister's remarks to the San José summit helped to shed some light on why he felt "the time has come for Canada to occupy the vacant chair at the OAS that has been reserved for us all these years."[20] There seemed to be a realization on the part of the Prime Minister that Canada had interests in the hemisphere that needed to be protected and promoted.[21] The onset of "interdependence," he argued, has left Canada with little choice but to confront the major issues—which impact directly upon Canadian interests—facing the hemisphere. As he indicated: "Interdependence is making us all partners in each other's burdens, participants in each other's prosperity, and architects of each other's dreams."[22] Stated differently, Canada could no longer avoid the "tentacle-like" implications of such major hemispheric issues as environmental destruction, drug-trafficking, foreign debt, and population movements. For the Prime Minister, the best means of dealing with these serious problems—which would inevitably require concerted hemispheric co-operation—was through the existing structures and procedures of the OAS. In his words: "It can unify us in the pursuit of solutions to these problems that we have in common."[23]

The then External Affairs Minister Joe Clark, like the Prime Minister, was keen on seeing a greater role for Canada in Latin America.[24] He was, according to some DEA officials, receptive to Latin American points of view as well as cognizant of Canadian interests in the region.[25] He was in agreement with those who argued that those interests have to take into account the fact that the world is becoming increasingly "regional" in nature. More specifically, that it is being divided into three major blocs or trade areas: Europe, the Pacific, and the Americas.[26] And if Canada did not want to be left passive on the sidelines, watching the process of global restructuring unfold, it would have to strengthen its ties with the hemisphere.

Clearly, one way of solidifying and consolidating these linkages was for Canada to join the OAS. This move was not only in line with Clark's desire for closer relations with Latin American countries, but it was also consistent with his vision of a "new internationalism" or "constructive internationalism" for Canada.[27] That internationalism, at least in Clark's eyes, should echo past experiences of "middlepowermanship"—namely, seeking Canadian involvement in multilateral institutions.[28] Emulating past exponents of liberal internationalism, he subscribed to the view that Canada is "a country whose skills and independence have helped breathe life into multilateral organizations."[29] Clearly, Clark believed that Canada—as a full-fledged member of the OAS—could make a positive contribution to the forum, employing its diplomatic expertise and its unique brand of pragmatism in hopes of minimizing confrontation within the forum.

Through this judicious use of its diplomatic skills, Clark also believed that Canadian officials could work to revitalize and strengthen the body. Clark was likely of the mind that these officials would be better situated to influence the OAS reform process from the inside rather than from a semi-detached position. While he admitted in his Calgary speech that the OAS could not by itself solve all the problems of the hemisphere, he pointed out that it could be transformed into a forum where meaningful political dialogue can take place.[30] And as he indicated in his testimony before the Standing Committee on External Affairs and International Trade (SCEAIT): "We are there because we can probably help the organization work more effectively and contribute to the general achievement of goals in the region."[31]

Clark's testimony before SCEAIT was instructive because it provided some insight into his thinking on the membership decision. He believed that joining the OAS was an effective means of symbolizing Canada's commitment to expand its ties with the region—especially from an economic standpoint. As he stated before the committee: "The long-term potential for trade with Latin America is tremendous."[32] He obviously felt that membership would position Canada to take advantage of future trade and investment opportunities in the region. This point was further reinforced when he later noted: "We think the fact of joining the OAS creates a sense of being part of the family in Latin America. We think it can lead to more constructive, durable trade links."[33]

This rhetoric about Canada's needing to feel a part of the hemispheric community also helps to explain why Clark felt that the time was ripe for joining.[34] These rhetorical flights reached a crescendo when Clark, speaking before the Permanent Council of the OAS, opined: "For too long, Canadians have seen this hemisphere as our house; it is now time to make it our home."[35] Behind the platitudes, Clark believed that the time had come for Canada, as a country of the Americas, to assume its hemispheric obligations and responsibilities.[36] In other words, he felt that Canada was duty-bound to confront—in partnership with other countries of the Americas—the myriad problems facing the Americas.

Many of these problems—such as good governance, debt, drugs, the environment, and development—have implications for Canada. Full membership in the OAS, according to Clark, would give Canada the opportunity to engage with both voice and vote on those issues which affected Canadian interests. As Clark explained,

We have a responsibility to be at the table when issues of importance to us are discussed, and we have an obligation to speak out when our interests are threatened or our values are under attack.[37]

Through admission into the OAS, then, he felt that Canada would be better able to not only protect its interests, but also to shape the formulation and implementation of various responses to major hemispheric issues.

THE FOREIGN POLICY BUREAUCRACY

The foreign policy bureaucracy, like the political leadership in Canada, was also a major force behind the government's decision to seek membership. Senior officials from the Latin America and Caribbean bureau and the South America Relations desk, in particular, were involved heavily in influencing the government's thinking toward the OAS.[38] But this involvement, to be fully understood, needs to be seen in the context of a growing "official level" interest in Latin America in general.

To some extent, the crushing debt crisis—beginning with Mexico's inability to make its payments in August of 1982, compelled officials in Ottawa to take the region more seriously. But it was the ongoing conflicts in Central America that actually galvanized Ottawa officialdom, along with an active and vocal non-governmental community.[39] In point of fact, groups such as OXFAM, the Inter-Church Committee for Human Rights, the Taskforce on the Churches and Corporate Responsibility, and the Canada-Caribbean-Central America Policy Alternatives (CAPA) strongly urged the Mulroney government to become more active in resolving the continuing wars in both Nicaragua and El Salvador.

In response to this growing public awareness and interest in Central America—as reflected most starkly in the number of submissions on this topic to the government's special joint committee on Canada's international relations in 1985-86—Ottawa decided to appoint a Roving Ambassador to Latin America and offered technical assistance and advice on verification matters under the terms of the Central American Peace Plan.[40] Then SSEA Joe Clark, in the face of U.S. opposition, visited the region—including a meeting with the Nicaraguan Foreign Minister—in the fall of 1987. Significantly, this increase in governmental attention led to the establishment, perhaps for the first time, of a cadre of foreign policy officials tasked specifically to formulate, analyze, and recommend policy options for the region. In short, the Central American imbroglio had engendered both a domestic public constituency and a bureaucratic enclave focusing specifically on matters south of the U.S.-Mexican border. And it was this bureaucratic enclave—namely, senior DEA officials from the Latin America and Caribbean Branch—that actually urged the Mulroney government to undertake a full review of Canada's relations with Latin America in late 1988.[41]

After months of discussion, analysis, and consultation, DEA officials cobbled together a comprehensive policy framework for Canadian-Latin American relations. By mid-September 1989 the final touches were made on what became known as Canada's long-term political strategy for Latin America. It was not until early November, however, that more details of the political strategy were revealed. In his remarks to the SCEAIT, SSEA Clark delineated some of the aspects of Canada's newly-minted policy strategy. The key objective underpinning this strategy, he noted, was "the development of democracy and the pursuit of economic prosperity within the region."[42] He went on to list a number of initiatives that the government was contemplating pursuing in the coming months:

Canada will host the annual meeting of the Inter-American Development Bank next April in Montreal. The Joint Ministerial Committee with Mexico will meet in Canada in January. The Prime Minister will be visiting Mexico in the first half of 1990. Canada will participate actively in the Central American peace process, and we will increase our bilateral aid program in the region, as the committee knows, by $100 million as our contribution to the much-needed reconstruction of Central America. We will also mount trade missions to the region to identify export opportunities in areas of Canadian advantage.[43]

Once Minister Clark had articulated Canada's long-term political strategy for Latin America, the responsibility for communicating it fell to the foreign policy bureaucracy. Officials from the Latin America and Caribbean Branch were charged with the task of informing the public of the "nuts and bolts" of the new policy framework. Ambassador Richard Gorham, a key proponent of the internal policy review (and, incidentally, still wearing the hat of Canada's permanent observer to the OAS during the review process) and the resulting political strategy, travelled the country lecturing at various universities and giving speeches to a host of interested associations and groups. According to Gorham, the elements of Canada's long-term strategy were fourfold: 1) full membership in the Organization of American States; 2) increased diplomatic representation in Latin America; 3) active and regular dialogue at both the Ministerial and Heads of Government levels; and 4) closer linkages and cooperation with the region through trade missions as well as enhanced institutional, cultural, and academic exchanges.[44]

In his remarks to the Halifax Branch of the Canadian Institute of International Affairs (CIIA), Gorham noted that Canada's membership in the OAS was only one component—albeit a central one—in the government's new political strategy toward the Americas. In later discussions, though, he hinted that OAS membership was the centrepiece of the strategy—and that the other elements were essentially constructed around the membership point. Still, he indicated that it was far more important to understand that Canada's relations with Latin America

required that we develop and maintain a more focussed and consistent long-term strategy and approach toward the area which accords it a higher priority than heretofore and recognizes that Canada is a nation of the Americas, not only in the geographic sense but politically, economically, culturally, and socially as well.[45]

Hence, it was only after the internal review, and the crafting of Canada's policy framework for Latin America in 1989, that officials recommended to the government that it should seek full membership in the hemispheric forum.[46] Clearly, the significance and import of this recommendation should not be overlooked or underestimated. Although the bureaucracy believed that the costs of membership outweighed the benefits in 1983, it had completely reversed its position by 1989.[47] There was a sense among a small clutch of officials, who were for many years opposed to the idea of membership, that it was time for Canada to accept a larger role within the inter-American community. According to one senior official, they came to the conclusion that "Canada is a nation of the Americas not only geographically but politically, economically and culturally."[48] And if one is to accept this premise, they felt, then it was only logical that Canada should join the OAS.[49]

Full membership in the hemispheric forum was also consistent with the view, espoused by senior foreign policy bureaucrats, that the dynamics of inter-American affairs had changed considerably. For example, they believed that the role or influence of the United States in the hemisphere, particularly in hegemonic terms, had noticeably declined. In fact, they felt that Washington, after the Falklands/ Malvinas war, the U.S. invasion of Grenada, and its support for the contra rebels in Nicaragua,[50] had become increasingly isolated from the inter-American community. As one senior official remarked: "The United States no longer plays such a dominant role in the OAS or in the hemisphere."[51]

In addition to this realization, these same officials acknowledged that Latin American political and economic life had taken on a new look.[52] They were especially cognizant of the growing role that Latin America was certain to play in international affairs (e.g. global trade talks, environmental concerns, and economic development questions). At the same time, they noticed that a number of Latin American countries were exhibiting clear signs of support for regional co-operation and consultation, particularly on issues such as debt, drug-trafficking, trade, and the environment.[53] These countries, led mainly by the Rio Group, also began to look more toward the OAS as the appropriate institutional framework within which to confront pressing hemispheric issues and to pursue their policy objectives. As a result, Latin American countries—especially after the ratification of the Protocol of Cartagena—began to take the organization more seriously.[54] All these factors, taken together, led foreign policy officials in Ottawa to conclude that the timing was propitious for Canadian membership.

In addition to these hemispheric considerations, DEA officials were convinced of the practical merits of seeking membership. They believed that joining the OAS would enhance Canada's relations with the Caribbean micro-states, which had advocated Canadian admission for a number of years. Not only would it send a positive indication of Canada's commitment to this area, but it would also open up new opportunities for Canadian-Caribbean interaction, co-operation, and understanding. Similarly, they felt that it would serve as a dramatic demonstration, particularly to Canada's Latin friends, of Canada's heightened awareness and interest in the region. Put another way, they were sure that membership would send out a strong signal that Canada's interests extended far beyond the U.S.-Mexican border.[55]

Furthermore, foreign policy mandarins recognized the importance of the OAS to the functioning of the inter-American system. A large part of this recognition was based on the fact that the major issues facing the region tended to transcend national borders and thus would invariably demand international or multi-nation co-operation.[56] And since the OAS was the principal political institution in the hemisphere—which brings together all (with the exception of Cuba) the members of the Americas to deal with these "international" questions—they felt that it was in Canada's interests to seek membership. They also believed that membership would enable Canada to play a larger role on those issues (e.g., the environment, human rights, debt, and emigration)[57] where its interests were at stake. In other words, having a seat at the OAS Council table would increase Ottawa's ability to shape those issues impacting directly upon Canada.[58]

Similarly, key foreign policy-makers believed that OAS membership would create a "window of opportunity" for Canada.[59] Or, more specifically, an opening through which Canada could secure increased economic and political benefits. They tended to work under the assumption that admission to the "club" was linked directly to improved trade relations between Canada and various Latin American countries.[60] In the words of one senior official, "For one thing, never again will Canadian businessmen be faced with the embarrassing question of why does Canada not become a member of the OAS."[61] Removing this stigma, then, was seen as a means of creating a better climate within which trade promotion and investment opportunities would be enhanced.

From a purely political standpoint, department officials were even more enthusiastic about OAS membership.[62] They were totally convinced that admission would enhance Canada's "influence" in Latin America. Stated differently, membership would place Canada in a better position to galvanize Latin American support in various multilateral fora—including the OAS, the UN, and the GATT—for Canadian positions on the environment, arms control and disarmament, and global trade talks. Additionally, there was a sense that admission would provide Canada with an opportunity to mould the policies of Latin American governments and thus enable it to influence events in the region. In short, officials believed that as a participating member state—brandishing its G-7 status and its distinction of being the second largest financial contributor to the organization—Canada would carry more weight in the region, and thus be better able to promote respect for human rights, democratic principles, and economic development.

On these issues and a variety of others, foreign policy mandarins generally felt that Canada could, as a full-fledged member, make a solid contribution to the OAS.[63] For instance, by adding Canada's name to the list of member states, they felt that it would immediately raise the prestige and profile of the forum. In addition, Canada had cordial and solid relations with all the members of the organization. This, in turn, could be used to reduce the level of polarization between the English- and Spanish-speaking members of the body—a key point given Canada's close ties with the English-speaking Caribbean countries. More important, it was thought that Canada, if it planned to influence the reform process at all, should seek membership as soon as possible. Within the institution, they believed that Canada would have a greater opportunity to shape it into an effective hemispheric forum.[64]

MAJOR DEVELOPMENTS IN THE REGION

Further reinforcing the mindset of DEA officials was the series of developments that had recently taken place in the region. Clearly, the onset of these dramatic changes played an important part in influencing both the bureaucracy and the political leadership in Canada. To be sure, the fact that Latin America was experiencing a major metamorphosis or transition period—particularly in the areas of democratization and "marketization"—weighed heavily on the minds of those involved in the decision-making process. As Joe Clark commented, "Democracy is sweeping Latin America. Dictatorships are now very much the exception."[65] In addition, many countries in the region were (and still are) introducing economic reform programmes and opening up their economies to outside competition.

These key developments, as mentioned, were largely in the political and economic realm. Politically speaking, a large number of countries, including Brazil, Argentina, Uruguay, Paraguay, and Chile, had already begun to institute sweeping democratic reforms. What were once implacable authoritarian or dictatorial regimes were, by the late 1980s, becoming fledgling democracies. While regular elections and political mobilization have not completely erased repression and human rights abuses, the fragile bloom of democracy appeared to be taking root.[66]

From an economic standpoint, the changes occurring in the region were equally dramatic. Many Latin American countries were moving away from import-substitution strategies to export-oriented economic policies. Countries such as Brazil, Mexico, and Argentina had implemented major economic adjustment programmes, encouraging foreign investment and wholesale privatization, cutting tariffs, and deregulating services.[67] Chile, Venezuela, Uruguay, and Peru, to name only a few, were also quick to introduce market reforms, eliminate subsidies, and prune the public sector.[68] In short, countries in the region were exhibiting a willingness to enter the world economy and to compete for export markets, investment dollars, and new technologies.

These dramatic steps were not only welcomed by the Canadian government, but they also helped to set the stage for Canada's admission to the OAS. Foreign policy officials, and, later, key decision-makers in the Mulroney government, saw these striking changes or "shocks" as particularly significant. They held out the possibility, if they were to become firmly entrenched, of creating new situations and new opportunities for Canada. Put another way, Canada would be better able—morally, economically, and politically—to deal with the wide array of Latin American countries espousing representative democracy, liberalized economies, and open societies. Changes of this nature, it was felt, could also breathe new life into multilateralism in general and the OAS in particular. And it was felt that through membership in this forum, Canada could work to nurture and encourage these positive developments.[69] The bottom line, then, is that these conditions were simply not in play when previous Canadian governments were examining the membership issue.

SUMMARY

The purpose of this chapter was not to justify or commend the Mulroney government on its decision to join the OAS. Instead, it sought to outline the various reasons why the Conservative government did decide to join the body in late 1989. In other words, it was intended to shed some much-needed light on a policy change that was an enigma to many. In some ways, it still is, since there is scant information on the exact role of the Prime Minister himself, the Prime Minister's Office (PMO), and the Bush White House. While it does go some way toward solving the mystery, a number of questions still remain. Those, however, will have to be answered by future research in this area.

In any event, the decision to join the OAS did not represent a fundamental or radical shift in Canadian foreign policy. One should not lose sight of the fact that successive Canadian governments, albeit in an incremental fashion, were moving closer to full membership. It would be more accurate to say that it marked a departure from the manner in which past Canadian governments conducted their relations with Latin America and the Caribbean. While it did amount to more than merely a change of emphasis, it did not signify a dramatic reorientation of Canada's overall policy approach toward the hemisphere. Indeed, Canada's policy objectives toward the hemisphere remained largely intact, while the "means" of helping to attain them was demonstrably altered. In some ways, the change in policy was consistent with the long tradition of Canadian foreign policy behaviour—namely, promoting hemispheric stability and security, joining international organizations and working with other like-minded nations to advance Canadian interests, and seeking counterweights to a decidedly asymmetric Canada-U.S. relationship.

Nonetheless, the change in government policy did reveal a number of interesting points about the nature of foreign policy-making in Canada. For instance, the decision to join the OAS was influenced by the changing dynamics of the external environment.[70] Dramatic changes taking place in Latin America—from the establishment of popularly-elected civilian governments to the introduction of across-the-board market reforms—served to create a more positive image in the minds of officials and decision-makers in Ottawa. Consequently, the OAS itself was viewed as a more workable and relevant body as well as one in which these regional developments could be fostered and consolidated. Although these changes did not singularly convince the government to join the organization, they did help to create a favourable climate for such a decision.

On a broader scale, this auspicious climate toward the OAS was also shaped by the changing nature of international politics itself. To be sure, the onset of the post-Cold War period has brought with it a conspicuous change in the international issue-agenda. The traditional "high politics" of war and security issues have been joined by the "low politics" of environmental degradation, narcotics, human rights, and debt. Governments can no longer hope to solve these intractable problems unilaterally, and thus are turning increasingly toward multi-national consultation and co-operation. With multilateralism experiencing a resurgence, officialdom in Ottawa viewed the OAS in a more favourable light.

The foreign policy bureaucracy, in particular, was a leading proponent of this view and of the decision to seek membership. Indeed, the very idea of joining was initiated, analyzed, and pushed by the department's Latin American specialists. And it was these same officials who formulated the documents—solely for cabinet perusal—that outlined the reasons and advantages of Canadian membership.[71] In short, DEA officials were active supporters, advocates, and players in the decision to join.

It is unlikely, though, that bureaucrats in External Affairs would have recommended membership without some knowledge that the Prime Minister and then SSEA Joe Clark were both supportive of this policy change. Put another way, if the Prime Minister or Clark had harboured serious reservations about such a move, it is unlikely that the government would have adopted the recommendation. It was important, then, that a favourable attitude and a genuine interest in joining the OAS existed at the highest levels of the Canadian government—especially with the Prime Minister himself. Hence, the making of this foreign policy change was less the result of "bureaucratic politics," domestic political pressures, or foreign prodding, than the product of top-level governmental commitment and a favourable external climate.

Perhaps the most important feature of the membership decision was the fact that it was the culmination of a decision-making process. To be sure, DEA officials had been reviewing and reevaluating the possibility of Canada joining the OAS months before the topic was broached by Prime Minister Mulroney in Kennebunkport. There were also lengthy discussions with other federal departments, and both the Prime Minister and Joe Clark discussed the issue on more than one occasion. Moreover, there were top level consultations with other hemispheric leaders and Latin American officials. Simply put, the decision to join the OAS was not a "bolt from the blue," but rather the result of a lengthy process of examination, consultation, and finally, implementation.

VII

Canada and the OAS: The Early Years

THE ACTUAL DECISION TO JOIN THE OAS WAS MERELY THE END OF the beginning.[1] From the time that Ottawa deposited its instrument of ratification of the OAS Charter, the real issue became the role Canada would play within the hemispheric forum. The focus quickly shifted away from the long-standing debate over membership to the more central question: what is Canada going to do now that it has joined the organization? Some analysts suggested that membership in the body would be a complete waste of time, if Canada failed to undertake constructive and creative initiatives.[2] Others contended that Canada's international experience, pragmatism, and mere presence at the OAS table would immediately strengthen the institution.[3]

In general, Canada has sought to delineate a modest, middling role for itself—neither over-active nor sheepishly reticent. After a pre-membership fumbling of the December 1989 U.S. invasion of Panama, which saw Prime Minister Mulroney slavishly offer his unequivocal support for the Bush administration's action, Canada's OAS mission settled into its new surroundings.[4] Canada's ambassador to the OAS, Jean-Paul Hubert, began his tenure in early January 1990—in the wake of the crisis in Panama. He joined a host of other OAS country representatives and supported a resolution which condemned the United States for forcibly entering the residence of Nicaragua's ambassador to Panama.[5] Six weeks later, a Canadian delegation, acting under the auspices of the OAS and the UN, participated as official observers in the February general elections in Nicaragua—which resulted in the defeat of the Sandinistas and the coming to power of UNO's Violeta Chamorro.

In early June Canada's Minister for External Relations, Monique Landry, attended the annual OAS General Assembly meeting in Asunción, Paraguay.[6] During the course of the gathering, Ms. Landry put forth a proposal—which was unanimously approved by member governments—calling for the establishment of a Unit for Democratic Development (later renamed the Unit for the Promotion of Democracy).[7] A second recommendation that urged member governments to stage a hemispheric summit at the head of state or government level was also endorsed. Additionally, Canadian representatives offered their firm support for a resolution geared toward reforming the financial quota system of the hemispheric body, in hopes of placing it on a more stable financial and administrative footing. At this same meeting, Canada was elected to the Inter-American Drug Abuse Control Commission (CICAD).

By year's end, Canada had moved in a variety of directions to solidify its OAS linkages. First, Canada joined the Inter-American Commission of Women (CIM) and participated in the Commission's XXV Assembly of Delegates, which was held in Washington in mid-October. Secondly, it was active on environmental issues, earmarking funds for an Amazon Basin project. Thirdly, Canadian Senator Gerald Ottenheimer was named to a high-level OAS Consultative Group on the Inter-American System, which was to look into ways of renovating and revitalizing the hemispheric forum. Lastly, Canadian officials, as part of an OAS observer team, monitored the late December elections in Haiti—which brought to power the country's first democratically-elected President, Jean-Bertrand Aristide.[8]

As its second year in the OAS began, Canada was still active on a number of fronts. It was involved in the OAS Sub-committee on the Environment, which was working on an action plan for the environment. And it was continuing its involvement in CICAD and the Consultative Group, while participating in a number of other inter-American agencies and specialized organizations.[9] It was, however, moving slowly on such critical questions as human rights, economic development, foreign debt, the drug trade, and securing peace in Central America. On the issue of Cuban reintegration into the OAS fold, Canada exhibited little interest in acting as an intermediary.[10]

Still, Canada made known its feelings on this point at the June 1991 General Assembly in Santiago, Chile. For the first time in a public forum, Canada called for the normalization of OAS-Cuban relations. As Canada's new Secretary of State for External Affairs, Barbara McDougall, noted in her remarks:

We look forward to the time when the vision of the founders of the OAS for a universal hemispheric forum can be realized and Cuba will retake its place in the Organization as a full member of the hemispheric family.[11]

Ms. McDougall also put forth a proposal in the area of hemispheric security and arms control. She indicated Canada's support for

a resolution on security condemning the proliferation of weapons of mass destruction in the world, as well as excessive build-ups of conventional arms, and establishing a working group to study this issue and report back to this assembly with recommendations for action.[12]

By sponsoring this resolution, Canada hoped to begin a process of meaningful dialogue on hemispheric arms control and disarmament matters.

Underpinning this resolution was the realization that the proliferation of both nuclear and conventional weapons—whether in a horizontal or vertical fashion—could only lead to increased international tensions and, ultimately, to regional conflicts. While Ottawa was not advocating the complete cessation of state interaction in "sensitive" technologies, it did seek to regulate and monitor these types of exchanges. The purpose of proffering this resolution, then, was essentially two-fold: first, to foster a better climate for attaining a sound foundation for hemispheric security, primarily through confidence-building measures, increased transparency, and regularized consultation in the acquisition and transfer of armaments; secondly, and perhaps more important, to divert the allocation of resources from war-making to more stabilizing activities—such as development, democratization, environmental protection, and the safeguarding of human rights.

To help realize these objectives, Canadian officials tabled a number of constructive suggestions to the OAS working group on hemispheric security.[13] In the area of nuclear weapons, Canada admonished OAS member states to sign the nuclear Non-Proliferation Treaty (NPT) or to take appropriate steps to bring into force the Treaty of Tlatelolco (which applies to Latin America).[14] In regards to the NPT, Canada also urged all governments to promote the extension of the treaty, which is up for renewal in 1995. Under the Treaty of Tlatelolco, the Canadian government supported the prohibition of nuclear explosions (including those for so-called peaceful purposes), while encouraging modification and strengthening of the treaty itself.

In terms of conventional weaponry, Ottawa was particularly concerned about the excessive build-up of these destabilizing armaments. It was worried about the negative consequences—such as heightened international tensions and increased internal repression—that such build-ups could foster. Canada hoped that the initiation of a programme to curb the stock-piling of conventional armaments, both within the hemisphere and without, would become a major priority for OAS member countries. As far as Canada was concerned, it believed that conventional weapons could be curbed through an OAS-wide commitment to both transparency and consultation.

Consequently, Canada put forth a proposal calling on all member governments to report their activities in this area to a yet-to-be-created non-discriminatory arms transfer register. In addition, the proposal advanced a supplementary idea of having OAS members exchange information on how each state actually governs the procurement and transfer of armaments. Canada supported the notion that regularized consultations and briefings could engender a better understanding not only of what types of weapons are stabilizing or destabilizing, but also of areas where arms build-ups are beginning to take place. Such a process of dialogue, Canada contended, could also be useful in terms of establishing practical guidelines for monitoring arms transfers, for developing more advanced techniques of regulation, and for creating a psychological climate of self-restraint.

On the question of chemical and biological weapons, the government also made a number of practical recommendations. Canada believed that the OAS could play a key role in invigorating the negotiations on a chemical weapons ban, now taking place within the Conference on Disarmament (CD). At the same time, it urged OAS member countries to introduce effective controls on chemical exports as well as on the very production facilities themselves. Lastly, it supported the introduction of confidence-building measures—such as trial inspections—in the area of chemical weapons.

Similarly, the government was concerned about the production and use of biological weapons and toxins. It was convinced that the OAS could provide valuable support for the Biological and Toxin Weapons Convention—which member states succeeded in doing at the Third Review Conference in September 1991. In this context, it called for OAS member governments to work toward the promotion of transparency, in conjunction with the Convention, and to take an active role in the Ad Hoc Group of Governmental Experts, which was established at the September Review Conference. On the issue of proliferation, the Canadian government proposed an informal discussion among OAS member states on finding ways of prohibiting transfers of such weapons and on enhancing regional co-operation (i.e., through scientific exchanges).

In all of these above-mentioned areas, Canada viewed both con-sultation and confidence-building as integral to any debate about hemispheric security. And it saw the consolidation of democratic principles and institutions within the inter-American community as a central component of any confidence-building regime. Accordingly, it called for discussions among OAS members to begin on the con-cept of transparency (in their military activities) and on those mech-anisms which would facilitate this openness. In addition, it proposed the creation of a new Committee on Cooperative Security—which would be composed of all member states—to promote debate and discussion, on a regular basis, of security matters. In this way, Canada was determined to see hemispheric security issues, whether of an immediate or long-term significance—accorded considerable politi-cal and institutional attention.

As of this writing, few if any of Canada's propositions in the security domain have been implemented. Many of its ideas, how-ever, are now under active consideration by an OAS working group. There was also a movement afoot, backed by Canada, to redefine the mandate of the Inter-American Defense Board (IADB). In this post-Cold War period, the IADB—which consumes roughly 3 per cent of the OAS operating budget—has become increasingly outdated. There have even been suggestions, expressed privately by some OAS offi-cials, that the board should be scrapped altogether. In any event, Canadian officials are quietly moving toward advocating a reorien-tation of the board's activities and *raison d'être*.[15]

These same Canadian officials have also come to view the whole human rights equation in the context of hemispheric security. As a result, Canada made known its intentions in June 1991 to take action in this area and to seek a seat on the Inter-American Court of Human Rights. It was unsuccessful, however, in its initial attempt to have Madam Justice Bertha Wilson appointed to the Inter-American Court. It is worth mentioning here that Canada has not signed the American Convention on Human Rights. This failure to ratify the convention stemmed in large part from the inability of Ottawa to secure provincial approval.[16] (Canada did move in late October to ratify the Convention on the Nationality of Women, the Inter-American Convention on the Granting of Political Rights to Women, and the Inter-American Convention on the Granting of Civil Rights to Women.)[17] While federal-provincial discussions on this impor-tant topic continued, the government quickly turned its energies to a major inter-American crisis.[18]

In the last three months of 1991, and well into 1992, Canada was active in arguably the hemisphere's biggest crisis since the U.S. invasion of Panama—specifically, the military overthrow of Haiti's President Jean-Bertrand Aristide. The ousting of Aristide by General Raoul Cédras on 30 September 1991, just one week after his elo-quent speech before the United Nations, washed away the seeds of Haitian democracy. While his seven months in power were criticized by some as politically naive, dictatorial, and erratic—particularly in terms of his alleged backing of *père lebrun* (the placing of a burning tire around the neck of his foes)—he still maintained the support of the poor and economically disadvantaged.

Not surprisingly, his removal from office, and hurried exile to Venezuela, was met with widespread revulsion in Haiti and through-out the inter-American community in general. The solid backing of Caribbean and Latin American states was due in large part to the fact that the OAS had pledged its firm support at the June 1991 General Assembly to involve itself in any

sudden or irregular interruption of the democratic political institutional process or of the legitimate exercise of power by the democratically elected government in any of the Organization's member states.[19]

Thus the goal of restoring democracy to Haiti was quickly elevated to the top of the OAS agenda.

External Affairs Minister McDougall set the tone of Canada's response to Aristide's ouster. She began by immediately stating "Canada's support of the legitimate government of President Aristide."[20] In addition to condemning the military coup, the federal government cancelled talks on determining future disbursements of development assistance to the tiny Caribbean country. Prime Minister Mulroney even went as far as to suggest that Canada had not ruled out the use of military force to bring about the reinstatement of Aristide. As he explained to the media, "We are examining all possible options that will help us help Haitians help themselves."[21]

Evidently, one of those options was pursuing a negotiated political settlement through the oas. In fact, Canada was at the forefront of trying to restore the constitutional government of Aristide. On 2 October 1991 Barbara McDougall met in Washington with the Foreign Ministers from other oas member governments for an emergency session on the Haitian crisis. By the end of the meeting, a toughly-worded condemnation of the coup was released, along with a rare consensus on an eleven-point resolution. Besides calling for "full restoration of the rule of law and of the constitutional regime, and the immediate reinstatement of President Jean-Bertrand Aristide," it recommended that all member countries "suspend their economic, financial and commercial ties with Haiti and any aid and technical cooperation except that provided for strictly humanitarian purposes."[22]

Furthermore, it proposed the creation of a high-level OAS delegation "to go to Haiti immediately and inform those who hold de facto power of the rejection by the American States of the interruption of constitutional order and of the decisions adopted in this Meeting," along with the suspension of any "military, police or security assistance of any kind and from the delivery of arms, munitions or equipment to that country under any public or private arrangement." The nine-member mission, which was composed of representatives from the United States, Canada, Venezuela, Bolivia, Costa Rica, Argentina, Jamaica, and Trinidad and Tobago, flew to Haiti on a Canadian Armed Forces Boeing 707.

When the delegation first arrived in Haiti on October 4, it met almost immediately with representatives of the three-man military junta in the conference room of the international airport. But after two days of hastily-arranged meetings, the OAS mission emerged from the conference room without any assurances from the junta that Aristide would be reinstated. In fact, on 6 October disgruntled Haitian soldiers disrupted the talks at the airport in a conspicuously threatening manner. In a frantic and highly-charged situation on the airport tarmac, members of the OAS mission hurriedly boarded the Canadian-supplied aircraft and headed back to Washington.[23] The next day, a steadfast OAS passed a resolution calling on all member governments to impose a trade embargo against the French-speaking Caribbean country, to freeze Haitian assets, and to establish a civilian observer group (known by its French acronym OEA-DEMOC) to help mediate the crisis. The civilian mission, which would be dispatched to Haiti once conditions there were suitable, was supposed to be composed of some five hundred observers and peacekeepers—who would have a mandate to monitor human rights, establish an independent judiciary, to "professionalize" the army, to install a civilian-controlled police force, and to strengthen and safeguard democratic institutions.[24]

With no appreciable progress on the restoration of Aristide, the OAS activated the civilian observer group in late October—naming former Colombian Foreign Minister Augusto Ramírez Ocampo to head the mission. Canada's deputy chief electoral officer, Jacques Girard, was made available to serve as Ocampo's assistant. On 7 November a team of OAS officials, led by Ocampo, was assembled and shortly thereafter departed for Haiti. For the most part, the fourteen-member delegation was instructed to meet with Haitian officials, military personnel, and business leaders to discuss the reinstatement of Aristide. After three days of discussions, both sides agreed to hold talks between Aristide and Haitian legislators in Cartagena, Colombia. But like most of the agreements between OAS representatives and Haitian authorities—including tentative agreements in mid-November 1991 and late February 1992—they proved difficult and problematic to implement.

At any rate, Canada's high-profile role in the Haitian crisis contrasts sharply with the cautious approach that marked its first eighteen months in the OAS.[25] This activism in the case of Haiti stemmed from the confluence of a variety of domestic and external factors.

First, the government's response was orchestrated and supported by the highest levels of the Canadian government—including the personal commitment of the Prime Minister himself. Indeed, Prime Minister Mulroney made the restoration of President Aristide an issue at both the Commonwealth and la Francophonie summits in late 1991.[26] He also lobbied other francophone members to introduce punitive sanctions against the military junta in Port-au-Prince. In addition, Mulroney participated in a formal press conference in Ottawa with Aristide—when he made a high-profile visit to Ottawa in early December—as well as engaged in some "telephone diplomacy" with Venezuelan President Carlos Andrés Pérez and U.S. President Bush.[27]

With the personal involvement of the Prime Minister, the Department of External Affairs was duly bound to respond in a diligent fashion. The issue became a priority for officials in the Latin America and Caribbean bureau and with the staff at the OAS mission in Washington. In some respects, it was viewed by the foreign policy bureaucracy—and perhaps the political leadership as well—as a "test case" of Canada's commitment to the OAS and to the principles of democratic pluralism. The point here was that the Haitian crisis—in contrast with a number of other hemispheric issues and problems—had the full backing of key political figures, and thus it received sufficient bureaucratic attention.

This support, it is worth noting, was made possible by a unique set of external circumstances. Clearly, the crisis in Haiti was a "safe" issue for Ottawa—one which would not be costly from a political standpoint. More specifically, it was a situation in which the government could play a leading role without offending the sensibilities of the United States or the countries of Latin America. The Bush administration did not view the crisis from a security-related or Cold War perspective. Latin American governments, for their part, were acutely aware of the fact that they were not immune to coup attempts and therefore wanted to send a pointed message to their own militaries. Consequently, Washington was perfectly content to work within the confines of the OAS—while Latin American leaders privately urged Canada to play a major role in the crisis.[28] In other words, there was virtually no pressure on the Mulroney government from the White House to adopt a certain position or line and little chance of Ottawa's being criticized by Latin American countries for siding with the "gringos."

It is also important to note that Canada's response to the crisis was a function of domestic considerations—perhaps even touching upon the national unity debate. Almost immediately, leaders of the French-speaking Haitian community, approximately 60,000 strong, petitioned the Prime Minister to lead a movement to have Aristide returned to power.[29] Moreover, External Relations Minister Monique Landry and Montreal Mayor Jean Doré—sensitive to the interests of their constituents—urged the government to play a leading role. In some respects, then, Canada's activism stemmed in part from political pressures emanating from the Haitian community in Montreal.

All these factors, when taken together, prodded the government to play a major part in the Haitian crisis. But if the external circumstances had been different—and the Prime Minister's popularity had not been hovering at 16 per cent—Canada would have undoubtedly been more timid. Indeed, one could ask if Ottawa would have responded in a similar fashion had it been Castro's Cuba rather than Aristide's Haiti? Put another way, the government's response should not be interpreted as a pointed demonstration of Canada's commitment to the OAS. This was simply an issue that allowed Ottawa to look good, and at very little cost politically and economically.

This perception that the behaviour of the Canadian government was affected by the nature of the issue or crisis at hand was, to a certain extent, borne out by the recent constitutional crisis in Peru. In this case, Canada's response was more circumspect and cautious, perhaps reflecting the subtle differences between the crises in Haiti and Peru. While External Affairs Minister McDougall did say that she was "very disturbed" by Peruvian President Alberto Fujimori's dissolution of Congress and the suspension of part of the constitution, there was none of the tough talk that followed in the wake of the crisis in Haiti. She noted that "Canada is committed to democracy and human rights in this hemisphere, and we will take every possible action, in concert with the Organization of American States (OAS), to support these essential values."[30] However, there was no immediate convocation of an emergency session of OAS Foreign

Ministers to discuss the crisis, even though Canada took over the rotating chairmanship of the Permanent Council in early April.[31] Officials in Ottawa were also non-committal on the question of cutting off aid to the South American country, preferring to wait for some direction from the OAS.[32]

When the *ad hoc* OAS Meeting of Foreign Ministers met in Washington some ten days later, Canada was represented by Minister McDougall. Her language this time was more forceful, stating that Fujimori's conduct was "unconstitutional, illegal and unacceptable." She also expressed Canada's support for a high-level OAS mission—led by Secretary-General Baena Soares and Uruguayan Foreign Minister Hector Gros-Espiell—to travel to Peru for talks with President Fujimori. Unlike a number of other Foreign Ministers, she indicated Canada's backing for possible sanctions against Peru. As McDougall explained: "In our deliberations today we will have to consider all the measures at our disposal, including sanctions." Later on in her remarks before the emergency session of Foreign Ministers, she restated that Canada will, if Fujimori proved intransigent, "press foreign ministers to develop a program of sanctions that will demonstrate that this organization is prepared to stand for democracy."[33]

Canada once again turned its attention to both Peru and Haiti in mid-May. At the OAS General Assembly in the Bahamas, it supported a resolution which called for the return of democracy in Haiti. Among the ten points contained in the resolution was a recommendation to "expand and intensify the monitoring of the trade embargo on Haiti" and a reaffirmation "that the OAS and its member states remain fully prepared to facilitate the reestablishment and strengthening of the democratic institutions in Haiti."[34] (It also backed a 22 May declaration expressing concern over the continual violation of human rights in Haiti.) In addition, the new measures proposed the banning of ships that do business with Haiti from all member countries, denying visas to supporters of the coup, and urging the European Community (EC) to refrain from trading with the military-backed provisional government in Port-au-Prince.[35]

Ms. McDougall, in her address before the Assembly, reiterated Canada's firm support for the return of democracy in Haiti. As she went on to explain: "The illegitimate regime in Haiti has thwarted every attempt to restore democracy to the Haitian people. Canada will continue to enforce sanctions, as we all agreed last October."[36] And in a veiled threat to the military-backed provisional government, she indicated that Canada "is determined that the impasse in Haiti not continue indefinitely."[37] She also criticized the current regime's treatment of the Haitian people and announced Canada's commitment to provide a further $5 million in humanitarian assistance.[38]

In the case of Fujimori's Peru, Canada was equally vocal and vigilant. Following President Fujimori's remarks to the assembly, it backed an OAS resolution calling for the restoration of full democracy in Peru. In addition to recognizing "the commitment made by the President of Peru to call immediate elections for a Constitutional Congress," the resolution urged "the Peruvian authorities to effect the return to the system of representative democracy at the earliest possible opportunity, with full respect for the principle of separation of powers and the rule of law."[39] While there was no mention of sanctions or a trade embargo, OAS members did agree to

keep open the *ad hoc* Meeting of Ministers of Foreign Affairs, there to receive, through the Permanent Council, information on the progress of the situation in Peru and, in particular, on compliance with the commitment to democratization.[40]

External Affairs Minister McDougall was particularly engaged by the crisis in Peru. Notwithstanding Fujimori's personal assurances, she was quick to remark: "He doesn't seem to understand yet the most fundamental attribute of democratic life and that is that you can't have a part-time democracy."[41] In her comments to the assembly, Ms. McDougall was firm when she stated: "We must continue to press the Government of Peru for a full and early return to democracy, and we must not shrink from further action if necessary."[42] As part of Canada's "further action," she noted that humanitarian assistance would continue, but "direct support to the government will be suspended until full democracy is restored. It will not be business as usual with this President."[43]

If the crises in Haiti and Peru are any indication, Canada has exhibited signs of taking its membership in the OAS very seriously. It has managed to play a visible and constructive role in both of these crises. It is important to remember, however, that both of these cases were instances were Canada could take a firm position without offending the sensibilities of either the United States or Latin American governments. Of course, the real test for Canada will come when it has to adopt a stance on a crisis that pits the United States against the majority of Latin American countries. Still, Canada has demonstrated its willingness to make its presence felt within the corridors of the OAS.

SUMMARY

When Canada joined the OAS in January 1990, a number of interested observers hoped that Canada would play a major role within the OAS. They tended to expect significant initiatives from a Canada that was now inside the body as opposed to outside looking in. They have been disappointed in Canada's response to the situation in Peru, and for that matter on a wide range of other hemispheric issues and problems.[44] They have also been less than satisfied with the government's creation of a Unit for the Promotion of Democracy and its role in the Haitian crisis. Such observers feel Canada must become far more active in the areas of human rights, environmental protection, OAS reform, development assistance, and the reintegration of Cuba.

Indeed, the Toronto-based Canada-Caribbean-Central America Policy Alternatives (CAPA)—in its second report on Canada and the OAS—urged the government to adopt a more active role within the body.[45] On the issue of human rights, it encouraged the government to press for much-needed reforms to the existing inter-American regime for human rights—specifically, to the Inter-American Commission on Human Rights and the nomination procedures for making appointments to the Inter-American Court. CAPA was also disappointed in Ottawa's approach toward combatting the problem of drugs. In particular, it criticized the federal government for simply adopting slavishly the goals and means of the discredited U.S. "war on drugs" strategy. Alternatively, it called upon Canada to

promote a policy that addresses the root socio-economic causes of drug production, including the problems of poverty, underdevelopment, and declining international terms of trade which lead peasant farmers towards coca cultivation.[46]

The CAPA report was also critical of the government's activity in the Caribbean region. In terms of the crisis in Haiti, the non-governmental organization—while noting Canada's leading role in returning Aristide to power—criticized the Department of External Affairs for severing all aid to Haiti, including those programmes organized by Canadian NGOs. Furthermore, it pointed out that "there has been little diplomatic activity by Canada at the OAS to encourage Cuban reentry."[47] The report challenged Ottawa's apparent intention to wait on the sidelines until Fidel Castro eventually departs the scene. It called upon the government to work with like-minded Latin American countries to secure Cuba's reintegration into the OAS family. By doing so, CAPA argued, Canada would be in a better position to benefit not only politically and economically, but also from a moral standpoint.[48]

Notwithstanding these criticisms, perhaps it would be fair to say that Canada's record of performance for this period can best be described as mixed. It has been involved in several areas of hemispheric import—including drugs, the environment, democratization, and security-related issues. Canada has played an important role in invigorating, as well as contributing in a positive fashion to, the issue of inter-American security. Not only has it been instrumental in placing the issue of security and arms control on the OAS agenda, but it has also put forth a number of practical and stabilizing suggestions in these areas. Canadian officials have come to believe that Canada's security interests are intimately linked to wider hemispheric (non-military) issues such as drug-trafficking, human rights violations, emigration, and environmental destruction.

Still, Ottawa has not maintained a high-profile or carved out a influential role for itself within the OAS. Nor has it shown any willingness to undertake any bold or innovative initiatives. This reluctance, in part, is due to the fact that Canada—as one of the new kids on the OAS block—does not want to be perceived as being too pushy or overbearing. Instead, Canadian officials have opted more for a behind-the-scenes, consensus-building, classic "quiet diplomacy" style of OAS interaction.

This penchant for a low-key role is also a function of several domestic considerations. First, there appears to be a lack of political will and commitment to hemispheric affairs at the ministerial and prime ministerial levels. It seems to take a major crisis in the hemisphere before the political leadership in Canada takes notice of the OAS. Secondly, there is little in the way of bureaucratic support not only within the Department of External Affairs, but also at the OAS mission in Washington. This lack of resources and analytical capabilities makes it extremely difficult to formulate creative policy ideas and options. Thirdly, Canada appears to be unwilling to engage in actions that might somehow adversely affect relations between Ottawa and Washington. Clearly, the federal government is not about to undertake any initiatives that could raise the ire of the White House or further complicate other "irritants" on the Canada-U.S. issue agenda.

Finally, Canada's ability to play a greater role in hemispheric issues is hampered by the dispositions of OAS members themselves. Member governments of the organization—always conscious and over-protective of the long-standing principle of non-intervention—have rarely exhibited a willingness to interfere in the internal affairs of a member state. This, in turn, makes it very difficult for Canada to undertake meaningful initiatives in the areas of human rights, the environment, and the drug trade. Although the task facing Canada is formidable, it is not insuperable. Ultimately, Canada will have to convince OAS member governments of the merits of adjusting their thinking to the changing dynamics of inter-American politics and to the need to interpret the non-intervention axiom more flexibly. For Canada to succeed in this regard, it will have to understand clearly both its capabilities and its constraints with respect to the organization.

Conclusion

ALTHOUGH THE DECISION BY THE MULRONEY GOVERNMENT TO join the OAS brought Canada's hemispheric relations more into focus, it was in some ways more of an ending than a beginning. Indeed, a host of Canadian governments—reaching back as far as the government of Sir Wilfrid Laurier—have flirted with the inter-American system. Many of them expressed an interest in developing contacts with the region and in exploiting any available trade and investment opportunities. And while there was a willingness on the part of some of these governments to join a select group of hemispheric bodies, there was also a firm reluctance to seek full membership in the major institutional entities of the inter-American community—namely, the Pan-American Union (PAU) and the OAS.

Canada's penchant for remaining aloof—or preferring the role of a dilettante—from these organizations was based on a number of real concerns and serious reservations. Initially, it was the active opposition of the United States and Ottawa's essentially British-directed foreign policy that effectively precluded Canada from seeking full membership.[1] In later years, Canadian governments, from Mackenzie King's onward, questioned the wisdom of joining such a weak and ineffective hemispheric forum. Almost invariably, concerns about U.S. dominance of the body, along with a noticeable lack of appreciation for things Latin American, and a preference for a more Atlantic- and Commonwealth-oriented foreign policy, led decision-makers in Ottawa to shy away from the hemisphere in general and its institutional off-shoots in particular. By the 1960s and early 1970s, fears of jeopardizing the overall Canada-U.S. relationship, a general disillusionment with the OAS itself (particularly in the wake of the 1962 suspension of Cuba and the 1965 U.S. invasion of the Dominican Republic, when it was clear that Washington sought to use the organization as an instrument in the conduct of its foreign policy), and the actual dollar cost of membership tended to convince officialdom in Ottawa of the merits of remaining outside the hemispheric body. Similarly, the mid-1970s and the early 1980s in Canada echoed many of the reservations that held currency during the 1960s and the early 1970s, with a general feeling that the perceived costs of full membership outweighed any possible benefits.

Debating these very costs and benefits engaged interested Canadians inside and outside of government. Obviously, the political leadership in Canada, along with the Department of External Affairs (DEA), discussed and deliberated upon the balance between the costs and benefits of OAS membership. Of course, the academic community—led by a small number of Latin Americanists—entered the fray with a bevy of arguments for and against membership. So, too, did the media, Parliament, and interest groups in Canada—but to a much lesser degree—proffer their own views on the advantages and disadvantages of joining. Regrettably, the Canadian public, for the most part, remained both uninformed and disinterested in the membership question and the OAS in general.

Notwithstanding an apathetic public, the Mulroney government reversed Canada's long-standing aversion to membership in the organization. With the requisite key political support at the top, and a supportive bureaucracy, the government moved quickly to reverse almost eighty years of non-membership. For a variety of reasons, then, the Conservative government felt that the time was ripe for occupying Canada's long-standing "empty chair" at the OAS Council table. Latin America's growing role in international affairs, the changing economic and political climate in the region (especially economic liberalization and democratization), the potential for a hemispheric trading bloc, and a determination to consolidate Canada's expanding linkages with the region all worked to paint a favourable picture of full membership in the forum. In a word, the perceived benefits of admission were interpreted at that time as outweighing any possible costs to Canada. Furthermore, many of the reasons and conditions that had worked against membership in the past were no longer as persuasive.

While the decision to seek admission does not represent a fundamental change in Canadian foreign policy, it does reveal a number of points about how the Mulroney government viewed Canadian-Latin American relations. First, the decision showed a commitment on the part of Ottawa to play a greater role in hemispheric affairs. Secondly, it signalled the government's recognition of the growing importance of Latin America to Canada.[2] Thirdly, it signified an attempt on the part of federal decision-makers to focus more political and bureaucratic attention on the region.[3] Finally, it illustrated the willingness of officials in Ottawa to risk—at least on some occasions—complicating Canada-U.S. relations for the sake of Canadian-Latin American relations.

Many observers have cautioned against full membership precisely out of fear that it would disrupt Canada's relations with the United States. But now that Canada has joined the hemispheric forum, the jury is still out on whether Canada will simply conduct its OAS business with an eye and a ear toward Washington—making sure not to enrage the White House. Not surprisingly, both Canada and the United States share similar views and positions on a variety of issues coming before the body (most recently on the choice of César Gaviria as the new OAS Secretary General).[4] Given this lack of sharp differences between the two countries, the likelihood for confrontation has been substantially reduced. This, in turn, has led to a situation in which the two neighbours find themselves in agreement on how to make the OAS more relevant, which issues should be given priority, and the future direction the organization should take.

This is not to suggest that Canadian and U.S. officials see "eye to eye" on all matters coming before the hemispheric forum. There are issues that both countries clearly disagree on, including budgetary matters (U.S. arrears in membership dues) and reforms to the Inter-American Defense Board (IADB). What is significant, though, is that these differences have not strained the overall relationship. Nor has there been any indication that Canada's independence of thought has been met with any overt or latent threats of retaliation. In short, the relationship continues to function—along with the Canada-U.S. "diplomatic culture"—in the face of these policy disagreements.

Still, there is no doubt that Canada's relationship with the United States does somewhat limit Ottawa's room for manoeuvring within the organization. The dictates of Canada-U.S. relations cannot but have implications for Canadian behaviour within the institution. The very magnitude of Canada's relations with the United States—politically, militarily, economically, culturally, and diplomatically—almost ensures a certain pause on the part of Canadian officials before embarking upon any bold initiatives within the OAS. For instance, Canada is unlikely to call for the total elimination of the IADB since it would not be well received by U.S. officials. If, moreover, a hemispheric issue arose where U.S. interests were clearly at stake, it is unlikely that Canada would adopt a position which was totally at variance with the view emanating from Washington.

The complexity and intertwining of the Canada-U.S. relationship, along with the importance attached to it by Ottawa, will undoubtedly place some limitations on Canadian officials. For example, policy-makers in Ottawa may be hesitant to pursue the reinstatement of Cuba into the OAS family for fear of enraging officialdom in Washington. Or, these same officials could find themselves in the unenviable position of having to support U.S. heavy-handedness in Latin America (as happened with Panama in 1989) so as not to jeopardize other outstanding issues or irritants on the Canada-U.S. political agenda. In short, government officials might be unwilling to sacrifice the overall Canada-U.S. relationship at the OAS altar.[5]

Perhaps more important will be the restrictions imposed upon Canadian officials by fiscal restraint and deficit-reduction pressures. Given the present financial realities, the government in Ottawa—irrespective of its political stripe—will be hard-pressed to find the fiscal resources necessary for Canada to be a full and contributing member of the hemispheric forum. In other words, budgetary considerations will make it more difficult for Canada to engage in the kinds of initiatives it might wish to undertake within the organization. Accordingly, a certain amount of prioritizing will have to take place to ensure that Canada gets the most out of the limited funds that it has available to its OAS mission. Issues such as the environment, human rights, and extreme poverty might be accorded less emphasis by a budget-conscious Canadian mission.

In addition, the nature of the OAS itself will impose certain constraints on Canada's ability to secure its objectives. For instance, some members are still firmly resisting Canadian initiatives to reform, strengthen, and revitalize the organization.[6] Particularly those member states that feel strongly about national sovereignty and non-intervention have responded in a lukewarm fashion to Canadian efforts to "modernize" the security institutions of the body. Some OAS officials have also been unwilling to make the body more responsive and disciplined in budget matters and spending priorities. It will take some time to get Canadians into positions, such as John Graham's at the UPD, in which they can accelerate the process of reform. In the meantime, Canada will have to content itself with the arrival of a new OAS Secretary General—and the potential for change which that brings—who will immediately begin a process of replacing many of those in executive positions.

On a less practical plain, Canada's ranking as a middle power within the international hierarchy of nations does not provide it with substantial "power" capabilities. With its small to middling power resources, Canada's influence within the OAS is likely to be modest. As former External Affairs Minister Joe Clark conceded, "you apply your influence in five or six places at different times and expect failure in most of them."[7] Of course, Canada will be unable to persuade or pressure OAS members to subscribe automatically to its vision of a revitalized hemispheric body. Limited political clout will also make it difficult for Canadian officials to shape the organization's agenda, as well as to influence decisions taken by member governments.

Another factor constraining Canada is likely to be the lack of political will in Ottawa. With national unity, recessionary and unemployment pressures, and a ballooning federal deficit all consuming the political leadership in Ottawa, the OAS might not receive the necessary attention from the highest levels of the Canadian government. Put another way, federal politicians—already under siege—would be loath to concentrate their energies on the country's international commitments when the domestic scene in Canada is in the throes of a deeply-rooted crisis. This lack of political commitment, in turn, cannot but constrain Canadian behaviour within the OAS. Indeed, Canadian diplomats' influence cannot be effective when their OAS counterparts are unconvinced of Canada's full support of the organization.

Placing further limits on Canada is the dwindling supply of support staff in the bureaucracy and diplomatic service. Under tight budgetary constraints, the Department of External Affairs (DEA) cut 250 positions a few years ago, including some responsible for South America.[8] When this reality is combined with the fact that the Canadian mission to the OAS is composed of only a small staff, competence is difficult to achieve.[9] The danger here is that Canada's voice—unless buttressed by thoughtful, sensitive, and pragmatic arguments—is likely to fall on deaf ears.

For example, if Canada tries to have environmental protection placed at or near the top of the OAS political agenda, it requires a solid understanding of the complexities of the Amazon rain forest issue. Simply to state publicly Canada's firm commitment to preserving the rain forest will not be enough. To be taken seriously, then, Canadian officials will need to be thoroughly briefed on the cultural, social, economic, and strategic realities of deforestation in Brazil. In order to do this, though, Canada will need officials and diplomats in Washington, and in the field, who can accumulate information and understand the full gravity of the situation.

These limitations should not be taken to mean that Canada's contribution to the OAS will be marginal at best and minuscule at worst. Rather, it simply means that Canada's behaviour within the organization needs to be understood in the context of certain inescapable realities. For the most part, Canada has sought to make its presence felt within the organization. While it has not always been successful—and obviously could be doing more—it has not been totally ineffective either. It does have a certain amount of weight to throw around—particularly when it comes to the smaller members of the organization—but it must do so in a discriminating and judicious fashion. Still, it continues to be active in a number of areas, including hemispheric security, democratic development, and OAS reform. In addition, it has expressed interest in issues involving the environment, drug-trafficking, and human rights. More recently, it has begun the process of trying to enhance the status of NGOs with respect to the hemispheric forum. This issue-agenda is unlikely to change in the foreseeable future—even if the government in Ottawa does.

Clearly, we will have to await the results of the Chrétien government's foreign policy review—and possibly the "action plan" which comes out of the December 1994 Summit of the Americas in Miami—to get a definite sense of how it intends to approach the OAS and the Americas as a whole from a policy standpoint.[10] In the absence of the review's final report, however, some general observations can be gleaned from the government's recent behaviour. Early indications seem to suggest that the new government is unlikely to lessen Canada's interest and commitment to the Americas.[11] If anything, one is likely to see increased emphasis on enhancing trade relations—with possibly less interest in the promotion of human rights—if the government's approach to China is any indication.

The coming into force of the NAFTA has obviously increased the profile and importance of Latin America in the eyes of official Ottawa and the Canadian business community. More specifically, Canadian businesses seem to be responding to possible investment and market opportunities in Mexico. And with recent presidential elections in Mexico—which reconfirmed the sixty-five-year rule of the Institutional Revolutionary Party (PRI)—free market reforms will continue and thus Canadian investors might become even more "bullish" on Mexico.[12] At the same time, the Liberal government will likely focus high-level political attention on Mexico, as a possible model for expanding relations with other countries in the region. To be sure, the Chrétien government has expressed an interest in extending the NAFTA to other countries of the Americas—most notably, Chile and Argentina.

It is possible that the Chrétien government sees its quest to broaden political and economic linkages with countries of the Americas in terms of utilizing Latin America as part of a broader "counterweight" strategy vis-à-vis the United States.[13] Accordingly, there is likely to be more emphasis placed on improving Canada's trade relations with Mexico and on opening new export markets in a small number of South American countries. Increased political attention toward the region is also likely to flow from the Chrétien government's version of the "Third Option." Thus, there will be more ministerial visits to the region as well as more bureaucratic attention focused on developments in the Americas.[14] Moreover, official visits at the head-of-government level are likely to increase in the coming years. (In fact, the President of Argentina, Carlos

Menem, paid an official visit to Canada in June of 1994.) In short, Latin America stands a good chance of becoming the "rising star" within Canada's foreign policy universe.

As for the OAS itself, one should not anticipate any major changes in this area. Given the government's interest at the 1994 OAS General Assembly in Brazil, and the energetic commitment of Secretary of State Christine Stewart, Canada's firm support of the OAS is unlikely to change in the near term. Thus, one should not expect any fundamental or radical shift in Canada's OAS policy approach— and in the issues that underlie that approach. There could, however, be some minor changes, such as an intensified effort to ratify the American Convention on Human Rights and to reintegrate Cuba back into the OAS fold. Overall, though, the focus is unlikely to be altered in any substantial fashion in the coming years.

The appointment of a junior minister for Latin America and Africa is an interesting, and perhaps significant, development in and of itself. While it is probably too early to judge the precise impact of this move, it does seem to suggest the Liberal government's determination to keep abreast of developments in the region. As for the OAS in particular, it could mean that Ms. Stewart will be responsible for overseeing Canada's OAS activities and subsequently reporting directly to the Foreign Minister on matters of pressing importance to Canada. Indeed, it was Stewart herself, and not Foreign Minister Ouellet, who attended the last General Assembly in Belem, Brazil. All of this, of course, is purely speculative at the moment—since no one is really sure of the significance of Ms. Stewart's appointment. What does seem certain is that without the minister's attention and the necessary political will, Canada is unlikely to reach its full potential within the OAS.

Postscript

As of the writing of this book, Canada has reached the five-year plateau as a full-fledged member of the OAS. Interestingly, a new Liberal government in Ottawa, an ongoing foreign policy review, and a new Canadian Ambassador (Mr. Brian Dickson) to the hemispheric forum has not altered in any substantive fashion Canada's role within the organization. In many ways, Canada's "OAS record" for 1993-1994 has been very reminiscent of the government's performance for its first three years of full membership—although perhaps not as vigorous.[1] For example, it has maintained a continuing interest in a core grouping of issues, including democratic development, OAS reform, human rights, and hemispheric security. Canadian officials, with perhaps less urgency and priority, have also focused their energies on a second set of issues—namely, economic cooperation, women's issues, drug trafficking, and the environment.

In light of Canada's expanding role within the OAS, and the growing significance of this political relationship, scholarly attention should be focused more closely on the emerging Canada-OAS dynamic.[2] And with a new government in Ottawa seemingly looking for "counterweights" to balance off its relations with the United States, along with a junior minister interested in OAS affairs, there is a strong possibility that the body will become more salient in the conduct of Canadian foreign policy. This, in turn, raises a number of important questions—only fitting, given Canada's achievement of its fifth anniversary within the hemispheric institution. Perhaps it makes sense to begin with some obvious queries, though they do not always lead us to obvious answers. For example, has Canada's recent role within the body remained relatively consistent with its earlier activities? More important, how does one explain or account for Canada's behaviour within the OAS from the very beginning? Lastly, what will likely be the future tone and direction of Canada-OAS relations under the government of PM Jean Chrétien?

CANADA-OAS RELATIONS FOR 1993-1994

Perhaps the most visible, and arguably the most challenging, aspect of Canada's presence within the hemispheric forum has been its contribution to resolving the crisis in Haiti. From the very beginning, Canada and the OAS have remained firmly committed to reestablishing the democratically-elected government of Jean-Bertrand Aristide.[3] And now with the 18 September agreement (dubbed the Carter accord), which calls for the *de facto* military government to step down no later than mid-October 1994, Canada continues to be involved.[4] Canada, along with other member states such as the United States and Venezuela, has played (and continues to play) an important role in securing the restoration of President Aristide— and in rebuilding the country in the post-military junta period. Prior to the recent negotiated settlement, brokered by former U.S. President Jimmy Carter, General Colin Powell (ret.) and Senator Sam Nunn, Canada co-sponsored a UN resolution in July 1994 (resolution 940) essentially authorizing the formation of a multi-nation force which could "use all necessary means to facilitate the departure of the military leadership." But with a U.S. invasion of the tiny island averted at the last moment, Canada will undoubtedly be called upon to participate in a peacekeeping operation, supplying soldiers, one hundred RCMP officers, and other specialists.[5]

Although the OAS had attempted a number of earlier diplomatic initiatives to resolve the crisis, they met with only minor success. At times, the military leadership has expressed its willingness to remove itself from power and to allow the return of President Aristide. Repeatedly, though, the military has reverted back to its initial position—namely, its steadfast refusal to step aside. For instance, the so-called Governors Island Agreement, which was reached in New York City in July 1993, called for Aristide's return to Haiti by the end of October. However, the *de facto* military regime—while initially agreeing to the terms of the pact, voided the deal and rejected any possibility of returning power to Aristide. While U.S. support for Aristide has wavered and flip-flopped from the very beginning,

Canada has remained committed to restoring the constitutional government of Aristide.[6] In any event, once Aristide is returned to power, he has agreed not to engage in any retaliation or reprisals against his foes, and he has given his commitment to hold presidential elections—in which he will not be participating—in December of 1995.[7]

The issues of concern for Canadian officials, such as Haiti, remain largely those that have dominated Canada's agenda since it joined the hemispheric forum in 1990. Still, both 1993 and 1994 were busy years for Canada's mission at the OAS and for officials at the Pearson Building in Ottawa—and not without their controversial moments.[8] For purposes of clarity, Canada's agenda within the OAS will be divided into two sets of issue areas.[9] The primary set of issues includes democratic development, OAS reform, human rights, and hemispheric security.[10] A second set of issues focuses on drug trafficking, economic co-operation, women's issues, and the environment. Canadian officials in both Ottawa and Washington have been active in all of these areas, but with arguably more vigour on the first set—perhaps reflecting the priorities of the Canadian government.[11] This is not to suggest that Canada has made only token efforts on the second set of issues, since it has sought to have its voice heard, as well as offering constructive ideas on these matters.[12]

One could look upon Ottawa's response to the May 1993 *auto golpe* (self-coup) in Guatemala as a demonstration of Canada's strong support for democracy in the Americas.[13] Canada supported a toughly-worded resolution, passed during an emergency meeting of the OAS Permanent Council, condemning the unconstitutional actions of Guatemalan President Jorge Serrano. Canada also participated in a 4 June Special OAS Foreign Ministers' Meeting in Washington to deal with the crisis in Guatemala. At that meeting, External Affairs Minister Barbara McDougall indicated "that Canada would accept nothing less than the full restoration of constitutional government in Guatemala."[14]

On the issue of democratic development, Canada continues to help Latin America prepare for and monitor elections. In the May 1993 elections in Paraguay, Canada contributed some $60,000 (Canadian) and five members to the OAS observer mission.[15] In late November Canada also contributed both personnel and financial resources ($35,000 Canadian) to the OAS-observed elections in Honduras.[16] Just one week later Canada participated in the presidential elections in Venezuela, which saw the return to power of former President Rafael Caldera and his Committee for Independent Political Organization (COPEI) party. In addition to providing $40,000 (Canadian), Canada sent a number of observers, including Canada's own John Graham—the then Executive Coordinator of the Unit for the Promotion of Democracy (UPD).[17]

While the unit was active in preparing for the May 1994 elections in Panama, Canada did not contribute any financial resources.[18] Despite the best efforts of some Canadian officials, including Mr. Graham himself, they were unsuccessful in having left-over funds from the Venezuelan mission transferred to the Panamanian effort.[19] Perhaps more significant was the unit's involvement in the June 1994 elections (and post-election activities) in the Dominican Republic. Despite a number of election irregularities, which were denounced by the UDP and Mr. Graham personally, the unit was successful in avoiding a major outbreak of post-election violence and instability. Mr. Graham, who worked tirelessly for some three months in the country, was a pivotal player in forging or mediating an agreement between the tainted government of Joaquín Balaguer and his chief political opponent, José Peña Gómez. Mr. Graham, along with U.S. officials and church authorities, was able to cobble together a difficult compromise, which would see electoral reform in the country, Balaguer stepping down after two years in office, and fresh elections in 1996 (without Balaguer reoffering for the presidency).

Canada's commitment to safeguarding democracy, then, has seemingly been firm from the time it took its seat in the OAS Council chambers.[20] Indeed, as the initial driving force behind the creation of the Unit for the Promotion of Democracy (UPD), Canada has sought to make its presence felt in this area. The unit has finally begun to find its feet, largely under the able stewardship of John Graham, a respected Canadian foreign service officer.[21] It has adopted a typically Canadian approach based on pragmatism and practicality, signified by fine-tuning its mandate and securing greater resources, developing contacts with regional parliaments, establishing linkages with the Inter-American Development Bank (IDB) and aid agencies in Canada and the United States, and fostering a positive relationship with a host of democratic institutions in Latin America. Moreover, it has been working in the area of election preparation and confidence-building in hopes of instilling some semblance, however small, of a civic or democratic culture in the region. Given the region's history of authoritarian and military regimes, of course, this will not be a particularly easy task. But perhaps one can take some encouragement from Paraguay's recent elections—though marked by some irregularities—which resulted in the country's first democratically-elected president in 182 years.[22]

Like democratic development in Latin America, the UPD has experienced some difficult and trying times—perhaps best characterized as growing pains. Its wide-ranging mandate of promoting representative democracy in the Americas was far too large for the resources made available to the unit. In fact, the UPD was initially staffed by a small group of officials from the Secretary General's office and thereby confined largely to electoral observation. Simply put, it was not financially or institutionally prepared to deal effectively with matters of democratic development and good governance. As one Canadian official caustically remarked: "The Unit was like a glob of green jelly."[23] In other words, it was an organizational entity entrusted with a remarkably large mandate, but with no sense of direction or purpose.

Canada, as part of its overall OAS reform efforts, has sought to place the unit on a firmer footing. Besides working on a more definite mandate and strategy, Canadian officials have made some strides toward fashioning a clear set of priorities that make sense, as well as a series of precise tasks that it can perform adequately.[24] Accordingly, three basic target areas have been delineated: civic education, electoral observation activities, and training for legislators and legislative staff. In terms of civic education, the unit is interested in transmitting or disseminating information about democratic processes and values.[25] The focus here will be on "curriculum enhancement for schools" (beginning with the Department of Education of Trinidad and Tobago) and "facilitating public service communication."[26]

Secondly, electoral-observation activities will be geared toward making "the electoral process more effective and transparent and to support the development of up-to-date civil registers."[27] Third, training for legislators and legislative staff will be directed "not only at the level of the national congress, but at state (provincial) and at municipal levels where alienation between society and the political/executive organs of the state is felt most acutely."[28] These training programs will focus on a variety of different, though related, areas—including the relationship between legislatures and the political executive, the drafting of legislation and regulations, and the "nuts and bolts" of the budgetary process. In addition, attention will be given to the following:

understanding and coping with the needs of the media; how to help institutions become more effective and transparent (not corrupt); and how to improve the effectiveness of a parliamentarian through computer technology.[29]

Canada's interest in OAS reform was also manifested in other institutional areas.[30] For instance, it was active in pushing for the amalgamation or merging of the body's Inter-American Economic and Social Council with the Inter-American Council for Education, Science, and Culture.[31] In an effort to ensure improvements in technical cooperation, Canadian officials believed that a single council would coordinate information more effectively, reduce inefficiency, and avoid duplication. At the 1993 OAS General Assembly, the Canadian delegation was successful in getting a resolution approved which called for the creation of the Inter-American Council for Integral Development.[32] According to the resolution, this newly-established council is intended "to promote cooperation among the American States for the purpose of achieving integral development and, in particular, helping to eliminate extreme poverty."[33]

In the area of human rights, Canada still remains interested and committed—at least from a rhetorical standpoint.[34] Canadian officials in Washington are cognizant of domestic support in Canada for, and concerns about, the protection of basic human rights in the Americas. Through the Unit for the Promotion of Democracy, these same officials are supportive of "good governance"—that is, ensuring that the military remains under civilian control, fostering professional and competent civil services in the region, urging adequate funding for social programmes, and promoting respect for and protection of fundamental human rights. This commitment was demonstrated most recently at both the 1993 and 1994 OAS General

Assemblies (in Managua, Nicaragua and Belem, Brazil) where the Canadian delegation played a role in forging the Declaration of Managua for the Promotion of Democracy and Development. In addition to a number of points on strengthening democracy in the region, the declaration called for a hemisphere-wide commitment to

address the problem of safeguarding human rights with renewed emphasis on the promotion of civil, political, economic, social, and cultural rights. Where violations of human rights are pointed out, educational and promotional activities should also be carried out to prevent situations in which human rights are threatened.[35]

More recently, Ms. Stewart pointed out that the

Inter-American Court and Commission are unique and extremely important mechanisms for protecting and promoting human rights in the region. The defence of human rights is one of the fundamental principles of the OAS and, as a membership, we must ensure that these institutions are given the wherewithal to execute their mandates fully, effectively and objectively.[36]

While Canada apparently remains vigilant about human rights, it has shown itself to be active in the area of hemispheric security. For example, the Canadian government continued its quest either to reform or to dismantle the Inter-American Defense Board—despite some opposition from the United States, Mexico and a number of South American countries.[37] Moreover, Canadian officials are working on creating the proper conditions for peace and security in the Americas—with particular emphasis on confidence-building measures modelled on those utilized in Central America (i.e. security agreements, greater transparency, and arms reductions). They have also expressed an interest in instituting mechanisms for conflict prevention and management, strengthening the global non-proliferation regime and offering support for the UN Conventional Arms Register—with the possibility of a separate register for the hemisphere. These same officials draw a clear connection between confidence-building in the region and political stability, economic progress, democratic development, and respect for human rights in the Americas.[38]

During the course of the Managua General Assembly, Canada demonstrated its commitment to this ascendant issue. It supported, for example, a resolution advocating the need to define the precise legal-institutional relationship between the Inter-American Defense Board and the Organization of American States.[39]   And in Ms. McDougall's prepared address to the Assembly, Canada's position on the IADB was made perfectly clear:

As a body that receives approximately $2 million each year from the OAS and yet remains largely outside the system, the board is long overdue for such a review. Canada will be guided in these discussions by the following principles: clear political and civilian control, strict guidelines for accountability, a revised and well-defined mandate flowing from this political process, and the allocation of a modest budget appropriate to these newly defined tasks. If this new role is not deemed acceptable, we would advocate that the board be abolished. The status quo is not acceptable to Canada.[40]

Ms. Stewart, in her remarks to the 1994 General Assembly, noted that the board is one of the bodies "most in need of reform" and that Canada "believes it is imperative that decisive action on this question—including issues of mandate and linkage—be taken by the OAS in the coming year."[41] Canada also supported another resolution at the Managua General Assembly establishing an Experts Meeting on Confidence and Security-Building Measures, under the auspices of the Special Committee on Hemispheric Security. This Meeting of Experts, which held its first meeting in November 1993, is mandated to examine/ensure that "security mechanisms and measures to promote confidence work toward preventing potential sources of conflict and thus assist efforts to safeguard peace and security."[42] Clearly, Canada has placed a fair amount of emphasis on enhancing hemispheric security through building confidence and urging regional cooperation.[43]

Hemispheric and regional cooperation has also played a crucial role in Canada's second set of issues. On drug-trafficking, for instance, Canada continued to host the RCMP seminar on drug enforcement and to participate actively on the Inter-American Drug Abuse Control Commission (CICAD).[44] In fact, Canada was part of a drafting group, along with Mexico, that devised and sent out a questionnaire (on the nature of the drug problem) to all member states. It was intended to collect information on the drug trade in Latin America and to recommend possible solutions for dealing with the problem of drugs.[45] Canadian officials have also been involved in trying to streamline CICAD in order to make it more efficient. They were especially concerned about the fact that countless proposals, some of a questionable nature, were being submitted for possible funding. As a result, Canada, along with Jamaica, put forth a resolution seeking to establish project guidelines for CICAD so as to reduce the endless flow of project proposals.

As of the end of 1994 Canada is continuing to press ahead with reforming and streamlining CICAD. Canadian officials are particularly active in reviewing the administrative processes and operations of the commission. (Mexico is engaged in a similar process with respect to CICAD's actual priorities.) They have examined how the commission functions, with special emphasis on all of its procedures, budget management, and project approval.[46] Essentially, Canada would like to see greater budget discipline and some semblance of "order to the books." As a result, Canadian officials have prepared a paper which recommends that the commission should work on the basis of a business plan—taking on new projects only when it is prepared to let some other initiative go.[47] Additionally, it has requested that some sort of chart for tracking various projects be instituted so as to know exactly how much money is being spent on those same projects.[48]

In terms of economic co-operation, Canada has shown a burgeoning interest in trade-related matters. Consequently, it has moved to revitalize the Special Committee for Consultation and Negotiation (CECON), long considered ineffectual and little more than a forum for criticizing the United States. While not exactly pushing the issue, Canada is an enthusiastic supporter of greater dialogue on economic liberalization and reduction of trade barriers. Accordingly, Canada has become active in the Special Committee on Trade (which is to replace CECON), which seeks to exchange information and to promote a better understanding of trade-related matters.[49]

At the first meeting of the Special Committee on Trade, held in Washington in May of 1994, some progress was recorded. First,

Canada's idea of an advisory group—comprised of representatives from nine member states (including Canada)—was accepted and made responsible for counselling the committee. The importance of being a member of this group (which will meet on a quarterly basis) can not be over-emphasized, since it will be looking at all the existing trade arrangements now operating in the Americas, identifying where these arrangements are compatible and complementary, reviewing the progress of the committee's work, and setting the agenda for hemispheric trade issues. The thrust of both the committee and the advisory group is to work toward the eventual removal of trade barriers hemispherically.[50]

Canada has been less active on women's issues and on the environment—perhaps reflecting their low priority. Still, Canadian officials continue to work co-operatively with other member countries within the Inter-American Commission of Women (CIM).[51] They have also been involved, with a number of other countries, in framing a draft convention on violence against women (known as the Inter-American Convention on the Prevention, Punishment and Eradication of Violence Against Women). It is hoped that this convention will be ready for signature by the June 1995 OAS General Assembly, and thus create a useful precedent for the fourth World Conference on Women to be held in Beijing in September of 1995.

On the environmental front, Canada has maintained a fairly low profile within the OAS—although this could change in 1995.[52] In any event, this cautious approach to environmental issues is due in part to the fact that Canadian officials are not particularly impressed with the body's less-than-dynamic Committee on the Environment. Canadian officials believe that the committee is not reaching its full potential and is desperately in need of a breath of new life. As part of a plan to revitalize the committee, these officials are considering dusting off the 1940 Environmental and Wildlife Convention to evaluate its applicability and whether it can be updated for the OAS.

In addition, Canada's OAS Ambassador, Brian Dickson, is currently chairing a working group on environmental issues. He will be striving to get the Environmental Committee back on track and organizationally relevant. To begin, the role of the OAS in the environment will be examined to see what it is now doing, what it can do better, what exactly is happening in the region from an environmental standpoint, how it can maximize its efforts (does it have any comparative advantage?), and how the OAS can tap into other institutions dealing with the environment and sustainable development. More specifically, Canada will be working toward examining the regional implications of Agenda 21 and the UN Commission on Sustainable Development (CSD)—which came out of the 1992 Rio Conference (UNCED). The idea here is to have the OAS feed into the UN's implementation processes for Agenda 21 and thus to fortify the work of the CSD. Canada, for its part, has recommended hosting a meeting in Ottawa of regional experts on environmentally sound technologies for some time in February of 1995.

A recently emerging issue for Canada, especially for 1995 and beyond, will be the role of non-governmental groups (NGOs) and their relation to the OAS. Following on the heels of the June 1994 OAS General Assembly, where the NGO question was discussed, a working group was created to study this issue. With the full backing of Secretary of State Christine Stewart, Canada is in the process of compiling a list of NGOs interested in OAS affairs and clarifying the rules on what status these groups can have *vis-à-vis* the organization. What Canada would like to see, even though it has been criticized by some segments of the Canadian NGO community, is enhanced status for these groups within the body. Simply put, they would like to see a more formalized way for these groups to comment on what the OAS is actually doing.[53] Canadian officials believe that the NGO community can be constructive in terms of providing valuable information, expertise, and a critical perspective on a wide range of issues.[54]

EXPLAINING CANADA'S BEHAVIOUR WITHIN THE OAS

Given Canada's recent record of performance within the OAS, one is struck by the continuity of interest in particular issues. Indeed, a very clear core of subjects—including OAS reform, democracy, good governance, hemispheric security and human rights—have dominated the energies of Canadian officials in both Washington and Ottawa since Canada's joining. This continuity raises an important analytical question: what explains why Canada has opted for these issues as opposed to another set? Stated differently, what are the factors that drive or underpin Canada's issue-agenda at the OAS?

In trying to account for Canada's OAS agenda, one runs the risk of overlooking at least one or two other pertinent reasons. This examination, while comprehensive in nature, is not intended to provide an exhaustive list of explanatory factors or variables. Instead, it will highlight a number of key sources or determinants of Canada's behaviour within the hemispheric body. For purposes of this section, a variety of historical, external, and domestic factors will be detailed and evaluated.

From a historical standpoint, this core set of issues is consistent with Canada's long-standing status as a middle power in the international system. To be sure, they are a contemporary reflection of Canada's past (middle power) concerns and capabilities. In point of fact, a good part of Canada's positive international image has been its focus on, and commitment to, improving the quality of life for the world's peoples—or, as its critics might refer to it, global "do-goodism."[55] Issues about good governance, human rights, and the environment clearly fall within the purview of this so-called "do-goodism" or what Cranford Pratt, for one, has positively labelled "humane internationalism."[56] In short, then, these issues are clearly in the spirit of Canada's storied middle power tradition.[57]

At the heart of this tradition was (and remains) preoccupation with international peace and security, along with the central goal of order-building. This concentration on establishing and maintaining a stable world order was applied to various regions in the world, which were capable of engendering regional conflict or "brushfire wars."[58] The point here was that Canadian officials believed that such regional "brushfires" held out the possibility of imperilling the world community in a wider global conflict. Canada's past concerns about regional instability—and its potentially wider implications—helps to place into context Ottawa's current focus on issues such as good governance, democratic development, and hemispheric security. Indeed, foreign policy officials, as evidenced by Canada's work on confidence-building measures within the OAS, are committed to fostering a stable and predictable order in Latin America.

Underscoring this quest for order-building both regionally and globally has been a keen awareness on the part of officialdom in Ottawa of Canada's middle power status and capabilities.[59] As a country of middling or medium resources and capabilities, though possessing a formidable and highly-skilled diplomatic corps, Canadian officials fully realize that Canada is not in a position to reshape or mould the existing world, or even regional, order to its liking. It simply does not possess the raw power or capabilities to impose an orderly and predictable order in the Americas.[60] Thus, it might try to work in concert with a number of other member countries in the OAS—including Mexico, Brazil, Chile, and Venezuela—on such issues as good governance, human rights, OAS reform, and hemispheric security, which are the foundation stones for just such a regional order.[61]

While this middle power penchant for order-building, combined with medium capabilities, offers some important insights into Canada's OAS issue-agenda, it does not provide a total explanation. For a fuller examination, it is useful to outline and to analyze the external as well as the domestic sources of Canada's OAS policy. From an external perspective, one needs to take into account the changing global architecture—due to such powerful forces and developments as globalization, growing interdependence, and the end of the Cold War. These changing circumstances have opened up new opportunities for countries such as Canada to take on greater responsibilities in world politics. Given a new window of opportunity provided by the OAS, and the onset of greater freedom of diplomatic manoeuvre, Canadian officials have responded by advancing a full and ambitious agenda. Canada's core set of issues, then, is partly a function of being confronted with, and wanting to take advantage of, this new political and diplomatic space resulting from these changing international realities.[62]

Advancing these types of issues within the OAS also accords with the policy preferences of the new Clinton administration in the United States.[63] This is not to suggest that officials in Washington have determined, or have sought to determine, Canada's agenda within the OAS. Rather, it is intended to convey the point that Canada's issue-agenda (including OAS reform) coincides with, and thus does not conflict with the general foreign policy thrust of the Clinton White House. Although there exists no hard evidence, officialdom in Ottawa would probably wish to avoid adopting a core set of issues likely to elicit a negative reaction from U.S. officials. There is, however, no clear or causal relationship between Canada's OAS agenda and the policy priorities of the White House. Stated differently, the role of the United States helps to shed some light on why perhaps a different series of issues was not selected by Canada; but it does not offer any insights or explanation for the nature and longevity of the current set.

More to the point, Canada's issue-agenda within the OAS is consistent not only with the Clinton Administration's policy thrust, but also with the issues emerging on the new global agenda. Indeed, the issues of "high politics," which dominated world politics in the 1950s and 1960s, have declined in importance when compared to the rise of questions about "low politics"—international trade, economic security, environmental degradation, and human rights.[64] Put another way, the global appeal and saliency of such issues as democratic development, sustainable development, and the protection of human rights has shaped Canada's focus within the OAS. With a seemingly world-wide consensus emerging around these fundamental issues, it was logical for Canada to seek their application on a regional basis.

Issues and problems within the region itself undoubtedly influenced Canada's selection of its core issues. Canadian officials were cognizant of the fact that continued abuses of human rights and basic freedoms, environmental destruction, and tenuous civil-military relations held out the possibility for political instability in the region. And with the fragile seedling of democracy still not firmly rooted in Latin America, along with the institution of painful neoliberal economic reforms, they saw the necessity of confronting these potentially explosive issues before they reached unmanageable proportions. Canada's OAS agenda, then, was partly a response to pressing developments within the region as well as a determination to address them in a meaningful and multilateralist fashion.

In addition to external determinants of Canada's issue-agenda, there are a number of domestic sources. For example, this core set of issues had the support and endorsement of then-Secretary of State for External Affairs Barbara McDougall.[65] She was very enthusiastic about Canada playing a leading role in promoting regional order and stability, hemispheric cooperation, consensus-building, and in mitigating conflict—all incidently classic middle power missions.

In her prepared address before the June 1993 OAS General Assembly in Managua, which was actually delivered by Stan Gooch, Assistant Deputy Minister for Latin America and the Caribbean, Canada's position was stated quite clearly. The Canadian government would continue to express a firm and unwavering interest in issues about democratic development, human rights, hemispheric security, and OAS reform. As the written text succinctly noted:

What were our priorities in joining? Why did we think the OAS and the region were important to Canada? What do we see as the primary areas of accomplishment over the last three and half years? All these questions can be answered in terms of three broad themes: democratic development and human rights, economic development, and co-operative security.[66]

In terms of OAS reform, the address referred to the fact that the organization "was becoming more open to reform, determined to become a more relevant organization, more responsive to the needs of its democratic members. We have tried to contribute to this process during our brief tenure in this organization, and we have already seen some very tangible and encouraging results.[67]

Canada's current Foreign Minister, André Ouellet, remains committed to the organization—but he is necessarily preoccupied with the ever-present question of national unity (especially given the recent election of a PQ government in Quebec).[68] He has basically left Ms. Stewart to handle the OAS in particular and Latin America in general. She has continued to promote the same OAS agenda as Ms. McDougall—but without the weight of a full cabinet position. Still, she has demonstrated a keen interest in the OAS and its activities—as witnessed by her appearance at the June 1994 OAS General Assembly. Again, she reconfirmed Canada's commitment to issues such as democratic development, good governance, sustainable development, security issues, and trade and economic integration.[69]

In addition to ministerial support, this list of issues had the backing of an internationalist-oriented foreign policy bureaucracy. Officials within the Latin America and Caribbean branch in particular view these issues as important and fundamental to getting the region situated on a more stable, orderly, and peaceful footing. Stability, according to officials, holds the key to unlocking the door to a "new hemisphere,"[70]—a hemisphere in which resources can be directed towards strengthening economies rather than for security purposes, and where a culture of democracy can take root without the fear of war. The issues articulated by Canadian officials in the OAS, then, are intended to create and maintain stability in the region so as to preclude a return to the Cold War days when civilian governments were losing out to military regimes.[71]

Canadian officials in Washington also recognized the fact that the OAS itself appears to view these issues as important. Not only did these same officials detect a need to deal seriously with them, but they were also in tune with a general consensus within the organization on their significance. A large majority of the member countries were in agreement on the fundamental importance of consolidating a stable and predictable regional order in the Americas. Being cognizant of this emerging co-operation, Canadian officials have sought to take advantage of this new window of opportunity within the OAS. This, in turn, helps to explain Canada's willingness to champion this core set of issues. As one senior Canadian official remarked pointedly: "The simple answer is that it needs to be done."[72]

Both ministerial and bureaucratic factors, when viewed together, suggest that official government interest in these issues is part of an overarching foreign policy.[73] Stated differently, these issues are consistent with a foreign policy marked by these same priorities and objectives. While one should be careful about describing Canadian foreign policy as increasingly based on ethical values, more attention does appear to be given to human rights and democratic development. More emphasis, for instance, is being accorded to human rights abuses in foreign countries, on the reporting of these abuses and the actors involved, and on Canadian missions abroad gathering information and preparing written reports on the state of human rights.[74]

Arguably, this increased government attention to human rights, and Canada's OAS policy in general, may also be the result of pressures from "civil society." More specifically, prevailing public attitudes in Canada have galvanized around the importance of promoting human rights, democratic development, and good governance in the conduct of Canadian foreign policy.[75] There is little disagreement, if any, amongst the Canadian public on the saliency of these issues. There have also been pressures (albeit on the decline today) on Ottawa from the non-governmental community, church groups, the attentive public, and the media to pay more attention to human rights concerns.[76] In short, Canada's agenda at the OAS reflects the government's intention to deal with issues and concerns that civil society views as important.

One should not, however, lose sight of the fact that Canadian foreign policy is based on some calculation of Canada's national interest. Both ministers at the political level and officials at the bureaucratic level are interested in promoting and advancing Canadian interests—be they economic, security-related, political, or symbolic.[77] The point here is that there exists a proximate affinity between Canada's OAS policy and Canadian interests, however narrowly-defined. Clearly, Canada has a genuine stake in encouraging stability and conflict-avoidance in the region, along with an open economic/trade environment in the Americas. This, in turn, will have positive and long-term implications for Canada's economic prosperity, job creation, and standard of living. Simply put, Canada's championing of these core issues is linked to the pursuit of Canadian interests—as determined by official Ottawa.

CONCLUSION

From the preceding discussion, a number of admittedly general observations can be made about Canada's five years in the OAS. To begin with, it seems clear that the agenda guiding Canadian action within the OAS has remained remarkably consistent over those years—although perhaps pursued with less vigour. Issues such as OAS reform, hemispheric security, democratic development, and human rights continue to occupy the energies of Canadian officials in both Ottawa and Washington. This agenda, however, could easily become over-crowded as a second tier of issue areas—including drug-trafficking, the environment, women's issues, and economic co-operation—grows in importance.

The consistency of this agenda derives from a variety of historical, external and domestic factors. Canada's traditional middle power status, and the attendant style of diplomatic behaviour, places Canada's OAS policy in its proper framework or context. Indeed, Canada's long-standing middle power concerns about order-building, conflict reduction, mediation, and multilateralism go a long way toward explaining Canada's behaviour within the hemispheric body. From an external standpoint, developments in the international system and within the OAS itself, coupled with a change of leadership in the United States and an emerging consensus in Latin America all helped to shape Canada's agenda.

One could also find insights on Canada's OAS agenda from an examination of the domestic environment. Ministerial endorsement, by way of illustration, should not be downplayed as a factor in establishing Canada's list of concerns. In addition, bureaucratic support for this agenda sheds some light on its staying power. It is probably fair to say that over-arching Canadian foreign policy objectives and a desire to promote Canadian interests in general factored into the calculations as well. Lastly, pressures from civil society—and its morally-infused concerns—undoubtedly played a role in fashioning Canada's issue focus.

An argument could be made that some of these same factors will no doubt affect the new Liberal government's approach toward the OAS. For this reason, one should not expect any fundamental shift in Canada's OAS policy, and the issues underpinning that policy. While it is possible that the proposed review of Canadian foreign policy espoused by the Chrétien government will recommend changes in this area, it is difficult to conceive of any major reorientation. There might, however, be changes around the margins—such as an intensified effort to ratify the American Convention on Human Rights and thereby set the stage for Canada to seek a seat on the Inter-American Commission of Human Rights.[78] Still, the overall focus is unlikely to be altered in any substantial manner.

The Liberal party's ubiquitous "Red Book," and the government's apparent willingness to remain committed to it, does seem to reinforce this impression. Prior to coming to power, the Chrétien team gave no indications that the importance of this agenda had dissipated. In fact, the section covering foreign policy indicates that a Liberal government would support "such goals as sustainable development, global economic prosperity, a capable defence, and the eradication of poverty and social inequality."[79] And it goes on to note the following: "We will continue to support democracy and respect for human rights worldwide and will provide for a more open foreign policy-making process at home."[80] Lastly, in an article in the journal *Canadian Foreign Policy*, André Ouellet states that he has a mandate to "ensure that the now famous Liberal Party Red Book of policies announced during the election campaign are implemented during the course of our first term in office."[81] Accordingly, the Chrétien government is not likely to wander far from the OAS path charted by its Conservative predecessors.

References

INTRODUCTION

1. This is taken from a speech given by de Montigny Marchand, Canada's former Under-Secretary of State for External Affairs, to the Americas Society in New York, 15 November 1990, 2.
2. The term "aloof" is used throughout the text to describe Canada's position toward the Organization of American States (OAS) and its predecessor, the Pan American Union (PAU). According to *The Concise English Dictionary*, the word "aloof" is defined in the following way: "To take no part in, keep away; remain by oneself, remain unsympathetic." This definition tends to capture aptly Canada's cautious and unenthusiastic approach toward the inter-American system's principal institutional entities.
3. Much to the chagrin of senior DEA officials, Mulroney informed the press of his discussions on the OAS, and in particular his government's intention to review the membership issue, with President Bush. Jennifer Lewington, "Mulroney, Bush vow action on drugs, trade," *Globe and Mail*, 1 September 1989, sec. A, p. 1. Foreign policy mandarins were perturbed by the fact that Mulroney spoke about the OAS at Bush's summer retreat in Kennebunkport, Maine rather than in official Ottawa. They were concerned about Mulroney's remarks in Kennebunkport creating the public perception that Canada was once again being pressured to adjust its foreign policy to the whims of the behemoth to the south. Confidential interview by author with former senior DEA official, 12 August 1991.
4. Brian Mulroney, Notes for an address, San José, Costa Rica, 27 October 1989, 5.
5. For the 1994-95 budget year the membership fee for Canada was assessed at $8.5 million (U.S.), with another $1.8 million (U.S.) going to the organization's voluntary fund for aid and development. With Canada contributing some 12.3 per cent of the overall OAS budget, it ranks as the second largest contributor, after the United States.
6. For a fuller treatment of this subject, see John W. Holmes, "Canadian External Policies Since 1945," *International Journal* 18 (spring 1963): 137-47; Jack Granatstein, *Canadian Foreign Policy Since 1945: Middle Power or Satellite* (Toronto: Copp Clark, 1973); Denis Stairs, "The Political Culture of Canadian Foreign Policy," *Canadian Journal of Political Science* 15 no.4 (December 1982): 669-90; Michael Hawes, *Principal Power, Middle Power, or Satellite?* (Toronto: York University Research Programme in Strategic

Studies, 1984); Kim Richard Nossal, *The Politics of Canadian Foreign Policy* (Scarborough: Prentice-Hall, 1985); Cranford Pratt, ed., *Middle Power Internationalism: The North-South Dimension* (Montreal: McGill-Queen's University Press, 1990); and Tom Keating, *Canada and World Order* (Toronto: McClelland & Stewart, 1993).

7. There is, of course, the possibility that because there is a junior minister now responsible for Latin America, the Minister for Foreign Affairs, currently André Ouellet, may focus his energies on other matters of Canadian foreign policy.

8. This section is not intended to be a detailed history of Canada's numerous ties with the inter-American system. Rather, it is designed to inform the reader of the fact that Canada has, over the years, established a wide variety of contacts with this hemisphere. This, in turn, helps to dilute the notion that the decision to join the OAS was akin to a "bolt from the blue."

9. Canada has been active in the United Nations, the Commonwealth, and La francophonie in dealing with such issues as African economic recovery, apartheid South Africa, and Third World debt. See, for example, John W. Holmes, "The United Nations in Perspective," *Behind the Headlines* 44 no.1 (October 1986): 1-24; Clarence G. Redekop, "The Mulroney Government and South Africa: Constructive Disengagement," *Behind the Headlines* 44 no.2 (December 1986): 1-16; and John Kirton, "Shaping the Global Order: Canada and the Francophone and Commonwealth Summits of 1987," *Behind the Headlines* 44 no.6 (June 1987): 1-17.

10. For a historical examination of Canadian-Caribbean relations, see James J. Guy, "The Caribbean: A Canadian Perspective," in *Canadian-Caribbean Relations: Aspects of a Relationship*, ed. Brian Douglas Tennyson (Sydney, Nova Scotia: University College of Cape Breton, 1990): 257-99.

11. Linda Hossie, "Caribbean leaders laud Canada's 'commitment'," *Globe and Mail*, 21 March 1990, sec. A, p. 11. By way of comparison, two-way trade in 1981 was roughly $477 million. See Statistics Canada, *Catalogue 65-202* (Ottawa: Minister of Supply and Services Canada, 1991): 4-5; and Statistics Canada, *Catalogue 65-203* (Ottawa: Minister of Supply and Services Canada, 1991): 4-5.

12. Linda Hossie, "$182 million in debt is forgiven, PM tells Caribbean countries," *Globe and Mail*, 20 March 1990, sec. A, p. 1.

13. As with the anglophone Caribbean, Canada's relations with Haiti, a predominantly French-speaking country, have been excellent. For many years, it was the largest single recipient of Canadian development assistance in the Caribbean. In 1988, though, Ottawa decided, largely in response to the nation's serious political difficulties, to channel its aid primarily through non-governmental organizations and multilateral agencies. More recently, aid figures show that Canadian assistance totalled more than $22 million for 1989-1990. See Rheal Sequin, "PM takes rights campaign to Paris," *Globe and Mail*, 18 November 1991, sec. A,

p. 1. A recent illustration of close Canadian-Haitian relations was given by the participation of Pierre Côté, Quebec's chief electoral commissioner and the head of the OAS observer team monitoring the December 1990 elections in Haiti. Moreover, the newly-elected president, Father Jean-Bertrand Aristide, received much of his formal theological training in Montreal. Given the nature of Canada's relations with both Haiti and the Commonwealth Caribbean, it is well-placed to exercise a fair amount of influence in the region.

14. It is, of course, simplistic to speak of Latin America as a single whole. Latin America includes a variety of peoples, with linguistic and cultural differences, and distinct political economies.

15. For a recent discussion of Canada's past and present involvement in inter-American affairs, see James J. Guy, "Canada Joins the OAS: A New Dynamic in the Inter-American System," *Inter-American Review of Bibliography* 34, no. 4 (1989): 500-11.

16. For a recent treatment of the trade dimension, see Wilson Ruiz, "A View from the South: Canadian/Latin American Links," in *Briefing* (Ottawa: North-South Institute, 1988): 1-5.

17. Statistics Canada, *Catalogue* 65-003.

18. See James J. Guy, "Canada and Latin America," *The World Today* 32 no.10 (October 1976): 384.

19. David Kilgour, "Canada and Latin America," *International Perspectives* (January/February 1986): 20. See also George W. Schuyler, "Perspectives on Canada and Latin America: Changing Context ... Changing Policy?" *Journal of Interamerican Studies and World Affairs* 33 no.1 (spring 1991): 31-33.

20. Linda Hossie, "Costa Rican summit celebrates democracy," *Globe and Mail,* 27 October 1989, sec. A, p. 4.

21. See Canadian International Development Agency, *Annual Report 1991-92,* August 1993: 8 and Canadian International Development Agency, *Annual Report 1992-93,* May 1994: 8.

22. In addition to opening a political dialogue with the leaders of these countries, Trudeau sought to sell such Canadian products as Dash-7 aircraft, CANDU reactors, and railway equipment. See George Radwinski, "Trudeau in Latin America Sets Stage for Closer Relations," *International Perspectives* (May-June 1976): 6-10, and J.L. Granatstein and Robert Bothwell, *Pirouette: Pierre Trudeau and Canadian Foreign Policy* (Toronto: University of Toronto Press, 1990), p. 274.

23. Linda Hossie, "Canada, Mexico enter 'new era' in relations," *Globe and Mail,* 17 March 1990, sec. A, p. 6.

24. Charlotte Montgomery, "Canada seeks to thaw frost in U.S.-Cuban relationship," *Globe and Mail,* 14 April 1990, sec. A, p. 7.

25. In 1992 total Canadian exports to other OAS member states (except the United States) amounted to some $3.2 billion, while imports from these same countries totalled $5.4 billion. For 1993, exports from Canada to

other OAS member states (omitting the United States) reached $3.6 billion and imports from these countries exceeded $6.3 billion. Department of Foreign Affairs and International Trade, *Canada-OAS Member States Trade Statistics*, June,1994, p. 2.

26. See Oxford Analytica, "Free trade faces challenges," *Globe and Mail*, 11 July 1994, sec. B, p. 9. For recent academic treatments of the NAFTA, see James Rochlin, *Discovering the Americas* (Vancouver: UBC Press, 1994), pp. 166-189; Peter Hakim, "NAFTA and After: A New Era for the United States and Latin America?" *Current History* 93 no.581 (March 1994): 97-102; and Guy Poitas and Raymond Robinson, "The Politics of NAFTA in Mexico," *Journal of Interamerican Studies and World Affairs* 36 no.1 (spring 1994): 1-35.

27. While it might be too early to tell whether the Americas will become a major area of focus for the Liberals, it does seem clear that Mexico will generate a fair amount of government attention.

28. See Casper Garos, *Canada-U.S. Free Trade: Background, Issues and Impact* (Amsterdam: VU University Press, 1990), p. 4.

29. Oxford Analytica, "Ottawa seeks harmonized trade practices," *Globe and Mail*, 12 September 1994, sec. B, p. 5.

30. For a sampling of these individuals, see footnote 31.

31. Humphrey, *The Inter-American System: A Canadian View* (Toronto: Macmillan, 1942) and Roussin, *Le Canada et le système interaméricain* (Ottawa: University of Ottawa Press, 1958). While I acknowledge the lack of French Canadian sources, I have interviewed Marcel Roussin, a pioneering scholar in Canada's relations with the inter-American system, as well as read many of his published works. Others have examined various aspects of Canada's ties with the inter-American system in general and Latin America in particular. See, for example, F.H. Soward and A.M. Macaulay, *Canada and the Pan American System* (Toronto: The Ryerson Press, 1948); Marcel Roussin, "Evolution of the Canadian Attitude toward the Inter-American System," *The American Journal of International Law* 47, no. 2 (1953): 296-300; John D. Harbron, *Canada and the Organization of American States* (Canadian-American Committee, 1963); W. Arthur Irwin, "Should Canada Join the Organization of American States?" *Queen's Quarterly* 72 no.2 (summer 1965): 289-303; David Edward Smith,"Should Canada Join the Organization of American States?: A Rejoinder to W. Arthur Irwin," *Queen's Quarterly* 72 no.1 (spring 1966): 100-114; J.C.M. Ogelsby, *Gringos From the Far North* (Toronto: Macmillan, 1976); D.R. Murray, "The Bilateral Road: Canada and Latin America in the 1980s," *International Journal* 37 no.2 (winter 1981-82): 108-31; Edgar J. Dosman, "Hemispheric Relations in the 1980s: A Perspective from Canada," *Journal of Canadian Studies* 19 no.4 (winter 1984-85): 42-60; James J. Guy, "Canada Joins the OAS: A New Dynamic in the Inter-American System," *Inter-American Review of Bibliography* 39, no. 4 (1989): 500-11; James Rochlin, "The Evolution of

Canada as an Actor in Inter-American Affairs," *Millennium* 19, no. 2 (1990): 229-48; and George W. Schuyler, "Perspectives on Canada and Latin America: Changing Context ... Changing Policy," *Journal of Interamerican Studies and World Affairs* 33 no.1 (spring 1991): 19-58. More recently, see Edgar J. Dosman, "Canada and Latin America: The New Look," *International Journal* 47 no.3 (summer 1992): 529-54; Jeffrey Haar and Edgar Dosman, eds., *A Dynamic Partnership: Canada's Changing Role in the Americas* (Miami: University of Miami, 1993); H.P. Klepak, ed., *Canada and Latin American Security* (Laval: Méridien, 1993) and James Rochlin, *Discovering the Americas* (Vancouver: UBC Press, 1994).

32. According to "conventional wisdom," Canadian foreign policy is formulated differently than, say, domestic policy in Canada. Public-policy formulation is influenced by, among other things, the political leadership, the bureaucracy, political parties, Parliament, the media, "attentive public," and public opinion. But as Kim Richard Nossal contends: "By contrast, foreign policy is formulated and conducted by government officials, mostly without any direct input by societal actors." Nossal, *The Politics of Canadian Foreign Policy* (Scarborough, Ont: Prentice-Hall, 1985), p. xii. For the most part, these officials tend to reside in two principal ministries or departments—namely, External Affairs and Finance. Individuals from each of these departments shape Canadian foreign policy by developing various policy options, positions, and recommendations for their political masters. The final decision on any particular foreign policy matter rests, of course, with the Cabinet and the political leadership in Canada. On this subject, see Harald von Riekhoff, "The Structure of Foreign Policy Decision-Making and Management," in *Canada Among Nations*, ed. Brian W. Tomlin and Maureen Appel Molot (Toronto: James Lorimer, 1987), pp. 14-30 and John Kirton, "The Foreign Policy Decision Process," in *Canada Among Nations*, ed. Maureen Appel Molot and Brian W. Tomlin (Toronto: James Lorimer, 1986), pp. 25-45. For a recent treatment of crisis decision-making, see P. Stuart Robinson, "Reason, Meaning, and the Institutional Context of Foreign Policy Decision-making," *International Journal* 49 no.2 (spring 1994): 408-33.

33. This examination of Canada-OAS relations fits nicely into what Arend Lijphart has referred to as "atheoretical case studies." See his "Comparative Politics and the Comparative Method," *American Political Science Review* 65 no.3 (Sept. 1971): 691.

34. Marcel Roussin, "Latin America: Challenge and Response," *Conference Proceedings* (Banff, Alberta: Banff Conference on World Development, 1964), p. 10.

CHAPTER I

1. Taken from Vicente Lecuña, *Cartas del Libertador* (New York, 1948), p. 55.
2. Some commentators note that other Latin Americans, including San Martín, Martínez de Rojas, and Bernardo Monteagudo, supported the idea of hemispheric co-operation and confederation. On this point, see J. Lloyd Mecham, *The United States and Inter-American Security, 1889-1960* (Austin: University of Texas Press, 1962), p. 29.
3. See Arthur P. Whitaker, *The Western Hemisphere Idea: Its Rise and Decline* (Ithaca: Cornell University Press, 1954), p. 26.
4. While there were earlier Hispanic-American Conferences, such as the Congress of Panama in 1826, delegates from the United States failed to reach Panama. For a useful discussion of these earlier conferences, see Ann Van Wynen Thomas and A.J. Thomas, Jr., *The Organization of American States* (Dallas: Southern Methodist University Press, 1963), pp. 6-12.
5. For further elaboration of this point, see Arthur P. Whitaker, *Western Hemisphere Idea*.
6. Increasing U.S. production levels also necessitated a greater demand for raw materials. Indeed, by the early 1900s, the bulk of U.S. imports from Hispanic America consisted of oils, iron, tin plate, and metal products. By way of comparison, total U.S. exports to Hispanic-American countries in 1850 amounted to some $9 million. By 1875, however, total U.S. exports had climbed to roughly $28 million, just over a three-fold increase. And by 1890, this export figure had increased dramatically to over $105 million. All these figures were drawn from William Spence Robertson, *Hispanic-American Relations with the United States* (New York: Oxford University Press, 1923), pp. 204-13.
7. In fact, from the period 1890-1914, trade between the U.S. and Hispanic America increased markedly. Imports from the Latin American republics, even for the years 1900 to 1914, grew by some $300 million. U.S. exports to the region, for the same period, increased from a modest $105 million to more than $273 million. As William Spence Robertson notes: "With the states of Central America the import and export trade of the United States had increased so markedly that, on the eve of the World War, the United States had a larger share in this commerce than either Great Britain or Germany." Ibid., p. 221.
8. Ibid., p. 278.
9. F.V. García-Amador, *The Inter-American System: Its Development and Strengthening* (Dobbs Ferry, New York: Oceana Publications, 1966), p. xx.
10. Robertson, *Hispanic-American Relations*, p. 210.
11. See Gaston Nerval, *Autopsy of the Monroe Doctrine: The Strange Story of Inter-American Relations* (New York, 1934), p. v.

12. Jerome Slater, "United States Policy in Latin America," in *Latin America: Its Problems And Its Promise*, ed. Jan Knippers Black (Boulder, CO: Westview Press, 1984), p. 221.

13. On this point, see Gordon Connell-Smith, *The United States and Latin America* (London: Heinemann Educational Books, 1974), pp. 107-45.

14. The term "American" is being used here solely for stylistic reasons. In general, Latin Americans find the loose usage of this term mildly insulting. To them, all the inter-American republics are part of the Americas and therefore they are all Americans. To avoid being slighted, they would prefer the term "norteamericano (-a)" instead of "americano (-a)."

15. Whitaker, *Western Hemisphere Idea*, p. 75.

16. See Jack Child, "The 1889-1890 Washington Conference through Cuban Eyes: José Martí and the First International American Conference," *Inter-American Review of Bibliography* 39, no. 4 (1989): 452-53.

17. See E. Bradford Burns, "The Continuity of the National Period," in *Latin America: Its Problems and its Promise*, ed. Jan Knippers Black (Boulder, CO: Westview Press, 1984), pp. 69-70.

18. See Gordon Connell-Smith, *The Inter-American System* (London: Oxford University Press, 1966), p. 23.

19. It is instructive to note that all of the participating republics were dependent upon customs duties as their major source of revenue.

20. See J. Lloyd Mecham, *United States and Security*, p. 53.

21. John P. Humphrey, *The Inter-American System: A Canadian View* (Toronto: Macmillan, 1942), p. 45.

22. Child, *Washington Conference*, p. 452.

23. Connell-Smith, *The United States and Latin America*, p. 112.

24. Connell-Smith, *The Inter-American System*, p. 44.

25. Ibid., p. 45.

26. The Second International Conference, held in Mexico City in 1901-02, was notable for its agreement on constituting a governing board for the International Bureau of American Republics, which consisted of the U.S. Secretary of State and the diplomatic representatives of Latin American governments. The following conference, which took place in Rio de Janeiro in 1906, was best remembered for its emphasis on the threat posed by U.S.—as opposed to European—influence in the hemisphere. For further elaboration of these two conferences, consult Connell-Smith, *Inter-American System*, pp. 45-51.

27. The building was erected largely with funds provided by Andrew Carnegie, who had been a U.S. delegate to the initial Washington Conference.

28. Given U.S. intervention in the Caribbean and Central America, Washington was fully in favour of not "politicizing" the PAU.

29. Up to this point, the PAU had been operating under a series of

resolutions, which could be modified at any time. For an excellent discussion of the various proposals for reform proffered by such countries as Mexico, see William Manger, "The Pan American Union at the Sixth International Conference of American States," *The American Journal of International Law* 22 no.4 (July 1928): 764-75.

30. At the 1945 Mexico conference further changes to the PAU were instituted. In addition to the fact that members of the Governing Board would no longer have to be accredited ambassadors to the United States, the chairmanship of the Board would be opened to Latin Americans. Furthermore, anyone holding the positions of Director General and Assistant Director of the PAU would not be eligible for re-election and should not be succeeded by a person of the same nationality. Again, this measure offered Latin Americans a greater opportunity to occupy a high profile position within the institution. For a discussion of this conference see Josef L. Kunz, "The Inter-American Conference on Problems of War and Peace at Mexico City and the Problem of the Reorganization of the Inter-American System," *The American Journal of International Law* 39 no.3 (July 1945): 527-33.

31. For a thorough analysis of the Sixth, Seventh, and Eighth conferences, see Thomas and Thomas, *Organization of American States,* pp. 21-24. In a general sense, though, there was a noticeable absence of any inter-American machinery for mutual defence. Furthermore, there were no adequate peace instruments for resolving hemispheric disputes or controversies. Lastly, the burgeoning inter-American system had completely failed to address the hemisphere's more pressing economic difficulties.

32. By the early 1940s, after more than forty-five years of inter-American dialogue and interaction, the hegemonic tendencies embodied in the Monroe Doctrine still remained the cornerstone of U.S. policy in the hemisphere. Over these years, a majority of Latin Americans developed a deep distrust and fear of U.S. power and influence. Clearly, U.S. intervention in Mexico (1914), Haiti (1915), the Dominican Republic (1916), Nicaragua (1926), and harassment of Cuba (1933) all caused resentment and left a bitter taste in the mouths of Latin American peoples. Furthermore, U.S. economic influence and control of Latin American resources, restrictions on Cuban and Panamanian independence, denial of the right of revolution to Central American republics, and a high tariff policy only served to reinforce this sense of U.S. domination and control.

33. Arthur P. Whitaker, *Western Hemisphere Idea,* p. 172.

34. This point is made by William Everett Kane. See his *Civil Strife in Latin America: A Legal History of U.S. Involvement* (Baltimore: The Johns Hopkins University Press, 1972), p. 150.

35. Quoted in J. Lloyd Mecham, *United States and Security,* p. 257.

36. Interestingly, there was no Marshall Plan for Latin America to help the economies of these states, distorted by the war, to adjust to peace-time conditions.

37. It is interesting to note that the Rio Treaty's hemispheric security zone—as delineated in Article 4—encompasses Canada. And as Thomas and Thomas explain: "If Canada were subject to armed attack arising against its territory or within its security zone, it could request the other American states as ratifiers of the Rio Treaty to come to its aid." Thomas and Thomas, *Organization of American States,* p. 81.

38. It does not, however, establish a form of military co-operation or a system of military forces under collective command.

39. Thomas and Thomas, *Organization of American States,* p. 249.

40. On this point, see Margaret M. Ball, *The OAS in Transition* (Durham, NC: Duke University Press, 1969), p. 26.

41. For a thorough analysis of the various articles, see Thomas and Thomas, *Organization of American States,* pp. 249-76.

42. According to Gordon Connell-Smith, a keen student of inter-American affairs, the "inter-American system" includes "certain treaties and agreements between the American nations; numerous inter-American institutions created to further common objectives and the observance of agreed principles; and a form of multilateral diplomacy through which the American states conduct a part of their international relations." Connell-Smith, *The Inter-American System,* p. xv.

43. Unless otherwise indicated, quotes are taken directly from the Rio Treaty itself. Organization of American States, *Inter-American Treaty of Reciprocal Assistance, Applications I* (Washington, DC: General Secretariat, 1973), pp. 423-30.

44. This point is made most forcefully by Jerome Slater. See his study, *A Revaluation of Collective Security: The OAS in Action* (Ohio: Ohio State University Press, 1965), pp. 24-25.

45. However, these same governments would receive more protection—from intra- or extra-continental aggessors—if the United States was bound to a collective security system. With the United States tied to the inter-American system, the treaty also provided Latin Americans with greater leverage over the U.S. behemoth. On this point, see Ibid., p. 37.

46. See John C. Dreier, *The Organization of American States and the Hemisphere Crisis* (New York: Harper & Row, 1962), p. 26.

47. The actual invocation of the Rio Treaty will be discussed more fully in chapter two.

48. The OAS Charter has, over the years, been reformed—including the "Protocol of Buenos Aires" (approved in 1967) and, more recently, the "Protocol of Cartagena de Indias" (approved in 1985).

49. Jerome Slater, *The OAS and United States Foreign Policy* (Ohio: Ohio State University Press, 1967), p. 39.

50. In fact, the U.S. delegation actually favoured limiting the scope of the OAS Charter. On this point, see Connell-Smith, *The Inter-American System,* p. 197.

51. The subsequent discussion of these three sections is not intended to be an exhaustive evaluation of the charter. Rather, it is designed to give the reader a clearer sense of what the document actually represents.

52. For a thorough treatment of these principles, see Ball, *OAS in Transition,* pp. 43-67.

53. Interestingly enough, it was the Cuban delegation which was actually the driving force pushing for inclusion of a statement condemning economic aggression.

54. The Permanent Council is composed of a single representative, with the rank of ambassador, from each of the member states.

55. For a recent evaluation of the commission, see Tom F. Farer, "The OAS at the Crossroads: Human Rights," *Iowa Law Review* 72 (1986-87): 401-13.

56. These Specialized Organizations exist in addition to a number of other important OAS agencies. For instance, the Inter-American Defense Board (IADB), which was established in 1942, is the principal agency in charge of planning the defence of the Western hemisphere. With its sizeable budget, it studies, plans, and recommends to governments measures to repel aggression. Moreover, it prepares and maintains plans for collective defence, and it engages in other military matters, training courses, liaison, and inspection trips. The Inter-American Court, the Inter-American Committee on Peaceful Settlement, and the Inter-American Statistical Institute are also official or semi-official agencies of the OAS. Furthermore, the Inter-American Development Bank (IDB), though considered part of the inter-American network, is not linked formally to the OAS. Still, it promotes the investment of capital for development purposes, uses its own capital to accelerate the process of economic development in member countries, and provides technical assistance for the formulation and implementation of development plans. Bank decisions are made on the basis of a weighted voting system. While the United States—with roughly 40 per cent of the shares in the bank—lacks the voting power to dictate every IDB decision, its vote is by far the most powerful. For an excellent discussion of these agencies, see Ball, *OAS in Transition,* pp. 365-407.

57. For a critical assessment of these organizations, see Thomas and Thomas, *Organization of American States,* pp. 131-33.

58. The strengths and weaknesses of the charter are examined more thoroughly in chapter two.

59. The most recent version of the charter, which incorporates the Protocol of Cartagena, contains 151 provisions.

60. It is instructive to note that the ineffectiveness of the American Treaty on Pacific Settlement resulted in the creation of the Inter-American Peace Committee. See Connell-Smith, *The Inter-American System,* p. 215. Also see Larman C. Wilson, "Multilateral Policy and the Organization of American States: Latin-American-U.S. Convergence and Divergence," in *Latin American Foreign Policies: An Analysis,* ed. Harold Eugene Davis and Larman C. Wilson (Baltimore: Johns Hopkins University Press, 1975), p. 54.

61. Those states which have not ratified the Pact of Bogotá are still bound by the earlier instruments that they have ratified and by the mechanisms for pacific settlement embodied in the Rio Treaty and the OAS Charter.

62. L. Ronald Scheman and John W. Ford, "The Organization of American States as Mediator," in *International Mediation in Theory and Practice,* ed. Saadia Touval and I. William Zartman (Boulder, CO: Westview Press, 1985), p. 198.

63. Critics of the pact were quick to point to the fact that some of its provisions essentially superseded the political prerogatives of the parties involved. If invocation of the treaty entailed conceding that kind of national sovereignty, they were simply not prepared to do so.

64. Ball, *OAS in Transition,* p. 428.

65. Connell-Smith, *The Inter-American System,* p. 209.

66. John C. Dreier, *Organization of American States and Hemisphere Crisis,* p. 37.

67. Disputes among Latin American countries, particularly in the area of bitter border controversies, were also a major source of discontentment and ill-will.

CHAPTER II

1. Quoted in Francis X. Gannon, "Will the OAS Live to Be 100? Does it Deserve To?" *Caribbean Review* 13 no.4 (fall 1984): 13.

2. Its ineffectiveness in dealing with the conflicts in Central America throughout the 1980s was another telling signal of its irrelevancy.

3. Obviously, the words "success" and "failure" pose some definitional problems. While they are difficult to quantify and are admittedly artificial, they do provide a means of classification. For purposes of this study, the term "success" denotes the fact that the OAS was a major player in an inter-American dispute, a useful and constructive institutional instrument, and a determining factor in bringing a particular dispute to a peaceful conclusion. As for the term "failure," it refers to cases where the hemispheric body was not a force to contend with in an inter-American dispute, where it was conspicuously dilatory and ineffective, and where it was unable to play a leading role in resolving a hemispheric conflict—despite its desire to do so.

4. It is important to emphasize the fact that there is little in the way of Canadian government documentation on the early period of the OAS, particularly from 1948-1957. The examination of copious archival material showed virtually no references to the early successes of the body. This is due, in part, to the fact that Canada's association with the organization—and especially the issue of membership—was not a major priority for the Liberal government of the day.

5. In addition, it is important—particularly from a foreign policy-making standpoint—to grapple with the strengths and weaknesses of the OAS. As

a member of the body, Canadian officials and diplomats should be cognizant of what the organization can and cannot do or where it can and cannot be effective. By recognizing what roles the OAS is best suited for, policy-makers in Ottawa will be able to formulate possible areas where Canada can make a valuable contribution.

6. The treaty received the fourteenth notice of ratification (thereby obtaining the requisite two-thirds) on 3 December 1948 when, incidently, Costa Rica deposited its instrument of ratification in Washington. See Manuel R. García-Mora, "The Law of the Inter-American Treaty of Reciprocal Assistance," *Fordham Law Review* 20 (March 1951): 1-20.

7. The Nicaraguan government, in turn, claimed that Costa Rican authorities supported the unsavoury Caribbean Legion, a band of mercenaries who threatened the peace of the region. For this dispute, see, Organization of American States, *Inter-American Treaty of Reciprocal Assistance Applications, I, 1948-1959* (Washington: Pan American Union, 1964), pp. 27-65. (Hereafter referred to as OAS *Applications, I*) Also see Robert D. Tomasek, "The Organization of American States and Dispute Settlement from 1948 to 1981—An Assessment," *Inter-American Review of Bibliography* 34, no. 1 (1989): 467.

8. Article 6, as mentioned in the previous chapter, refers to the convening of the Organ of Consultation in cases where the sovereignty of an American state has been violated "by an aggression which is not an armed attack or by an extra-continental or intra-continental conflict, or by any other fact or situation that might endanger the peace of America."

9. It is instructive to note that the 1948 Costa Rican-Nicaraguan controversy focused international attention upon the OAS. It was clear that its actions in this case would ostensibly set the standard for future inter-American disputes. In short, the institution was under enormous pressure to meet this initial challenge head-on, to produce a favourable settlement, and to prove to its critics that it was a viable international organization.

10. Charles G. Fenwick, "Application of the Treaty of Rio to the Controversy between Costa Rica and Nicaragua," *The American Journal of American Law* 43 no.2 (April 1949): 330.

11. Edgar S. Furniss, "The Inter-American System and Recent Caribbean Disputes," *International Organization* 4 no.4 (November 1950): 588.

12. The committee was composed of members from Mexico, Brazil, Colombia, and the United States. The delegation flew to the region on an aircraft placed at the disposal of the Committee by the U.S. government. See OAS *Applications, I*, p. 32.

13. This Commission of Military Experts was sent to the area to ensure that the border between the two countries was closed. Secondly, it was empowered to verify that rebels on both sides put down their weapons and phased out their illegal activities. Several months later, it reported to the council that the Costa Rican government had disarmed the

Caribbean Legion and indicated that Nicaragua had closed its border with Costa Rica and was interning any remaining pockets of the revolutionary movement. Ibid., p. 33.

14. Ibid., pp. 38-42.

15. Dreier, *Organization of American States and Hemisphere Crisis*, p. 60.

16. For a look at this case and others, see Robert D. Tomasek, "Caribbean Exile Invasions: A Special Regional Type of Conflict," *Orbis* 17 no.4 (winter 1974): 1354-82.

17. *OAS Applications, I*, p. 125.

18. Santo Domingo, in response, charged that Haiti, along with Cuba and Guatemala, was supporting hostile activities against the Dominican government. Furniss, *Inter-American System and Recent Caribbean Disputes*, pp. 586-87.

19. Thomas and Thomas, *Organization of American States*, p. 299.

20. For the actions of the council, see *OAS Applications, I*, pp. 129-32.

21. Ibid., p. 134.

22. Ibid., p. 136.

23. For a fuller elucidation of the various recommendations, see Thomas and Thomas, *Organization of American States*, pp. 300-01.

24. It is important to remember that these notable successes had little impact on Canadian attitudes toward the body. Given Canada's unenthusiastic response to these cases, it is conceivable that officials simply did not view the OAS as a significant institutional entity. Their relative indifference tends to confirm the view that Canada-OAS affairs were not a major foreign policy priority.

25. *OAS Applications, I*, p. 168.

26. Peaceful observation flights, never before used as an inter-American peace measure, took place over regions that were reportedly strafed and bombed from aircraft flying out of the north (read Nicaragua). See Ibid., p. 170 and Tomasek, "Organization of American States and Dispute Settlement," 467.

27. The Investigating Committee was composed of representatives of Mexico, Brazil, Paraguay, Ecuador, and the United States. Once the council decided to establish an air patrol, under the direction of the committee, the governments of Ecuador, Mexico, Uruguay, and the United States made planes available. *OAS Applications, I*, p. 172.

28. At one point, the committee threatened possible sanctions, which would have been an unprecedented action under the Rio Treaty. However, with the departure of the invading forces, this idea was quickly shelved. Ibid., p. 174 and Tomasek, "Organization of American States and Dispute Settlement," 467.

29. After the dispute was resolved, Costa Rica returned the planes to the United States. Mecham, *The United States and Inter-American Security, 1889-1960*, p. 404.

30. *OAS Application, I*, p. 201.

31. It is instructive to note that the OAS was not committed to condemning or punishing the illegal actions of Nicaragua. Rather, it was more interested in bringing Nicaragua back into the OAS fold and normalizing relations between the two countries.

32. Slater, *OAS and United States Foreign Policy*, p. 73.

33. Dreier, *Organization of American States and Hemisphere Crisis*, p. 62.

34. Gordon Connell-Smith, *The Inter-American System* (London: Oxford University Press, 1966), p. 237.

35. While most of the disputed area was mainly jungle borderland, some reports indicated that a portion of it contained oil deposits. From a historical standpoint, the territory in question was the subject of an arbitrated award in 1906, in which the King of Spain supported the claim by Honduras. Nicaragua, however, never accepted the validity of the award. See Tomasek, "Organization of American States and Dispute Settlement," 468.

36. See C. G. Fenwick, "The Honduras-Nicaragua Boundary Dispute," *American Journal of International Law* 51 (1957): 762.

37. *OAS Applications, I*, p. 246.

38. The committee was comprised of representatives and military experts from Argentina, Bolivia, Mexico, Panama, and the United States. Ibid., p. 248.

39. Ibid., p. 250.

40. Tomasek, "Organization of American States and Dispute Settlement," p. 469.

41. *OAS Applications, I*, p. 300.

42. Mecham, *United States and Inter-American Security*, pp. 419-21 and Lloyd J. Mecham, *A Survey of United States-Latin American Relations* (Boston: Houghton Mifflin, 1965), pp. 185-87.

43. Dreier, *Organization of American States*, pp. 72-73.

44. It would be an understatement to say that Trujillo was disliked by his own people. While the military dictator was staunchly anti-communist, he was despised and shunned by the wider Latin-American community. Slater, *OAS and United States Foreign Policy*, p. 205.

45. The committee was composed of representatives from Argentina, Mexico, Panama, Uruguay, and the United States. Ball, *The OAS in Transition*, p. 453.

46. Ibid., pp. 453-54.

47. Slater, *OAS and United States Foreign Policy*, p. 189.

48. The United States, which had valued Trujillo's anti-communist disposition, opposed the adoption of sanctions. Dreier, *United States and Inter-American Security*, p. 421.

49. Ball, *OAS in Transition*, p. 454.

50. It also retained discretion to study the feasibility and desirability of extending the trade sanctions to other articles.

51. Since the United States was the Dominican Republic's largest trading partner, the new sanctions were, for the most part, unilateral. Reportedly, Washington turned on the Trujillo regime in an effort to secure future Latin American support against Castro's Cuba. See Mecham, *United*

States and Inter American Security, p. 421.

52. Dreier, *Organization of American States and Hemisphere Crisis,* p. 98.

53. Ball, *OAS in Transition,* p. 454.

54. Ronald St. John Macdonald, "The Organization of American States In Action," *University of Toronto Law Journal* 15 (1963-64): 371-72.

55. It is worth reiterating here that these OAS successes did not register in any discernible fashion on officials in Ottawa and diplomats in the field. One could argue, of course, that Canada's foreign policy at this time was geared more toward Western Europe and the creation of the North Atlantic Treaty Organization (NATO). In addition, the government of Louis St. Laurent—as later chapters will illustrate—exhibited little interest in moving Canada into the inter-American orbit.

56. Interestingly, in cases where the OAS proved to be ineffective—as opposed to those occasions when it played a constructive role—there was a fair degree of Canadian reaction.

57. Prior to the actual onset of the Guatemalan crisis, the Tenth Inter-American Conference was held in Caracas, Venezuela in March 1954. At this conference, the United States delegation pressed for, and succeeded in obtaining, a firm declaration on anti-communism. In the words of Arthur P. Whitaker: "Guatemala was not mentioned by name, but the reference was clear." Arthur P. Whitaker, "The Organization of American States," *Yearbook of World Affairs* 13 (1959): 129. For a fuller discussion of the Caracas conference, see Connell-Smith, *Inter-American System,* pp. 229-31. For an excellent analysis of the Guatemalan crisis itself, see Piero Gleijeses, *Shattered Hopes: The Guatemalan Revolution and the United States, 1944-1954* (Princeton, NJ: Princeton University Press, 1991).

58. It is important for contextual reasons to understand the prevailing international climate at the time of the Guatemalan crisis. First, the Korean War, which was in many ways portrayed as a struggle against communist forces, had recently come to a close. Secondly, the final chapter of the McCarthy era was just being written. With rabid anti-communism flourishing in the United States, the Eisenhower administration was very sensitive to any hint of communist infiltration in the Western hemisphere. In the eyes of the Eisenhower White House, the Arbenz government, even in the face of scanty evidence, was decidedly communist. And its view was clear: since the risk from any possible spread of communist influences in the region would be great, the Arbenz government would have to be removed. For a critical assessment of U.S. interference in Guatemala, see Stephen Kinzer and Stephen C. Schlesinger, *Bitter Fruit: The Untold Story of the American Coup in Guatemala* (Garden City, NY: Doubleday, 1982); Philip B. Taylor, "The Guatemalan Affair: A Critique of United States Foreign Policy," *American Political Science Review* 50 no.3 (September 1956): 787-806; and William Everett Kane, *Civil Strife in Latin America* pp. 186-97. For a more favourable view, see Dreier, *Organization of American States and Hemisphere Crisis,* pp. 52-54.

59. In some respects, the actions of the OAS were more in line with an anti-communist alliance than a collective security arrangement.

60. Thomas and Thomas, *Organization of American States*, p. 310.

61. Taylor, "The Guatemalan Affair," 800-01.

62. Kane, *Civil Strife in Latin America*, pp. 194-95.

63. By limiting the jurisdiction of the UN, Washington could effectively head off any pressure from within the world body to curb or thwart the U.S.-sponsored invasion. Secondly, it would prevent the Soviet Union, which was sympathetic to the Arbenz government, from utilizing its veto in the Security Council. In the OAS, though, the Eisenhower administration would be better able to control events and more likely to generate support and backing for the intervention. Washington was, in effect, using the "try the OAS first" argument to bolster its position on freezing out the UN. Interestingly enough, the majority of Latin American governments espoused the view that American states could, if they so wished, appeal directly to the Security Council before approaching the OAS. On this point, see Inis L. Claude, "The 'Try OAS First' Issue," *International Conciliation* 547 (March 1964): 61.

64. Ibid., 30.

65. Ibid., 30.

66. Arthur P. Whitaker, *Western Hemisphere Idea*, p. 131.

67. As Slater further indicates: "It had not even helped in the post-hostilities negotiations, which were dominated by the United States." Slater, *OAS and United States Foreign Policy*, pp. 126-27.

68. Thomas and Thomas, *Organization of American States*, p. 310.

69. Dreier, *Organization of American States and Hemisphere Crisis*, p. 62.

70. House of Commons, *Debates*, 19 June 1954, 6278.

71. Ibid., 6279.

72. House of Commons, *Debates*, 23 June 1954, 6519.

73. National Archives of Canada, "Tenth Inter-American Conference," 1 April 1954, File RG-25 2226-40, 28:3.

74. Ibid., 3.

75. Ibid., 3.

76. National Archives of Canada, "Organization of American States," 28 April 1954, File RG 25 2226-40, 28:1.

77. National Archives of Canada, "Canadian Membership in the O.A.S.," 13 May 1954, File RG 25 2226-40, 28:6.

78. National Archives of Canada, "Organization of American States," 9 June 1954, File RG 25 2226-40, 28:1.

79. Ibid., 3.

80. See, for example, Jerome Slater, "The Limits of Legitimization in International Organizations: The Organization of American States and the Dominican Crisis," *International Organization* 23 no.1 (winter 1969): 54-58; and A.J. Thomas and Ann Van Wynen Thomas, "The Dominican Republic Crisis 1965: Legal Aspects," in *The Dominican Republic Crisis 1965*, ed. John Carey (Dobbs Ferry, NY: Oceana Publications, 1967), pp. 1-83.

81. For a more detailed discussion of the Dominican crisis, see, Abraham F. Lowenthal, *The Dominican Intervention* (Cambridge, MA: Harvard University Press, 1972). It is instructive to note that in February 1963, a freely-elected chamber of deputies as well as a senate was installed in Santo Domingo. At the same time, Juan Bosch was proclaimed the first popularly-elected president in Dominican history. Seven months later, he was overthrown in a bloodless coup, which was orchestrated primarily by the military and the Dominican upper class. By 1965, though, the country began experiencing the instability of a pro-Bosch revolution. The Cabral government was unable to quell the unrest and young military officers subsequently began agitating for the restoration of the former constitutional government of Bosch.

82. It is important to note that at the time of the U.S. intervention, Cuban-U.S. relations were in a disastrous state, Cold War diplomacy was flourishing, and the threat of "international communism" was foremost in the minds of U.S. decision-makers. Indeed, the possibility that the Dominican Republic could turn out to be "another Cuba" was a potent force underpinning U.S. policy toward the Caribbean country. See Slater, *The OAS And United States Foreign Policy,* p. 52; and Michael J. Kryzanek, "The Dominican Intervention Revisited: An Attitudinal and Operational Analysis," in *United States Policy in Latin America,* ed. John D. Martz (Lincoln, NE: University of Nebraska Press, 1988), pp. 140-41.

83. Evidently, the OAS was not consulted beforehand by the United States and, more important, was only brought into the picture after Washington had secured its primary objectives. The White House was well aware that it would have been unable to muster the two-thirds majority needed to authorize the invasion. Moreover, President Johnson regarded the hemispheric body as largely inconsequential. His view was succinct: "The OAS can't pour p*** out of a boot if the instructions were written on the heel." Quoted in Robert D. Schulzinger, *American Diplomacy in the Twentieth Century* (Oxford: Oxford University Press, 1984), p. 279.

84. Ball, *OAS in Transition,* p. 472.

85. Ibid., p. 473.

86. Thomas and Thomas, "The Dominican Republic Crisis, 1965," 37.

87. The United States, in pressing for its creation, viewed the IAPF as an effective hedge or defence against any outside communist threat. Latin American governments, for their part, saw the force as more of a defence against Washington. Simply put, they hoped that the IAPF would remove from the United States the self-imposed task of protecting the hemisphere from extra-continental aggression. There were, however, some concerns among the Latins that the establishment of "collective intervention" would create a dangerous precedent in inter-American diplomacy. In other words, that OAS backing would, in effect, legitimize what was essentially a unilateral U.S. operation. Needless to say, there was no serious movement afoot within the OAS to revise the charter to incorporate a permanent force. The creation of the IAPF, as Ball notes, "had been

the best way to make the best of a bad business, not something to be desired for its own sake." Ball, *OAS in Transition*, p. 480.

88. The Special Committee was widely regarded as a complete failure. After about two weeks in Santo Domingo, it resigned in a cloud of controversy and returned to Washington. For more details of the Committee's failings, see Jerome Slater, *Intervention and Negotiation: The United States and the Dominican Crisis* (New York: Harper & Row, 1970), pp. 81-84.

89. The Ad Hoc Committee that negotiated the final settlement was influenced by Ellsworth Bunker, the U.S. representative. According to Slater, "there is no doubt that Bunker dominated the Committee, planned its general strategy, and was the source of almost all its initiatives." Slater, "The Limits of Legitimization in International Organizations," 61.

90. Not surprisingly, most Latin Americans and their governments viewed U.S. intervention with anger and dismay. As Connell-Smith explains: "The intervention was a profoundly humiliating experience for Latin Americans, recalling the worst humiliation of the past." Connell-Smith, *The United States and Latin America*, p. 245. There were some states, however, which actually encouraged and backed U.S. interference (e.g. El Salvador, Honduras, and Nicaragua). But, for the most part, it was viewed as a flagrant and painful reminder of Washington's proclivity for violating the cherished principles of non-intervention. It would be an understatement to suggest that the invasion left a bitter taste in the mouths of Dominicans and, for that matter, the majority of Latin Americans.

91. Slater does praise the OAS for pressing for a ceasefire, helping to keep the lines of communication open, and for playing a useful "lightning rod" role. Slater, "The Limits of Legitimization," 61-62.

92. Ibid., 64.

93. Ibid., 64.

94. See, for example, Jerome Slater, "The Decline of the OAS," *International Journal* 24 no.3 (summer 1969): 497-506.

95. Slater, "The Limits of Legitimization," 68.

96. House of Commons, *Debates*, 3 May 1965, 831.

97. Ibid., 831.

98. House of Commons, *Debates*, 10 May 1965, 1108-09.

99. House of Commons, *Debates*, 12 May 1965, 1203.

100. House of Commons, *Debates*, 28 May 1965, 1786.

101. Former Director of the Latin American division, 1964-66, Interviewed by author, 29 January 1992.

102. Archives, Department of External Affairs, "Dominican Miscellany," 16 December 1965, File 20-4-OAS-4-1, 4:3-4.

103. Archives, Department of External Affairs, "Canada and the OAS," 31 May 1966, File 20-4-OAS-4-1, 4:1.

104. Archives, Department of External Affairs, "Membership in the Organization of American States," 29 June 1966, File 20-4-OAS-4, 2:3.

105. The purpose of this discussion is not to uncover which country has legal ownership or rights to the disputed territory. For a legal perspective, see Raphael Perl, ed., *The Falklands Dispute in International Law and Politics: A Documentary Source Book* (New York: Oceana Publications, 1983). Nor will it describe the military actions of Britain or Argentina. See Max Hastings and Simon Jenkins, *The Battle for the Falklands* (New York: Norton, 1983). Rather, it is concerned with outlining the role that the OAS played throughout the crisis. See Barbara Crossette, "O.A.S. Unable to Agree on Falkland Resolution," *New York Times*, 13 April 1982, sec. A, p. 16; Bernard Gwertzman, "President appeals to Falkland foes to show restraint," *New York Times*, 21 April 1982, sec. A, p. 1; and Barbara Crossette, "O.A.S., by 17-0, calls for a truce in the Falklands," *New York Times*, 28 April 1982, sec. A, p. 1.

106. The Reagan administration lobbied hard to have the session meet under OAS Charter procedures. Washington was hoping to utilize the votes of the English-speaking countries of the OAS, most of which had not ratified the Rio Treaty and were allies of Britain. It is also worth mentioning that the Reagan administration's abstention in the Falklands/Malvinas case marked the first time that the Rio Treaty was invoked without the backing of the United States.

107. This lack of support for Argentina can be explained by several factors. First, Argentina has traditionally been disliked by many Latin American countries for a number of reasons, not least of which were its designs on regional leadership. Secondly, these same nations were very uneasy about the fact that Argentina was willing to resort to force to settle a long-standing territorial dispute. Grave concerns about establishing a dangerous precedent weighed heavily on the minds of Latin America's political leadership. Perhaps more important, though, was the fact that none of these countries were prepared to jeopardize their interests for the sake of Argentinean claims to a group of islands, particularly when the government in question had been condemned by human-rights groups throughout the world for its policies of institutionalized terrorism.

108. Though the details are sketchy, it did criticize the European Community for imposing punitive measures against Argentina. Barbara Crossette, "O.A.S., by 17-0, calls for a truce in the Falklands," *New York Times*, 28 April 1982, sec. A, p. 1.

109. "Excerpts from O.A.S. resolution on the war," *New York Times*, 30 May 1982, p. 16.

110. Jack Child, "War in the South Atlantic," in *United States Policy in Latin America*, ed. John D. Martz (Lincoln, NE: University of Nebraska Press, 1988), p. 216.

111. While most Latin American governments refrained from offering any assistance, Brazil reportedly lent Argentina some reconnaissance aircraft. But no country severed diplomatic or commercial relations with the United Kingdom. Interestingly enough, Chile was actually singled out by

some observers as a major source of military intelligence for the British. See Gordon Connell-Smith, "Latin America and the Falklands Conflict," *Year Book of World Affairs 1984* 38 (1984): 85.

112. Connell-Smith, "Latin America and the Falklands Conflict," 88.

113. Carlos Andrés Pérez, speech to the OAS in Washington, 27 April 1990, 2.

114. See Gwynne Dyer, "Self-interest still thicker than blood," *Montreal Gazette*, 1 June 1982, sec. B, p. 3.

115. Gerald Regan, former Liberal Cabinet minister, interviewed by author, 21 January 1992.

116. Ibid.

117. Former Canadian permanent observer to the OAS, interviewed in confidence by author, 27 January 1992.

118. Former senior official in the Latin America and Caribbean bureau, interviewed in confidence by author, 20 January 1992.

119. Former Canadian permanent observer to the OAS, interviewed in confidence by author, 27 January 1992.

120. It certainly reinforced the proverbial argument against seeking membership in the body because of the Rio Treaty. It pointed to the risks of Canada's joining the organization and finding itself in the awkward position of having to take a stand under the terms of the security pact. Former senior official in the Latin America and Caribbean bureau, interviewed in confidence by author, 20 January 1992.

121. Former senior official in the Latin America and Caribbean bureau in the early 1980s, letter to author, 27 January 1992.

122. Ibid.

123. Confidential paper on Canada and the OAS, 1983, p. 24.

124. Ibid., p. 24.

125. Ibid., p. 24.

126. The decidedly pro-British stance adopted by Washington at the time of the Falklands/Malvinas conflict was, for many Latin American governments, a major slap in the face. With the Reagan administration openly siding with Thatcher, imposing sanctions against Argentina, and providing covert military support for the British task force, it was no wonder that Latin American officials felt a deep sense of betrayal. It was quite evident that Pan-Americanism was sacrificed at the altar of North Atlanticism. For an excellent discussion of these and other points, see Jack Child, "War in the South Atlantic," 228-29.

127. For details of the invasion and its aftermath, see Richard L. Millett, "The Aftermath of Intervention: Panama 1990," *Journal of Interamerican Studies and World Affairs* 32 no.1 (spring 1990): 1-15; and Raul Leis, "Panama: The Other Side of Midnight," *NACLA Report on the Americas* 23 (April 1990): 4-6.

128. While Canada was not an "official" member of the OAS at the time of the U.S. invasion, it had already proclaimed its intention to join. It was unlikely, therefore, that the government would have reversed its decision

in light of the developments in Panama. In fact, Prime Minister
Mulroney, before consulting with officials in External Affairs, indicated
his support for U.S. actions. Former senior DEA official, confidential
interview by the author, 20 August 1991; Linda Hossie, "Is Lester
Pearson smiling on the Tories?" *Globe and Mail*, 17 October 1991, sec.
A, p. 1; and Ross Howard, "Critics anticipate diplomatic problems after
endorsement," *Globe and Mail*, 22 December 1989, sec. A, p. 4.

129.   See Eloy Aguilar, "Embassies encircled in hunt for Noriega," *Globe and
        Mail*, 22 December 1989, sec. A, p. 1.

130.   The vote was twenty in favour, one opposed, and six abstentions. Five
        representatives, including El Salvador, Costa Rica, and Honduras, were
        absent when the vote was taken. "Washington's action 'deeply regretted'
        OAS resolution says," *Globe and Mail*, 23 December 1989, sec. A, p. 5.

131.   For a critical analysis of the U.S. response to Panama, particularly from an
        international legal standpoint, see Charles Maechling, Jr., "Washington's
        Illegal Invasion," *Foreign Policy* 79 (summer 1990): 113-31.

132.   Latin American reaction to the invasion was swift and overwhelmingly
        critical. Officials viewed the intervention as reminiscent of the days of
        "gunboat diplomacy" and "an era that was thought to have been sur-
        passed in inter-American relations." The Peruvian government even went
        as far as to recall its ambassador in Washington. Venezuela condemned
        U.S. intervention and, in a released statement, "awaits the withdrawal of
        the invading forces of the United States." Brazil criticized Washington
        and issued a statement maintaining "its support of people's self-determi-
        nation and deeply laments this event." Mexico added, in a toughly
        worded response, that "fighting international crimes is no excuse for
        intervention in a sovereign nation." See James Brooke, "U.S. denounced
        by nations touchy about intervention," *New York Times*, 21 December
        1989, sec. A, p. 24; and "Latin American leaders condemn U.S. move,"
        Globe and Mail, 21 December 1989, sec. A, p. 5.

133.   Pérez, speech to the OAS, 3.

CHAPTER III

1.   For a useful discussion of some of these matters, see J.C.M. Ogelsby,
      Gringos From The Far North (Toronto: Macmillan, 1976).

2.   In 1893 Canada was represented at the First Pan-American Medical
      Conference held in Washington. See Marcel Roussin, "Canada: The Case
      of the Empty Chair," *World Affairs* 116 no.1 (spring 1953): 15.

3.   John P. Humphrey, *The Inter-American System: A Canadian View*
      (Toronto: Macmillan, 1942), p. 44.

4.   R. Craig Brown, "Some Honest Differences of Opinion: Latin America,"
      Writings on Canadian-American Studies, vol. 2 (Ann Arbor, MI.:
      Michigan State University, 1967), p. 3.

5. F.H. Soward and A.M. Macaulay, *Canada and the Pan American System* (Toronto: Ryerson Press, 1948), p. 218.

6. Eugene H. Miller, "Canada and the Pan American Movement," *International Journal* 3 no.1 (winter 1947-48): 28.

7. It is unclear whether Ottawa was consulted beforehand or if it even approved of Root's actions.

8. Heath Macquarrie, "Canada and the OAS: The Still Vacant Chair," *Dalhousie Review* 48 no.1 (spring 1968): 1.

9. Miller, "Canada and the Pan-American Movement," 35; and Marcel Roussin, "Evolution of the Canadian Attitude towards the Inter-American System," *American Journal of International Law* 47 no.2 (1953): 298.

10. Until about 1914, rarely did Latin America absorb as much as 3 per cent of Canada's total exports. And Canada imported an even smaller percentage of the region's total exports. See Humphrey, "The Inter-American System," 2.

11. P.E. Corbett, "Canada in the Western Hemisphere," *Foreign Affairs* 19 no.4 (July 1941): 781.

12. While the business community in Canada was generally uninterested in the region, some Canadian banks, public utilities, and insurance companies were involved in the area. Chartered banks such as the Royal and the Bank of Nova Scotia had numerous branches throughout Latin America. As well, Brazilian Traction, Light and Power (later Brascan) was particularly active in Brazil's mining sector.

13. See Iris S. Podea, "Pan-American Sentiment in French Canada," *International Journal* 3 no.4 (autumn 1948): 334-37.

14. David R. Murray, "On Diplomatic Unrelations," in *Canada and the Latin American Challenge*, ed. Jorge Nef (Guelph: Ontario Co-operative Programme in Latin American Studies, 1978), p. 171.

15. Humphrey, *The Inter-American System*, p. 5.

16. Canada's admission to the League of Nations in 1919 was a factor precipitating some preliminary discussions on possible Canadian participation in the Pan American Union. Following World War I, the issue was first raised in the House of Commons in February 1923, where Prime Minister King responded by saying: "We have not received an invitation to join such Union. When it comes we will consider it." House of Commons, *Debates*, 21 February 1923, 496.

17. See, for example, National Archives of Canada, "The Attitude of the United States towards Canadian Entry into the Pan-American Union," 20 January 1943, RG 25 B-3, File 148, 2152:1-2; and National Archives of Canada, "Pan American Union: General File:1943," 7 January 1943, RG 25 B-3, File 148, 2152:2.

18. National Archives of Canada, "Canada and the Pan-American Union," 15 December 1942, RG 25 B-3, File 148, 2152:11.

19. Douglas G. Anglin, "United States Opposition to Canadian Membership

in the Pan-American Union: A Canadian View," *International Organization* 15 no.1 (winter 1961): 3.

20. National Archives of Canada, "Pan-American Union: General File: 1928-1937," 9 January 1928, RG 25 B-3, File 148, 2152:1-2; and Soward and Macauley, *Canada and the Pan-American System*, p. 23.

21. This is not to suggest that officials such as O.D. Skelton and Vincent Massey were unaware of the Pan-American Union. On the contrary, senior officials like Skelton, Under-Secretary of State for External Affairs, were aware of the potential commercial advantages of joining the body. But he was also cognizant of "the rivalries between the United States and the Latin-American countries, and of the fact our entrance into the Union is desired by our Latin-American friends in order that we may serve as a counterpoise to the United States, we are of the opinion that, for the present at least, it would not be desirable to join." Alex I. Inglis, ed., *Documents On Canadian External Relations 1926-1930* (Ottawa: Information Canada, 1971), 4:676.

22. Ogelsby, *Gringos from the Far North*, p. 16

23. Miller, "Canada and the Pan-American Movement," 33.

24. National Archives of Canada, "Canadian Entry into Pan-American Union," 24 November 1941, File RG 25 2226-40, 134:3.

25. The Peruvian delegation was concerned about having to change the convention of the Union of American Republics to accommodate Canada, which was not a republic. Ibid., 4.

26. Anglin, *United States Opposition*, 4.

27. See "The Attitude of the United States," 1; and Vincent Massey to O.D. Skelton, in *Documents On Canadian External Relations 1926-1930*, ed. Alex I. Inglis, (Ottawa: Information Canada, 1974), 4:677.

28. National Archives of Canada, "Pan-American Union: General File: 1943," 16 January 1943, RG 25 B-3, File 148, 2152:1-2.

29. Canada, House of Commons, *Debates*, 30 March 1939, 2421.

30. National Archives of Canada, "Canadian Entry into Pan American Union," 24 November 1941, RG 25 File 2226-40, 134:1-2.

31. In some respects, this lack of Canadian interest and awareness of things Latin American is reflected in the trade figures for that period. Prior to the outbreak of World War II, Latin America accounted for less than 3 per cent of Canada's total business abroad. See Vincent Massey, "Canada and the Inter-American System," *Foreign Affairs* 26 no.4 (July 1948): 697. Indeed, Canada's exports to Latin America in 1938 consisted of a paltry $33 million. Ogelsby, *Gringos From the far North*, p. 27.

32. Security concerns, highlighted by the outbreak of war, were also factors changing Canada's attitude toward inter-American affairs in general. Not only were Canadian officials worried about an overt threat to North American security interests, but they were also concerned about the possibility of a Nazi foothold in Latin America. National Archives of Canada, "Pan-American Union: Canadian Entry: 1945," 17 March 1945,

RG 25 B-3, File 628, 2127:1; and National Archives of Canada, "Canada and the Inter-American System," 16 February 1945, RG 25 B-3, File 628, 2127:15. Canada, it has been argued, actually entered into the inter-American system through its endorsement of the declaration produced at Ogdensburg, New York in August of 1940. The wording of the agreement, according to Humphrey, implies that Canada has interests and responsibilities "that extend to at least the equator and include, therefore, not only the North American republics of Mexico, Guatemala, Honduras, El Salvador, Nicaragua, Costa Rica and Panama, but three republics and a number of colonies in the Caribbean sea, and Colombia, Venezuela, the Guianas, and parts of Brazil and Ecuador in South America." Humphrey, *The Inter-American System*, pp. 17-18.

33. National Archives of Canada, "The Attitude of Canada to the Pan-American Union," 7 February 1942, RG 25 B-3, File 148, 2152:5-6.

34. It is interesting to note that Canada's trade with Latin America was governed principally by treaties negotiated by Britain. In the case of Argentina, trade between the two countries was governed by a treaty Britain had signed in 1825.

35. Corbett, *Canada in the Western Hemisphere*, p. 779.

36. National Archives of Canada, "Canada and the Pan-American Union," RG 25 File 4889-40, 3182:2; and Ibid., p. 1.

37. David R. Murray, ed., *Documents on Canadian External Relations, 1939-1941* (Ottawa: Information Canada, 1974), 7:1104-06.

38. Prior to World War II, Canada had no formal diplomatic relations with any of the countries of Latin America. By the end of the war, Canada had established legations in most of the major countries in Latin America. By the end of 1940 Canada had incipient diplomatic relations with the so-called "ABC" powers—Argentina, Brazil, and Chile. Some four years later, Canada had diplomatic legations in Peru and Mexico. The process of establishing relations with the major Latin American countries was the result of perceived trade advantages as well as from pressures emanating from the accredited countries themselves. David R. Murray, ed., *Documents on Canadian External Relations 1939-1941* (Ottawa: Information Canada, 1974), 1:45-89.

39. For an excellent treatment of Canada's incipient diplomatic contacts with Latin America, see D.R. Murray, "Canada's First Diplomatic Missions in Latin America," *Journal of Interamerican Studies and World Affairs* 16 no.2 (May 1974): 153-72.

40. Officialdom in Ottawa, although flirting with strengthening contacts with the inter-American community, was still more interested in solidifying ties with Western Europe and the British Commonwealth.

41. National Archives of Canada, "Pan American Union: General File: 1942," 15 December 1942, RG 25 B-3, File 141, 2128:1; and National Archives of Canada, "Pan-American Union: General File: 1943," 24 February 1943, RG 25 B-3, File 148, 2152:2.

42. National Archives of Canada, "Canadian Entry into the Pan-American Union," 31 October 1941, RG 25 File 2226-40, 134:17; and David R. Murray, ed., *Documents on Canadian External Relations 1939-1941* (Ottawa: Information Canada, 1974), 1:1108.

43. King makes reference in his private papers to Norman Robertson's putting pressure on him to have Canada attend the conference. *The Mackenzie King Diaries 1932-1949* (Toronto: University of Toronto Press, 1980), p. 1164.

44. National Archives of Canada, "Canada and the Pan-American Union: Summary," 21 November 1941, RG 25 File 2226-40, 134:1-2.

45. Officials in DEA based their support for Canadian admission at this time primarily on commercial and security concerns. There were some fears that a German attack against Canada could be launched from somewhere in the Americas. Commercially speaking, they began to view the region as a potentially lucrative market for Canadian goods and services. See Escott Reid to Norman Robertson in National Archives of Canada, "Pan-American Union," File 2226-40, 134:1; Escott Reid to Hugh Keenleyside, Ibid., 1-2; and "Canada and the Pan-American Union," Ibid., 1-4. Also see James Rochlin, "Canada, the Pan-American Union and the Organization of American States" (paper presented at the Canada-Latin America Opportunities Conference, Calgary, 6 May 1991), 4-5.

46. H. Hume Wrong, National Archives of Canada, "Legation in Washington to SSEA," RG 25 File 2226-40, 134:1-4.

47. National Archives of Canada, "Canada and the Pan-American Union," 15 December 1942, RG 25 B-3, File 148, 2152:6-7.

48. Hume Wrong, in *Documents on Canadian External Relations, 1942-1943,* ed. John F. Hilliker (Ottawa: Supply and Services Canada, 1980), 9:903.

49. National Archives of Canada, "Canada, the Pan-American Union and the United States," 13 April 1942, RG 25 File 2226-40, 134:1-3.

50. John F. Hilliker, ed., *Documents on Canadian External Relations, 1942-1943* (Ottawa: Supply and Services Canada, 1980), 9:904.

51. U.S. officials were also concerned about the possibility that membership might open the door for Canada to compete with the United States for Latin American markets. Additionally, they were concerned that Canada's admission to the PAU would spur Ottawa to demand the same kinds of concessions that Washington was prepared to offer the countries of South America. Ibid., 905-906.

52. Anglin, "United States Opposition," 12.

53. King's support for admission was predicated more on the advice from External Affairs than on his own personal view, which tended to question the merits of joining. He wrote in his diary, "I was agreeable to having Canada represented there if an invitation were extended but made clear I thought we should ascertain the views of the U.S. Gov't first." *Mackenzie King Diaries, 1932-1949,* 1164; and National Archives of Canada, "Canada and the Pan-American Union," RG 25 File 4889-40, 3182:3.

54. In response to a question in the House of Commons, King noted: "I am convinced that Canadian participation in such an organization could be based only upon a wide general appreciation in this country of the purposes and responsibilities of the pan-American union. I am not convinced that such appreciation now exists." House of Commons, *Debates*, 4 August 1944, 5912-13.

55. John F. Hilliker, ed., *Documents on Canadian External Relations, 1944-1945* (Ottawa, Supply and Services Canada, 1990), 2:1152-53; and Donald M. Page, ed., *Documents On Canadian External Relations, 1946* (Ottawa: Supply and Services Canada, 1977), 12:1221-22.

56. One of the principal reasons was that some officials preferred to focus more on the creation of a world body. National Archives of Canada, "Report on Canadian Representation in and Relations with Latin American States," RG 25 File 7145-40, 3291:9-11.

57. See Canadian Institute of Public Opinion, *Gallup Poll of Canada*, 12 January 1944, 1.

58. See "72 P.C. Canadians haven't heard of Pan-America union," *Toronto Daily Star*, 12 January 1944.

59. John W. Holmes makes the point that Canadian officials were finding it increasingly difficult to get along with their Latin American counterparts. Holmes, "Our Other Hemisphere: Reflections on the Bahia Conference," *International Journal* 27 no.4 (autumn 1961-62): 416.

60. In March 1945 Lester B. Pearson, then Canadian Ambassador to the United States, indicated to Norman Robertson that "this formal joining of a Pan American Union was not a question which could be decided at the present time; that, in any event, we should wish to see how world organization plans, with their relationship to regional groupings, were worked out at San Francisco." National Archives of Canada, "Pan-American Union: Canadian Entry: 1945," RG 25 B-3, File 628, 2127:1; and Donald M. Page, ed., *Documents on Canadian External Relations, 1946* (Ottawa: Supply and Services Canada, 1977), 12:1219-20.

61. Quoted in John W. Holmes, *The Better Part of Valour: Essays on Canadian Diplomacy* (Toronto: McClelland and Stewart, 1970), p. 228.

62. Pearson indicated that "we are satisfied that our relationships of friendship and mutual interest with the other American countries will continue to grow irrespective of membership or non-membership in any formal organization." p. 3. For more details of Pearson's speech to the *Herald Tribune* Forum in New York, see Canada, Department of External Affairs, "Canada in the Americas," *Statements and Speeches*, 47/7, 8 March 1947, p. 3.

63. James J. Guy, "Canada Joins the OAS: A New Dynamic in the Inter-American System," *Inter-American Review Of Bibliography* 39, no. 4 (1989): 501.

64. In his 23 April 1947 diary entry, after he met with Truman in the White House, King noted the following: "I spoke about the Pan-American

Union. I said I thought it was just as well not to have that pressed too strongly at present and hoped there would be no official invitations sent without a word with our government first." 23 April 1947, *Mackenzie King Diaries, 1932-1949,* p. 371.

65. Ogelsby, *Gringos from the Far North,* p. 300.

66. For discussion of Canada's North Atlantic foreign policy orientation, see John W. Holmes, *The Shaping of Peace and the Search for World Order, 1943-1957* (Toronto: University of Toronto Press, 1982), 2:98-122; and James Eayrs, *In Defence of Canada: Growing Up Allied* (Toronto: University of Toronto Press, 1980), 4:68-128.

67. National Archives of Canada, "Extract from Minutes of Press Conference Held by the Prime Minister," 12 February 1949, RG 25 File 2226-40, 11:1.

68. Ibid., 2.

69. In fact, in a March 1949 letter from External Affairs to the Canadian Minister to Cuba (E.H. Coleman), it pointed out: "There has been no change in the policy of the Canadian Government regarding participation in the Organization of American States since the then Prime Minister made a statement of policy in the House on August 4, 1944." National Archives of Canada, "Canada and the Organization of American States," 11 March 1949, RG 25 File 4900-B-40, 3.

70. House of Commons, *Debates,* 27 March 1953, 3341.

71. Ibid., 3341.

72. House of Commons, *Debates,* 8 March 1954, 2749.

73. It would be wrong, of course, to argue that every foreign service officer (FSO) was opposed to Canadian membership in the OAS. For a positive response to admission, see, National Archives of Canada, "Canada and the Organization of American States," 9 October 1956, RG 25, File 2228-40, 28:1-2. Most of my archival research (for the period 1949-1957), however, tended to show that Canadian officials were generally against joining the body. The reasons for this included a reluctance to have to side with either the United States or Latin American countries, unwillingness to be used by the U.S. Government to counteract anti-U.S. propaganda in Latin America, and the general sense that the organization itself was largely ineffective. See, for example, National Archives of Canada, "The Organization of American States—OAS," RG 25 File 2226-40, 28:4-7; and National Archives of Canada, "Canada and the Organization of American States," RG 25 File 2228-40, 28:1-3.

74. Donald Barry, ed., *Documents on Canadian External Relations, 1952* (Ottawa: Supply and Services Canada, 1990), 18:1594.

75. Ibid., 1394.

76. National Archives of Canada, "The Organization of American States," RG 25 File 2226-49, 28:1.

77. National Archives of Canada, "Canada's Relations with the O.A.S.," RG 25 File 2228-40, 28:2.

78. National Archives of Canada, "Annual Review of Events in Peru for the Year 1956," RG 25 File 4900-B-6-40, 3.

79. The St. Laurent government's polite detachment from the OAS was confirmed in a June 1958 DEA letter to the newly-appointed Canadian Ambassador to Peru, Alfred J. Pick—one year after the Diefenbaker government assumed office in Ottawa. As the letter explained: "The present government has had no occasion to take a public stand vis-à-vis the Organization, but it may help you to know that in August 1957, Cabinet decided that, for the time being, the previous policy of this question should be considered, i.e. that is Canada is not seeking an invitation to become a member of the O.A.S. and would prefer not to receive one." National Archives of Canada, "Letter of Appointment for new Ambassador to Peru," 23 June 1958, RG 25 File 4900-B-6-40, 1-2.

80. Trevor Lloyd, *Canada in World Affairs, 1957-1959* (Toronto: Oxford University Press, 1968), p. 228.

81. While he tended to support membership, Smith was also aware of the potential drawbacks that membership would have on Canada's relations with the United States and Commonwealth countries as well as on an already over-burdened foreign service. "Canada may join Organization of American States," *Washington Post*, 6 March 1959.

82. External Affairs Minister Green believed that increased contact with Latin America could pay dividends in the world body. For instance, he felt that Canada, with the support of the Latin American delegations, would be well-positioned to secure its UN objectives—namely, arms control, disarmament, and peacekeeping. George Bell, "Canada and the OAS: Going Around the Buoy Again?" in *Canada, the Caribbean, and Central America*, ed. Brian Macdonald (Toronto: The Canadian Institute of Strategic Studies, 1986), p. 104.

83. J.C.M. Ogelsby, "Canada and the Pan-American Union: Twenty Years On," *International Journal* 24 no.3 (summer 1969): 573.

84. Richard A. Preston, *Canada In World Affairs, 1959-1961* (Toronto: Oxford University Press, 1965), p. 177. Two-way trade between Canada and the republics of Latin America was, by the late 1950s, experiencing steady—if unspectacular—growth. In 1959 Canadian exports to the region amounted to some $172 million. Imports from Latin America, for the same year, stood at roughly $340 million. See R.M. Will, "Economic Aspects of Canadian-Latin American Relations," *International Journal* 15 no.4 (autumn 1960): 350.

85. See J.A. Hume, "Canada Invited to Take Part in 'Operation Pan-American,'" *Ottawa Citizen*, 19 May 1960; and Michael Johnson, "New Canadian Interest Appreciated by Latins," *Montreal Star*, 13 June 1960.

86. "Canada Weighing Closer Latin Ties," *New York Times*, 20 March 1960.

87. Archives, Department of External Affairs, "Excerpt from Statement on International Affairs Passed by the Fourth Constitutional Convention of the Canadian Labour Congress," File 20-4-OAS-4, 1.

88. See H. Basil Robinson, *Diefenbaker's World: A Populist in Foreign Affairs* (Toronto: University of Toronto Press, 1989), pp. 200-01.

89. This official visit was not only emblematic of the increasing political and economic importance of Mexico, but also of the region in general. Editorial, "New hemisphere role for Canada," *Toronto Daily Star*, 25 April 1960, p. 3.

90. John D. Harbron, "Prime Minister's Press Conference, 23 April 1960," and "Mexico may buy Canadian steel," *Globe and Mail*, 25 April 1960, sec. B, p. 1.

91. "Latin America Unit to form close ties is set up by Ottawa," *Globe and Mail*, 31 May 1960, sec. A, p. 4.

92. The Toronto *Globe and Mail*, when hearing of the correction, felt that the prime minister's misquoted comments were far more appropriate. "Improving the truth," *Globe and Mail*, 17 January 1961, sec. A, p. 6. Also see "Ottawa unconcerned over PM's 'statement,'" *Ottawa Journal*, 13 January 1961, sec. A, p. 7.

93. Ogelsby, *Gringos from the Far North*, p. 315.

94. President Kennedy believed that Canada would be a welcome addition to the inter-American family. According to his address to the House of Commons, he felt that Canadians would bring to the organization valuable diplomatic skills and resources as well as an intelligent and thoughtful viewpoint. House of Commons, *Debates*, 17 May 1961, 4964. Perhaps Diefenbaker's coolness toward OAS membership flowed from his intense dislike of President Kennedy himself. He certainly did not appreciate Kennedy's "push" for Canadian membership in the body during their May 1961 meeting and in his subsequent speech to the House. See Lawrence Martin, *The Presidents and the Prime Ministers* (Toronto: Doubleday, 1982), pp. 181-211; and Knowlton Nash, *Kennedy and Diefenbaker: The Feud that Helped Topple a Government* (Toronto: McClelland and Stewart, 1990), pp. 107-42.

95. For Diefenbaker's reaction, see Robinson, *Diefenbaker's World*, 206-07. In his memoirs, Diefenbaker makes only a passing reference to Kennedy's pressure tactics. According to a DEA document, Canadian officials were preparing themselves to discuss the question of Cuba, although no specific mention was made of the OAS. National Archives of Canada, "List of topics for discussion between the President and the Prime Minister," 20 April 1960, File 18-1-A-USA, 3492:1-4. See also Knowlton Nash, *Kennedy and Diefenbaker*, pp. 114-16.

96. House of Commons, *Debates*, September 1961, 8203.

97. Ogelsby, "Canada and the Pan-American Union," 576.

98. Nevertheless, it is worth noting that the Diefenbaker government initiated several moves with regard to inter-American affairs. First, Canada became a full member of the Pan American Institute of Geography and History—a specialized agency of the OAS—in 1960. Secondly, Canada opted for membership on the United Nations

Economic Commission for Latin America (ECLA) in October of 1961. Lastly, the government had established diplomatic relations with all of the countries of Latin America by the end of 1961.

99. In the early 1960s officials in External Affairs were interested in maintaining commercial relations with Cuba, regardless of Castro's ideological predilection. They were also concerned that if Canada opted to join the OAS, it could have negative implications for Canada's Cuba policy. For instance, they were uneasy about the prospect of Canada, once it did become a member, being pressured into signing the Rio Treaty and thus compelled to sever relations with Cuba. In an August 1964 letter from the Canadian Embassy in Mexico, the Ambassador reconfirmed these concerns by noting that "unless we are prepared to subject our Cuban policy to an agonizing reappraisal, it would seem wiser to postpone membership until the problems presented by Cuba are less intractable in nature." Archives, Department of External Affairs, "Possible Entry of Canada into the Organization of American States," File 20-4-OAS-4-1, 3:4. Also see Archives, Department of External Affairs, "Canadian Position re OAS Resolutions on Cuba," File 20-4-OAS-1, 1-3.

100. House of Commons, *Debates*, 22 October 1961, 806-07.

101. House of Commons, *Debates*, 22 October 1962, 804-06.

102. Archives, Department of External Affairs, "Political and Military Implications of Membership in the OAS," File 20-4-OAS-4, 2:9.

103. Peyton V. Lyon, *Canada in World Affairs 1961-1963* (Toronto: Oxford University Press, 1968), p. 527.

104. Archives, Department of External Affairs, "Canada and the OAS," File 20-4-OAS-4-1, 1:11. Canada, along with Mexico, were the only two countries of the Americas not to sever relations with Castro's Cuba.

105. Archives, Department of External Affairs, "Possible entry of Canada into the Organization of American States," File 20-4-OAS-4-1, 2. This sense of frustration was detected by a Canadian diplomat in Ecuador when he stated: "Latin Americans have always been puzzled, sometimes hurt, by what seemed to them our reluctance to accept a preferred (sic) invitation to join with the other states in the Western Hemisphere in the only organization formed to deal with its regional problems." Archives, Department of External Affairs, "Canada and the OAS," File 20-4-OAS-4-1, 3:1.

106. For his views in favour of membership, see House of Commons, *Debates*, 27 April 1961, 4086; and House of Commons, *Debates*, 11 September 1961, 8203.

107. While there is nothing in Pearson's memoirs about any discussions with Kennedy on the OAS, newspaper accounts tended to be less than crystal clear on this matter. According to the *Ottawa Journal*, the issue of OAS membership—to be discussed—was conspicuously absent from the official communiqué. Richard Jackson, "Speeding plans for warheads says Pearson," *Ottawa Journal*, 13 May 1963, sec. A, p. 1. An article in the

New York Times, however, claimed that "Mr. Kennedy did not raise the question; a Canadian source denied emphatically that Mr. Pearson had given any understanding on the subject." Tom Wicker, "Canada confirms she will accept atom arms soon," *New York Times,* 12 May 1963, sec. A, p. 1. According to a DEA file, however, Pearson stated that "the Canadian Government would move cautiously to examine the implications of OAS membership, that membership was not a matter of first priority, and that he personally thought that Canada could assist with aid to former British colonies." Archives, Department of External Affairs, "Statements Concerning Canada's Joining the OAS Made at the Hyannisport Meeting," File 20-4-OAS-4-1, 1.

108. House of Commons, Debates, 20 May 1963, 65.

109. Department of External Affairs, *Press Release* A.18, 2 May 1963, p. 30. Martin was himself on record as supporting Canadian entry. Within Cabinet, though, he was rumoured to have had difficulty convincing his colleagues of the merits of doing so. See, for example, House of Commons, *Debates,* 11 September 1961, 8201; and Paul Martin, *A Very Public Life* (Ottawa: Deneau Publishers, 1983), p. 268.

110. "Canada to watch Americas talks," *Globe and Mail,* 3 May 1963, sec. A, p. 1.

111. From a trade standpoint, Canada's exports to the region jumped from roughly $175 million in 1959 to approximately $327 million in 1964. G.V. Doxey, "Canada and the Organization of American States," (paper presented at a conference on the Caribbean and Latin America, Kingston, Jamaica, March 1967), 27. It is worth noting that the Pearson government did give active consideration to the idea of appointing a Canadian Liaison Officer to the OAS—to demonstrate Canada's interest in the OAS and in inter-American affairs in general. Archives, Department of External Affairs, "Appointment of Liaison Officer to the OAS," File 20-4-OAS-4, p 1.

112. Department of External Affairs, "Signature of Agreement between Canada and Inter-American Development Bank," *Press Release* 89, 4 December 1964, 1.

113. Although Prime Minister Pearson was reported to have endorsed the idea of Canadian membership in the OAS in late 1965, he soon backed away from this position. House of Commons, *Debates,* 19 January 1966, 15. In response to a question on membership—following the announcement that some Caribbean countries were contemplating joining the OAS—he indicated that "I said I hoped it would be possible for us to act in unison with the other Commonwealth governments in this hemisphere. Trinidad-Tobago having announced their intention of joining ... with Barbados following up if it does apply within the next month or two, it looks as though my hope will not be realized." House of Commons, *Debates,* 20 February 1967, 13215.

114. C. Knowlton Nash, "Canadian thumbs turned down to U.S. Latin OAS pleading," *Financial Post,* 16 April 1966. Nash also noted that Latin

American governments, particularly in the wake of the Dominican crisis, were no longer unanimous in their support of Canadian membership.

115. See John F. Hilliker, *Canada's Department of External Affairs*, vol. 1, *The Early Years, 1909-1946* (London: The Institute of Public Administration of Canada, 1990), p. 231.

116. The outbreak of the Korean War in 1950, a manifestation of the Cold War, also distracted Canadian attention away from inter-American developments.

117. In fact, Pearson refused to endorse or support U.S. intervention in the Dominican Republic. In the House of Commons, he stated that "we have not received sufficient evidence from the United States authorities—and we are in touch with them on this matter—to justify any conclusion on our part at this time." Quoted from "Canada has wait-and-see attitude, Pearson indicates in Commons," *Globe and Mail,* 4 May 1965, sec. A, p. 8.

118. It is possible to argue that if DEA were truly supportive of membership in the OAS, it could have moved to mould this opinion in favour of join-ing—as in the cases of Canada's entry to the UN and NATO. It is equally possible that political leaders simply pointed to the lack of public support as an excuse to hide their own personal doubts about the usefulness of Canadian membership in the hemispheric body.

119. While Latin American governments were angered by Canada's unwilling-ness to sever relations with Cuba and its reluctance to join the OAS as a full member, they were still supportive of the idea of Canadian membership.

120. John Sokol, "Latin America Wants Canada in the OAS," *The Commentator* 6 no.5 (May 1962): 19-20.

CHAPTER IV

1. For an illustration of this point, see D.R. Murray, "The Bilateral Road: Canada and Latin America in the 1980s," *International Journal* 37 no.1(winter 1980-81): 108-131.

2. See, for example, John D. Harbron,"Canada and Latin America: Ending a Historic Isolation," *International Perspectives* (May-June 1972), 25-29; John D.Harbron, "Canada Draws Closer to Latin America: A Cautious Involvement," in *Latin America's New Internationalism:The End of Hemispheric Isolation,* ed. Roger W. Fontaine and James D. Theberge (New York: Praeger Publishers, 1976), pp. 109-42; James John Guy, "Canada and Latin America," *The World Today* 32 no.10 (October 1976): 376-86; and J.C.M. Ogelsby, "A Trudeau Decade: Canadian-Latin American Relations, 1968-1978," *Journal of Interamerican Studies and World Affairs* 21 no.2 (May 1979): 187-208.

3. "Justice Minister's wit delights supporters," *Globe and Mail,* 5 April 1968, p. 8.

4. Canada, Department of External Affairs, "Canada and the World," *Statements and Speeches*, 68/17, 29 May 1968, 3.

5. Quoted in Peter C. Dobell, *Canada's Search for New Roles: Foreign Policy in the Trudeau Era* (London: Oxford University Press, 1972), p. 115.

6. Influencing Trudeau's thinking on this subject were Cabinet colleagues Gérard Pelletier and Mitchell Sharp. As Secretary of State and Secretary of State for External Affairs respectively, they were key supporters of broadening relations with Latin America. See Bruce Thordarson, *Trudeau and Foreign Policy: A Study in Decision-Making* (Toronto: Oxford University Press, 1972), pp. 45-47.

7. Curiously, in 1969 the government decided, for budgetary reasons, to close Canadian missions in Uruguay, Ecuador, and the Dominican Republic as well as reducing staff at the remaining twelve missions in the region by some sixteen members. At the same time, it sought to expand contacts with francophone Africa and to establish full diplomatic relations with the Vatican. This tended to indicate that broadening relations with Latin America was not the government's top priority. Dobell, *Canada's Search for New Roles*, p. 116.

8. Ogelsby, *Gringos from the Far North*, p. 32.

9. Mitchell Sharp, former Secretary of State for External Affairs, interview by author, 12 January 1992.

10. Government of Canada, *Foreign Policy for Canadians* (Ottawa: Queen's Printer, 1970), p. 20.

11. Ibid., p. 20.

12. Ibid., p. 20.

13. Ibid., p. 20.

14. Drawing closer to the inter-American system did not, however, include joining the Inter-American Development Bank (IDB). According to the booklet on Latin America, "membership in the Bank would absorb a relatively high proportion of Canada's total development assistance budget" and, for that reason, "the Government does not contemplate joining the Bank at the present time but will keep this possibility under review." Ibid., p. 28.

15. Ibid., p. 23-24.

16. Ibid., p. 24.

17. Ibid., p. 32.

18. Ibid., p. 32.

19. Department of External Affairs, "Canada and Latin America—A Period of Mutual Discovery," *Statements and Speeches*, 70/10, 30 June 1970, 4.

20. Ibid., 4.

21. Ibid., 3.

22. Department of External Affairs, "Canada Seeks Closer Links with Latin America," *Statements and Speeches*, 71/14, 13 April 1971, 2.

23. Department of External Affairs, "Permanent Observer Status to the Organization of American States," *Communiqué* 5, 2 February 1972: 30.

The status of permanent observer represented an innovation in the organizational structure of the OAS. Not only was Canada the first country to apply for such status, but it also made a special plea to the organization for its creation.

24. Quoted in *International Canada* (October 1970), 215.

25. The principal function of the mission was to act, largely for political reasons, as a monitoring or listening post. In addition, it was to assist any agencies of the Canadian government in their dealings with the various specialized agencies and organizations of the OAS. According to Kenneth B. Williamson, a former Canadian permanent observer, it also functioned to "offer information and advice, undertake liaison, make arrangements, manifest a Canadian presence and communicate Canadian points of view." Williamson, "Canada and the Inter-American System: A Matter of Choice," (unpublished paper, 1983), 3.

26. Department of External Affairs, "Head of Canadian Delegation to the General Assembly of the Organization of American States," *Communiqué* 5, 2 February 1972: 30.

27. Ibid., 30.

28. In late April Alfred J. Pick was appointed Canada's first permanent observer to the OAS.

29. The government chose to join the IDB, despite earlier reservations, for a variety of reasons. As a full member, Canada would become an eligible source of supply for goods and services financed through loans from the Fund for Special Operations. It also gave Canada access to information that could enable Canadian consulting firms to gain contracts flowing from loan funds. Furthermore, the shift from a bilateral to multilateral footing would have the salutary effect of loosening the "tied-aid" predilection of previous development assistance programmes. In addition, it allowed the government to have more control over the actual projects funded by Canada's contribution. The government also saw IDB membership as a means of informing Canadians about Latin America, particularly in terms of opening up new trade and investment opportunities. Lastly, membership made Canada's contribution less bureaucratically cumbersome than it had been before Canada joined the IDB. On the decision to join the IDB, see J.C.M. Ogelsby, "Latin America," *International Journal* 33 no.2 (spring 1978): 403; Stephen J. Randall, "Canadian Policy and the Development of Latin America," in *A Foremost Nation: Canadian Foreign Policy and a Changing World,* ed. Norman Hillmer and Garth Stevenson (Toronto: McClelland and Stewart, 1977), p. 214; and Ogelsby, "A Trudeau Decade," 192-93.

30. Department of External Affairs, "Notes for Statement by Mr. Paul St. Pierre, Parliamentary Secretary to the Secretary of State for External Affairs," *Statements,* 15 April 1972, 3.

31. The move to join the IDB was consistent with the Trudeau government's desire to establish contact with the social and economic—as opposed to

the political—institutions of the inter-American system. It also signalled Canada's apparent willingness to confront issues which could bring it into conflict with the United States. Some observers thought that IDB membership was an important step because membership in the bank was almost the same as that of the OAS. See James Guy, "The Growing Relationship of Canada and the Americas," *International Perspectives* (July-August 1977): 4. In any event, joining the IDB would require Canada to commit some $100 million over three years and place another $202 million on standby.

32. Department of External Affairs, "Canadian Membership in the Inter-American Development Bank," *Communiqué* 31, 3 May 1972, 2.

33. Ibid., 2.

34. In early October 1972 Canada announced that it would become a member of the Inter-American Institute of Agricultural Sciences. Ambassador Pick deposited Canada's instrument of ratification and thereby enabled its membership to take effect one month later. According to a DEA communiqué, "Canadian participation in the work of the Institute marks one further step in the implementation of Canada's policy to develop a more substantive and meaningful relationship with the Inter-American Family of Organizations and with our Hemisphere as a whole. Department of External Affairs, "Canada Joins Inter-American Institute of Agricultural Sciences," *Communiqué* 72, 4 October 1972, 30.

35. Department of External Affairs, "Canada Forges Another Link with Latin America," *Statements and Speeches* 72/9, 10 May 1972, 4.

36. Department of External Affairs, "Notes for the Statement by Mr. Pierre de Bané, Parliamentary Secretary to the Secretary of State for External Affairs, *Communiqué* 43, 9 April 1973, 2.

37. Trudeau's tour was the first major trip to Latin America by a Canadian prime minister. Besides seeking to strengthen relations at the political level and to outline Canada's position on various foreign policy issues, Trudeau was also interested in selling Canadian Dash-7 aircraft, CANDU reactors, and railway equipment. Indeed, Mexico, Cuba, and Venezuela—the three countries he visited—purchased roughly half of Canada's total exports to the region ($1.2 billion in 1975). See George Radwanski, "Trudeau in Latin America Set Stage for Closer Relations," *International Perspectives* (May/June 1976): 6-10.

38. See, for example, James J. Guy, "The Growing Relationship," 6.

39. See "The Odd Couple," *Time*, 9 February 1976, 47.

40. Quoted in *International Canada*, January 1976, p. 4.

41. "Canada to Reconsider Joining the OAS," *Cambridge Daily Reporter*, 31 January 1976, sec. A, p. 1 and "Trudeau begins final leg of tour," Halifax *Chronicle-Herald*, 30 January 1976, sec. A, p. 2.

42. Quoted in *International Canada*, (September 1977), p. 200.

43. "Canada won't join alliance but 'we're moving closer,'" *Toronto Star*, 10 September 1977.

44. There is some evidence, by no means conclusive, that the short-lived Clark government, if it had survived that infamous vote of non-confidence, may have opted for full membership in the OAS. Evidently, External Affairs Minister Flora MacDonald was favourably disposed toward the hemispheric body. It was thought that she was prepared to bring a positive recommendation on the membership issue before the full Cabinet. Former Cabinet minister in the Clark government, interviewed by author, 24 August 1994. For Ms. MacDonald, Canada could only press ahead with the issue of human rights, a long-standing hemispheric problem, if it were a member of the OAS and thereby eligible to join the Inter-American Commission on Human Rights. Former DEA official, interviewed in confidence by author, 4 June 1991. It is also true that Ms. MacDonald requested a review of the OAS membership issue, which External Affairs had just begun when the Liberals were returned to power. When Mark MacGuigan took over as SSEA, he did not see any purpose in continuing the review of Canada's policy toward the OAS. Former senior DEA official, interviewed in confidence by author, 27 January 1992.

45. It is important to note that the Standing Committee on External Affairs and National Defence (SCEAND) was examining the totality of Canada's relations with Latin America and the Caribbean, and not just the question of OAS membership.

46. Just before he left the External Affairs portfolio in September 1982, MacGuigan indicated that it was time for Canada to join the OAS. After discontinuing the review of Canada's policy toward the OAS in the early 1980s, he now believed that non-membership placed certain limitations on Canada's involvement in Latin America. For him, Canadian-Latin American relations had matured to the point where membership in the hemispheric forum was the next logical step. He also pointed out that Canada, as distinct from the United States, would be able to enhance the organization by bringing to it a different set of values. See John Gray, "MacGuigan says it's time to join OAS," *Globe and Mail,* 10 September 1982, sec. A, p. 9.

47. House of Commons, Standing Committee on External Affairs and National Defence, Sub-Committee on Canada's Relations with Latin America and the Caribbean, *Minutes of Proceedings,* 9 June 1981, 61.

48. Ibid., 64-65.

49. Ibid., 65.

50. House of Commons, Standing Committee on External Affairs and National Defence, *Canada's Relations with Latin America and the Caribbean: Final Report,* (1982), 19-21.

51. Ibid., 22.

52. With one abstention, seven members of the sub-committee voted in favour of the recommendation to seek admission. There were four members who voted against it.

53. Quoted in Donat Pharand, "Canada and the OAS: the Vacant Chair Revisited," *Revue générale de droit* 17 no.3 (summer 1986): 439.
54. During the early 1980s the Liberal Cabinet did not appear to have any "appetite" for discussing Canadian membership in the OAS. Gerald Regan, former Cabinet Minister, interview by author, 21 January 1992.
55. The membership question was never a high priority on the Trudeau government's policy agenda. External Affairs Minister Allan MacEachen's comment at a 1984 press conference in Bogotá confirms this observation. When questioned by a reporter about the issue of possible Canadian membership in the hemispheric forum, he responded by saying that "I don't have it at the forefront of my agenda." Quoted in Pharand, "Canada and the OAS," 439.
56. This writer is not suggesting here that domestic political issues—in and of themselves—prevented the government from opting for full membership.
57. See Mitchell Sharp, "Canada-U.S. Relations: Options for the Future," *International Perspectives,* (September-October 1972): 1-24.
58. Stephen Clarkson, *Canada and the Reagan Challenge* (Toronto: James Lorimer, 1982), pp. 3-5.
59. With many countries in Latin America dominated by military governments—particularly during the 1960s and 1970s—this did little to improve the prospects of OAS membership for Canada.
60. The 1982 Falklands/Malvinas War did little to reassure Western governments of the region's interest in stability and prosperity.
61. Editorial, "Le Canada et l'OEA," *Cité Libre* 15 (October 1964): 2-3.
62. Former DEA official, interviewed in confidence by author, 19 June 1991. It is true that the percentage of total Canadian exports to Latin America went from 4.5 per cent in 1970 to 5.2 per cent in 1980. See Murray, "The Bilateral Road," 117. In dollar terms, Canada's exports to Latin America went from $540 million in 1970 to $1.8 billion in 1974. Similarly, imports from the region, over the same period, increased from $553 million to $1.2 billion. Guy, "Canada and Latin America," 379.
63. By the early 1980s Trudeau's interests had moved in other directions. During the 1980-81 period, he was actively championing North-South issues, pushing for meaningful dialogue between developed and developing countries. By 1983, though, Trudeau had ventured into the area of arms control with his quixotic "peace initiative." Clearly, the issue of OAS membership was not at the top of his agenda at this time.
64. Former DEA official, interviewed in confidence by author, 4 June 1991.
65. Mitchell Sharp, interviewed by author, 12 January 1992. Sharp was sceptical about joining the organization for a number of reasons, including the fact that he thought Canada could play a more constructive role in the hemisphere outside of the OAS. He also believed that it was ineffectual, that it could bring Canada into conflict with the United States, that it was composed of a host of authoritarian/dictatorial govern-

ments, and that it would not be in the best interests of Canada. Some of these concerns were also shared by former Liberal Trade Minister Gerald Regan, interviewed by author, 21 January 1992.

66. Former Canadian permanent observer to the OAS, letter to author, 8 January 1991.

67. External Affairs seemed to be satisfied with Canada's opting for observer status and hoped that this step would put the nagging question of membership to rest. This, in turn, would enable Canada to forge ahead with broadening contacts, across a wide range of areas, with Latin America as a whole. See Victor Huard, "Quiet Diplomacy or Quiet Acquiescence?: Canadian Policy in Central America since 1945," *Canadian Journal of Latin American and Caribbean Studies* 13, no. 26 (1988):111.

68. It is also clear that DEA, which suffered under Trudeau's down-grading of the department's significance, was not going to push an issue to which the Prime Minister was not fully committed. Already reeling from an earlier set-back in urging the government to maintain Canada's troop-strength in Europe, it was not about to expend what goodwill it had left on the membership issue.

69. Some officials in DEA were opposed to joining the OAS on the grounds that Canada's bilateral relations with countries in the region might suffer, particularly on the commercial and trade side. The handling of Cuba by the OAS, for instance, did little to convince DEA bureaucrats of the benefits accruing from admission. They also believed that any Canadian influence in the Americas would likely stem not from multilateral linkages, but from close, bilateral relations with the major countries in the region. There was a sense that joining the OAS would have the harmful effect of minimizing the importance of cultivating bilateral relations. Former DEA official, interviewed in confidence by author, 19 June 1991.

70. Officials in the Department of Finance, like some mandarins in DEA, were opposed to the idea of admission on financial grounds. They were strongly against Canada's taking on any new financial commitments in the foreign policy realm. They were quite satisfied with Canada's membership in a number of other international organizations. Former DEA official, interviewed by author, 14 June 1991.

71. This point was made earlier by John W. Holmes, "Our Other Hemisphere: Reflections on the Bahia Conference." *International Journal* 27 no.4 (autumn 1961-62): 416.

72. Thordarson, *Trudeau and Foreign Policy,* p. 43.

73. Quoted in Murray, "The Bilateral Road," 111.

74. Ogelsby, "A Trudeau Decade," 191.

75. See James Rochlin, "The Evolution of Canada as an Actor in Inter-American Affairs," *Millennium: Journal of International Studies* 19, no. 2 (1990):235.

76. Quoted in Murray, "The Bilateral Road," 112.

77. House of Commons, Standing Committee on External Affairs and National Defense, *Canada's Relations with Latin America and the Caribbean,* 23.

78. "A club we need not join," *Toronto Star,* 4 December 1982.

79. "Perils in membership," *Globe and Mail,* 6 December 1982.

80. On this point, see Kim Richard Nossal, "Analyzing the Domestic Sources of Canadian Foreign Policy," *International Journal* 39 no.1 (winter 1983-84): 1-22 and his *The Politics of Canadian Foreign Policy* (Scarborough, Ont: Prentice-Hall, 1985), pp. 33-70.

81. Quoted in Murray, "The Bilateral Road," 111.

82. For instance, it was raised by the President of Mexico on an official visit to Canada in 1973. In 1976 it was raised by President Pérez of Venezuela during Trudeau's visit to that country.

83. It is unlikely during this period that Washington would have applied any firm pressure on Canada to seek admission. With the possible exception of the Carter administration, U.S. governments from 1968-1983 were not particularly keen on the OAS.

84. House of Commons, Standing Committee on External Affairs and National Defence, *Canada's Relations with Latin America and the Caribbean,* 65.

85. There was also a sense that the move to permanent observer status was undertaken, in part, so that Canada would appear "friendly" in the eyes of Latin Americans. Mitchell Sharp, interviewed by author, 12 January 1992.

86. There was a feeling, though, that once Canada opted for observer status, it would eventually have to seek full membership in the OAS. Interview with Mitchell Sharp, 12 January 1992.

87. In fact, by the early 1980s the Trudeau government had embarked upon a policy of "concentrated bilateralism" with respect to Latin America.

88. Quoted in Pharand, "Canada and the OAS," 439.

CHAPTER V

1. R. Craig Brown, *Writings on Canadian-American Studies,* vol. 2 (Ann Arbor, MI: Michigan State University, 1967), p. 4.

2. An informal CBC radio poll on the issue of membership, taken in late 1961, clearly demonstrated the level of interest in the question in the early 1960s—generating a total of three for and three against. J.C.M. Ogelsby, "Canada and the Pan-American Union: Twenty Years On," *International Journal* 24 no.3 (summer 1969): 578.

3. Ibid., 579.

4. Editorialists entered the fray after it was reported, erroneously as it turned out, that Diefenbaker had remarked that Canada had no intention of joining the OAS.

5. House of Commons, *Debates,* 17 May 1961, 4964.

6. Clearly, the October 1962 missile crisis also brought the membership issue to the fore in Canada.

7. Ogelsby, "Canada and the Pan-American Union," 584.

8. John W. Holmes, "Canada and Pan-America," in *The Better Part Of Valour: Essays on Canadian Diplomacy,* ed. John W. Holmes (Toronto: McClelland and Stewart, 1970), p. 235.

9. As mentioned in a previous chapter, Howard Green, Diefenbaker's Secretary of State for External Affairs, was in favour of membership. He felt that such a step would be important in terms of mustering sufficient UN support (especially those countries from Latin America) for Canadian proposals on arms control and disarmament.

10. John G. Diefenbaker, *One Canada: The Years of Achievement, 1957-1962* (Toronto: Macmillan, 1976), p. 171.

11. Bernard Dufresne, "Links to China, OAS Opposed by Diefenbaker," *Globe and Mail,* 4 October 1965, sec. A, p. 1.

12. See George Bell, "Canada and the OAS; Going around the Buoy Again?" in *Canada, The Caribbean, And Central America,* ed. Brian Macdonald (Toronto: The Canadian Institute of Strategic Studies, 1986), p. 104.

13. In his memoirs, Pearson does not make a single reference to Canada and the OAS. By the 1966-67 period, it seemed clear that he was not truly convinced of the merits of joining the hemispheric forum. See, for example, House of Commons, *Debates,* 1 June 1967, 822; and House of Commons, *Debates,* 11 March 1968, 7469.

14. According to Alfred Pick, a former senior official in the Latin American division, Martin had inserted this "ultimate destiny" idea into his address—which was essentially written by Pick—on his own. Alfred Pick, interviewed by author, 27 January 1992. For Martin's speech, see Department of External Affairs, "Canada and Latin America," *Statements and Speeches,* 67/21, 31 May 1967, 3. More recently, Martin's favourable view of the OAS was reconfirmed in a newspaper interview. Jack Cahill, "Mulroney lauded for joining club of American states," *Toronto Star,* 29 October 1989, sec. B, p. 4.

15. According to Ogelsby, who had interviewed Pelletier, he was against joining. See his "A Trudeau Decade," 169.

16. Mitchell Sharp, former External Affairs Minister, interviewed by author, 12 January 1992, "Canada receives overture from OAS," *Montreal Gazette,* 6 February 1969, sec. A, p. 26; and John Harbron, "Growing pressures on Canada to Seek Hemispheric Identity," *International Perspectives* (May-June 1974): 34.

17. Sharp was also convinced that Latin America held out few opportunities for increasing the level of Canadian exports. Sharp, interviewed by author, 22 January 1992.

18. House of Commons, Standing Committee on External Affairs and National Defence, *Canada's Relations with Latin America and the Caribbean: Final Report,* 22.

19. Gerald Regan, former Liberal Cabinet Minister, interviewed by author, 21 January 1992. For an excellent account of Trudeau's quixotic peace initiative, see C. David Crenna, ed., *Pierre Elliot Trudeau: Lifting the Shadows of War* (Edmonton: Hurtig, 1987), pp. 63-114.

20. In February 1983 MacEachen was quoted as saying: "I need to be convinced that it is a real plus and that we are going to help Canada's interests by joining." "Canada will not join the OAS," Halifax *Chronicle-Herald,* 23 February 1983, sec. A, p. 2.

21. Quoted in Donat Pharand, "Canada and the OAS: The Vacant Chair Revisited," *Revue générale de droit* 17 no.3 (summer 1986): 439.

22. It was really not until the early part of the Mulroney government's second term in office that the issue of membership in the OAS received serious consideration at the official level. The nature and extent of this attention is discussed more fully in the next chapter.

23. Department of External Affairs, *Competitiveness and Security: Directions in Canada's International Relations,* 42.

24. See, for example, Andrew Cohen, "Canada's Foreign Policy: The Outlook for the Second Mulroney Mandate," *Behind the Headlines* 46 (summer 1989): 3-5. Also, Lawrence Martin, *The Pledge of Allegiance* (Toronto: McClelland and Stewart, 1993).

25 In an early 1960s survey of Canadian ambassadors in Latin America, 50 percent of them expressed opposition to the idea of Canada's joining the OAS. See Gerald Clark, *Canada: The Uneasy Neighbor* (Toronto: McClelland and Stewart, 1965), p. 65. Much of the information on External Affairs was gleaned from extant sources, confidential interviews with former DEA officials, and academics with an interest in Latin America.

26. Former deputy head of the Latin American division, 1969-1971, interviewed by author, 29 January 1992.

27. Former DEA Assistant Under-Secretary of State (Economic), interviewed by author, 29 January 1992.

28. Former director of the Latin American division, interviewed by author, 29 January 1992.

29. In the wake of the Cuban suspension and subsequent breaking off of diplomatic relations, officials in Ottawa were convinced that Canada should avoid this type of situation by remaining outside the OAS. Archives, Department of External Affairs, "Mexico, Cuba, and the OAS," File 20-4-OAS-4-1, 2:2; and Archives, Department of External Affairs, "Political and Military Implications of Membership in the OAS," 9.

30. Archives, Department of External Affairs, "Implications for Canada of Joining the OAS," 20 January 1967, File 20-4-OAS-4, 2:1-5.

31. Government of Canada, *Foreign Policy for Canadians* (Ottawa: Queen's Printer, 1970), p. 23.

32. Ibid., p. 22.

33. See John Best, "External Affairs seems to have won anti-OAS battle," *London Free Press,* 24 April 1984. Throughout the 1980s the business

community remained largely silent on the issue of OAS membership. In addition, interest groups in Canada—perhaps because of their focus on events unfolding in Central America—expressed little or no comment on the question. The same was also true for Latin American countries, which were likely still frustrated and tired of hearing the same old polite, but unenthusiastic, responses.

34. Ambassador Richard V. Gorham (speech to the Organization of American States, Washington DC, 7 September 1988), 18.

35. After a 1983 DEA internal review of the membership issue, officials recommended that Canada should not seek admission. There was a belief that the perceived costs of membership, on the whole, outweighed any of the potential benefits. Former DEA official, interviewed in confidence by author, 12 August 1991.

36. Richard Gorham, Department of External Affairs, "Some Preliminary Thoughts about Latin America and the Organization of American States," 11 May 1988, 8.

37. Later, the Cartagena group was formed to deal with the region's crushing debt problem.

38. Ogelsby, "Canada and the Pan-American Union," 578.

39. See House of Commons, Debates, 17 May 1962, 2:1608.

40. Peter Stollery, letter to Globe and Mail, 22 January 1983.

41. Maurice Dupras, "Canada and the OAS," International Perspectives (January-February 1984): 16.

42. Ibid., 17.

43. Ibid., 17.

44. See, for example, a letter to the Canadian-American Committee from Donald Gordon, Chairman of Canadian National Railways, 21 September 1961, 1-2. It is also important to remember that by 1978 Latin America represented just 5 per cent of Canada's overall global trade. David R. Murray, "The Present and Future Significance of Latin America for Canada," unpublished paper, 13 December 1979, 8.

45. Former senior DEA official, interviewed in confidence by author, 20 August 1991.

46. On this point, see Robin W. Winks, "Canada and the Three Americas: Her Hemispheric Role," in Friends So Different, ed. Lansing Lamont and J. Duncan Edmonds (Ottawa: University of Ottawa Press, 1989), p. 259. Interestingly enough, the Canadian Labour Congress, though a minor player, was in favour of membership. As one of its statements noted: "We cannot afford at this delicate stage in international relations to remain outside the community of nations in the Americas." Quoted in Kenneth McNaught, "Canada's Pan-American Hot Seat," Saturday Night Magazine, August 1961, 15.

47. Jack Ogelsby, letter to author, 17 August 1991.

48. See John Sokol, "Latin America Wants Canada in the OAS," The Commentator 6 no.5 (May 1962): 19.

49. Ibid., 20.

50. Also see "Canada and OAS," *Vancouver Sun,* 24 May 1961, sec. A, p. 4; and "Leave 'Well Enough' Alone," *Edmonton Journal,* 20 May 1961, sec. A, p. 4.

51. "Canada in the OAS?" *Globe and Mail,* 15 March 1960, sec. A, p. 6.

52. Ibid., 6.

53. "Canada and the OAS," *Globe and Mail,* 6 May 1963, sec. A, p. 6.

54. "The Punta Del Este meeting," *Calgary-Albertan,* 14 August 1961.

55. *Time* was more favourably disposed toward Canadian membership in the OAS.

56. Ian Sclanders, "The case against Canadian membership in the OAS," *Maclean's Magazine,* 15 June 1963, 4.

57. Ibid., 4.

58. Interest groups also remained largely silent on the question. With little chance of the government's changing its course on the OAS, these "sources" of foreign policy-making had no reason to engage in any sustained debate. As for foreign governments, the arguments they had used in the 1960s were offered again in the 1970s—the only possible exception being the valuable contribution that Canada, as a full member, could make to the process of reforming and revitalizing the hemispheric body.

59. Forsey, letter to *Globe and Mail,* 10 February 1976, sec. A, p. 6.

60. According to an External Affairs media analysis, 95 per cent of the media coverage was negative toward the 1982 sub-committee recommendation. David R. Murray, "Hard Realities: Canadian-Latin American Relations at the End of the Trudeau Era" (lecture given at the National Defence College, Kingston, Ontario, 28 March 1984), 20.

61. Editorial, "Perils in membership," *Globe and Mail,* 6 December 1982.

62. Editorial, "A club we need not join," *Toronto Star,* 4 December 1982.

63. This author focuses mainly on the academic community for several reasons. First, it was the principal constituency or policy network examining in detail the membership question. Secondly, officials in DEA would occasionally consult or sound out Latin Americanists in Canada on their views of possible Canadian admission. Lastly, many of the arguments flowing from academia—both pro and con—were indicative of the kinds of positions that characterized the whole OAS membership debate.

64. John D. Harbron, *Canada and the Organization of American States* (Canadian-American Committee, 1963), p. 21.

65. He also made the point that Canada is an "American nation" and therefore belongs in the OAS. According to Irwin, Canada has shared with the Americas common cultural and spiritual antecedents as well as "the travail of pioneering a new world, of shaping political, economic and social institutions to a new world environment, and of wresting by one means or another political independence from colonial status." W. Arthur Irwin, "Should Canada Join the Organization of American States?" *Queen's Quarterly* 72 no.2 (spring 1965): 294. A close examination of the

Irwin paper is useful because it was widely circulated, prior to being published, among Canada's embassies and missions in Latin America for comment. See, for example, Archives, Department of External Affairs, "Canada and the OAS," File 20-4-OAS-4-1, 3:1-3.

66. Ibid., 298.

67. Ibid., 298.

68. In particular, he argued that the military/security component of the OAS should not deter Canada from seeking membership. "Membership in the OAS and acceptance of the Rio Pact," according to Irwin, "would not involve commitments in the military field inconsistent with our obligations either to the United Nations or to NATO." Ibid., 295.

69. Ibid., 294.

70. Ibid., 295.

71. Ibid., 295.

72. Ibid., 295.

73. Ibid., 301.

74. Ibid., 300.

75. Irving Brecher and Richard A. Brecher, "Canada and Latin America: The Case for Canadian Involvement," *Queen's Quarterly* 74 no.1 (autumn 1967): 469.

76. Ibid., 468.

77. Ibid., 470.

78. Harbron, *Canada and the Organization of American States*, p. 22.

79. Ibid., p. 26.

80. David Edward Smith, "Should Canada Join the Organization of American States?: A Rejoinder to W. Arthur Irwin," *Queen's Quarterly* 73 no.1 (spring 1966): 107.

81. Ibid., 108.

82. As for relations with the United States, Smith believed that membership would only complicate matters even further. In his words: "United States dominance of NATO has presented problems for Canada which could be expected to increase in an organization as oriented toward Washington as the OAS." Ibid., 109.

83. Ibid., 111.

84. Ibid., 102.

85. Ibid., 114.

86. Ibid., 107.

87. John W. Holmes, who seemed to be undecided on the question of membership, did challenge the idea that Canada, a northern expanse, should be considered an "American nation." He quipped that "it is hard to think that anyone seriously believes Canada has more in common with Argentina than with Norway or New Zealand." Holmes, "Canada and Pan-America," 237.

88. He hinted at the fact that there might be certain advantages to Canada maintaining its steadfast aloofness from the hemispheric forum. He made the point that Canada's Cuba policy was tolerated by the United States

precisely because it was outside the framework of the OAS. Brown,
Writings on Canadian-American Studies, 7.

89. Brown, *Writings on Canadian-American Studies,* 9.
90. McNaught, "Canada's Pan-American Hot Seat," 15-17.
91. Ibid., 17.
92. Ibid., 17.
93. Thompson and Swanson, *Canadian Foreign Policy: Options and Perspectives* (Toronto: McGraw-Hill Ryerson, 1971), p. 101.
94. D.R. Murray, "On Diplomatic Unrelations," in *Canada and the Latin American Challenge,* ed. Jorge Nef (Guelph: Ontario Co-operative Programme In Latin-American Studies, 1978), p. 171.
95. James John Guy, "Canada and Latin America," *The World Today* 32 no.10 (October 1976): 386.
96. John D. Harbron, "Canada and Latin America: Ending a Historic Isolation," *International Perspectives* (May-June 1972): 28.
97. Quoted in J.C.M. Ogelsby, "Canada and Latin America," in *Canada and the Third World,* ed. Peyton V. Lyon and Tareq Y. Ismail (Toronto: Macmillan, 1976), p. 193.
98. Pharand, "Canada and the OAS," 447.
99. Ibid., 444.
100. Ibid., 441.
101. He also reiterated the argument that joining would be in Canada's economic interest. As he explained: "The OAS could thus provide Canada with a suitable framework for the implementation of its economic policy in the region and the intensification of trade with the member states." Ibid., 446.
102. Ibid., 445.
103. Robert Jackson, "Canadian Foreign Policy and the Western Hemisphere," in *Governance in the Western Hemisphere,* ed. Viron P. Vaky (New York: Praeger, 1983), p. 126.
104. Ibid., p. 126.
105. See, for example, Stephen Banker, "The Changing OAS," *International Perspectives* (May-June 1982): 23; and Edgar J. Dosman, "Hemispheric Relations in the 1980s: A Perspective from Canada," *Journal of Canadian Studies* 19 no.4 (winter 1984-85): 58.
106. David R. Murray, "The Bilateral Road: Canada and Latin America in the 1980s," *International Journal* 37 no.1 (winter 1981-82): 112-13.
107. See, for example, Edgar Dosman and David Pollock, "Canada, Mexico and the North-South Dialogue: The Need for Audacity," in *Relations Between Mexico And Canada,* ed. Omar Martínez Legorreta (El Colegio de México, Centro De Estudios Internacionales, 1990), pp. 280-81.
108. Dosman, "Hemispheric Relations in the 1980s," 59.
109. This reference to "semi-permanent sleep" was borrowed from a letter from David R. Murray, 14 June 1990.

CHAPTER VI

1. Much of the discussion in this chapter is drawn from Peter McKenna, "Canada Joins the OAS: Anatomy of a Decision," in *America and the Americas,* ed. Jacques Zylberberg and Francois Demers (Sainte-Foy, Québec: Laval University Press, 1992), pp. 253-69.

2. Since government documentation on this decision is unavailable for public perusal, this chapter relies extensively on confidential interviews and written correspondence with key policy-makers in the Department of External Affairs.

3. See Brian J.R. Stevenson, "Canada and the OAS: A New Era Emerges?" (CAPA Working Paper, 1991), 3; and Bob Hepburn, "Americas club may be going bust just as Canada prepares to join," *Toronto Star,* 15 October 1989.

4. Apparently, officials in External Affairs were angry that Prime Minister Mulroney informed the press of his discussions with Bush on the possibility of Canadian membership in the OAS. Former senior DEA official, interviewed in confidence by author, 12 August 1991.

5. See, for example, Stephen J. Randall, "Think twice before joining the OAS," *Globe and Mail,* 26 October 1989, sec. A, p. 7; Jeffrey Simpson, "The folly of joining the OAS," *Globe and Mail,* 4 October 1989, sec. A, p. 6; Allan Gotlieb, "Arguments against joining the OAS form a tired old refrain," *Globe and Mail,* 23 October 1989, sec. A, p. 6; and Donat Pharand, "Greater world role awaits Canada in the Americas," *Globe and Mail,* 3 October 1989, sec. A, p. 8.

6. Jeffrey Simpson, "Folly of Joining."

7. DEA official in Washington, interviewed in confidence by author, 5 March 1991.

8. Stevenson, "Entering the Inter-American System: Canada and the OAS in the 1990s" (unpublished paper, March 1991), ii.

9. The decision to seek full membership in the hemispheric body was made by the full Cabinet on 4 October 1989. Former senior DEA official, letter to author, 14 July 1991.

10. The Conservative government's 1985 foreign policy review makes only a single reference to the OAS. Furthermore, there is no mention of the organization in the Department of External Affairs report, *Canada's International Relations: Response of the Government of Canada to the Report of the Special Joint Committee of the Senate and House of Commons* (Ottawa: Minister of Supply and Services Canada, 1986).

11. Notes for an address by The Right Honourable Brian Mulroney, 27 October 1989, 5.

12. Canada did not officially become a member of the OAS until 8 January 1990, when Ambassador Jean-Paul Hubert formally signed the charter.

13. This was recently reconfirmed in an interview with a long-time Conservative MP and Mulroney caucus member. He indicated, in quite

strong terms, that SSEA Clark probably took his lead on the membership issue from Mulroney himself. Interviewed in confidence by author, 24 August 1994.

14. Joe Clark, Secretary of State for External Affairs, quoted in House of Commons, Standing Committee on External Affairs and International Trade, *Minutes of Proceedings and Evidence,* no. 25, 8 November 1989, 13.

15. It is conceivable that both Clark and Mulroney saw Latin America as an area in which the Conservative government—particularly if it undertook such an initiative as joining the OAS—could clearly differentiate itself from the foreign policy of previous Liberal governments.

16. Stevenson, "Canada and the OAS," 3.

17. Recently, he was the driving force behind Canada's sudden granting of diplomatic recognition to the three Baltic republics. See Ross Howard and Graham Fraser, "Ottawa extends recognition to Baltics," *Globe and Mail,* 27 August 1991, sec. A, p. 6.

18. See Hugh Winsor, "Mulroney calls shots on Gulf policy," *Globe and Mail,* 18 January 1991, sec. A, p. 1.

19. It is possible that the prime minister's thinking was influenced by the prospect of increased economic benefits for Canada. In May of 1989 a group of Brazilian businesspeople urged him to be more involved in Latin America, especially with such major players as Brazil, Mexico, and Venezuela. Apparently, they suggested that there would be potential economic dividends for Canada if it opted for full membership in the OAS. Former DEA official, interviewed in confidence by author, 12 August 1991.

20. Mulroney, Notes for an address, 5.

21. Some have speculated that the prime minister would not have accepted the invitation to participate in the hemispheric summit unless he had something substantial to say about Canada's place in the inter-American community. In this way, the summit served to move the government toward full membership. Former Canadian permanent observer to the OAS, letter to author, 8 January 1991; and J.C.M. Ogelsby, "Membership a waste of time, money unless Canada takes initiatives," *London Free Press,* 12 January 1990, sec. A, p. 11.

22. Mulroney, "Notes for an address," 4.

23. Ibid., 4.

24. Simon Fisher, "Canada seeks larger Latin American role, Clark says," *Globe and Mail,* 22 June 1989, Sec. B, p. 8.

25. Clark's contact with other foreign ministers from Latin America, particularly those of the Rio Group, helped to shape his favourable view of the region. He had also visited a number of Central American countries— including Sandinista Nicaragua—in the fall of 1987. At the same time, Latin American officials were privately urging him to bring Canada into the OAS family as a full member. Former DEA official, interviewed in

confidence by author, 12 August 1991.

26. Hugh Winsor, "Joe Where?" *Globe and Mail,* 17 November 1990, sec. D, p. 1.

27. This "new" internationalism appears to refer to an increased desire on the part of Canada to work more actively through multilateral organizations (i.e., UN, Commonwealth, NATO, G-7, GATT, CSCE, and La francophonie) to deal with such issues as apartheid, trade liberalization, Third World poverty, and arms control and disarmament. Perhaps it was a realization that the issues cluttering the world agenda are now increasingly "international" in scope. See John Kirton, "Canada's New Internationalism," *Current History* 87 no.527 (March 1988): 101-04, 134; Andrew Cohen, "Canada's Foreign Policy: The Outlook for the Second Mulroney Mandate," *Behind the Headlines* 46 no.1 (summer 1989): 1-3; and Tom Keating, "In Search of a Foreign Policy," in *Social Democracy Without Illusions,* ed. Richards, R. Cairns, and L. Pratt (McClelland and Stewart, 1991), pp. 158-60.

28. Joe Clark, "Canada's New Internationalism," in *Canada and the New Internationalism,* ed. John W. Holmes and John Kirton (Toronto: Canadian Institute for International Affairs, 1988), pp. 3-11.

29. Joe Clark, Secretary of State for External Affairs, Notes for a speech to the University of Calgary on Canadian policy towards Latin America, 1 February 1990, 3.

30. Ibid., 6-7.

31. Joe Clark, quoted in *Minutes of Proceedings and Evidence,* 18.

32. Ibid., 8.

33. Ibid., 28.

34. Evidently, Clark was not deterred by the prospect of Canada's having to disagree publicly with the United States. In an exchange with NDP member Bill Blaikie he stated: "If from time to time the United States does something in the OAS that we think is flagrantly outrageous, we will say so, as we have done in the past." Ibid., 19.

35. Joe Clark, Secretary of State for External Affairs, Notes for remarks at the meeting of the Council of the Organization of American States, Washington, DC, 13 November 1989, 1.

36. Joe Clark, quoted in *Minutes of Proceedings and Evidence,* 7.

37. Ibid., 10.

38. There was some consultation with business groups, academics, and non-governmental organizations at a colloquium held at Carleton University in early May 1989.

39. See Liisa North, ed., *Between War and Peace in Central America* (Toronto: Between The Lines, 1990), pp. 47-52; and James Rochlin, "Aspects of Canadian Foreign Policy towards Central America, 1979-1986," in *Towards a New World Order,* ed. J.L. Granatstein (Toronto: Copp Clark, 1992), pp. 191-94.

40. Richard Gorham, former Roving Ambassador to Latin America, interviewed by author, 4 August 1992. Representatives of the Canadian military were also involved in the UN Observer Group in Central America (ONUCA) and on the UN Observer Mission in El Salvador (ONUSAL), now in operation.

41. Former senior official in the Latin America and Caribbean Branch, interviewed in confidence by author, 5 August 1992.

42. Joe Clark, quoted in *Minutes of Proceedings and Evidence*, 11.

43. Ibid., 11.

44. Gorham outlined these points in his speech to the Canada-Brazil Chamber of Commerce. See "Canada's New Policy Initiatives in Latin America" (remarks, Montreal, Québec, 16 April 1990), 8-9.

45. Gorham, "The Organization of American States (OAS): What is it and Why Did Canada Join?" Halifax, Nova Scotia, 16 May 1990, 9-10.

46. For many years, the Latin Americanists in DEA were professionally demoralized and disillusioned with the lack of official government interest in the region. It is possible that joining the OAS was not only an way of grabbing the attention of the minister, but also an institutional means of getting the government to pay more attention to the region. They hoped that Latin America would become a sort of "fourth pillar" of Canadian foreign policy, after the United States, Europe, and Asia-Pacific. Former DEA official, interviewed in confidence by author, 12 August 1991.

47. After reviewing Canada's policy toward Latin America in 1982-83, the department advised the then Secretary of State for External Affairs Allan MacEachen not to seek full membership in the OAS.

48. Ambassador Richard V. Gorham, "Canada's New Policy Initiatives in Latin America" (remarks to the Canada-Brazil Chamber of Commerce, Montreal, 16 April 1990), 7.

49. Former senior DEA official, interviewed in confidence by author, 20 August 1991.

50. Officials also informed their political masters of the fact that Canada, despite its support for the Sandinista government and the Central American peace process in general, suffered absolutely no serious repercussions from the United States.

51. Ambassador Richard V. Gorham, "The Organization of American States (OAS): What is it and Why Did Canada Join?" (notes for remarks at a luncheon meeting of the Canadian Institute of International Affairs, Halifax, N.S., 16 May 1990), 17.

52. By 1988 Canada had become increasingly involved in both the Contadora/Esquipulas peace process, culminating in the sending of Canadian Armed Forces (CAF) personnel to participate in the UN/OAS peacekeeping force (ONUCA). While this growing involvement was not a central reason underpinning the government's decision to join the OAS, it

did create a positive atmosphere for such an eventuality. Former senior DEA official in the Latin America and Caribbean bureau, interviewed in confidence by author, 27 January 1992. For a discussion of Canada's participation in the Contadora peace process 1983-1986, see John Graham, "Shaping Stability in Central America," in *Canada and the New Internationalism*, ed. John Holmes and John Kirton (Toronto: University of Toronto Press, 1988), pp. 35-40.

53. By the mid-1980s a number of alternative approaches had been created to deal with the region's myriad difficulties—including the Contadora/Esquipulas Group, the Cartagena Group, and the Rio Group.

54. Canadian officials were well aware that under the Cartagena reforms to the OAS, both Guyana and Belize would have been eligible for full membership in December 1990. (The two countries subsequently became official members in January 1991). If they were to opt for full membership at that time, Canada would have been the only country of the Americas who was not a full-fledged member of the body. This possibility, and the potential embarrassment for Ottawa, was not lost on foreign policy mandarins.

55. There was a sense that if Canada refrained from joining altogether, it would seriously call into question the credibility of Ottawa's stated intention of strengthening its relations with the region. Former DEA official, interviewed in confidence by author, 20 August 1991.

56. There was also a firm belief that the failure of U.S. policy in Central America and the use of military force in general, along with a hemispheric issue-agenda requiring multi-nation attention and collaboration, had seriously called into question the efficacy of unilateralism.

57. Recently, the implications of large-scale migratory flows of economic refugees were explained in pointed fashion by Mexican President Carlos Salinas de Gortari. See Madelaine Drohan and Peter Cook, "Trade or face immigrant flood, Salinas warns," *Globe and Mail*, 5 April 1991, sec. B, p. 1.

58. For instance, officials felt that membership would give Canada a greater say on how the debt problem would be approached, especially on the form which the various proposals for tackling it would take. They were well aware of the fact that Canadian chartered banks have outstanding loans to a number of Latin American and Caribbean countries totalling more than $27 billion. This figure was taken from Claude Isbister, "Third World Debt: IMF and the World Bank," *Behind the Headlines* (March 1987): 10.

59. Former senior DEA official, interviewed in confidence by author, 20 August 1991.

60. Officials were aware that Latin America held out the possibility of representing a sizeable market for Canadian goods and services. To be sure, it is projected that by the year 2000, there will be some 600 million people in the region. Already, two-way trade in 1988, which amounted to more than $6.7 billion, was equivalent to Canada's trade with China

and a host of South East Asian countries combined. Gorham, "Canada's New Policy Initiatives," 18.

61. Ibid., 17.

62. Latin American specialists within DEA played down somewhat the trade side of the OAS membership equation. In part, this was done to allay the fears of other officials within the department, who were concerned about the possibility of resources being shifted to Latin America at the expense of Europe and Asia-Pacific. Former DEA official, interviewed in confidence by author, 20 August 1991.

63. They also knew that this contribution could be made without having to sign the Rio Treaty and thus assume the attendant military/security obligations. For all intents and purposes, the security pact, especially after the Falklands/Malvinas conflict, had fallen into disrepute.

64. Former senior DEA official, interviewed in confidence by author, 20 August 1991.

65. Joe Clark, Notes for a speech on Canadian policy towards Latin America, 2.

66. For a fuller discussion of these developments, see José Alváro Moisés, "Democracy Threatened: The Latin American Paradox," *Alternatives* 16 no.2 (spring 1991): 141-60; and Peter H. Smith, "Crisis and Democracy in Latin America," *World Politics* 43 no.4 (July 1991): 608-34.

67. See, for example, James Brooke, "Collor plan now turning to privatization, payroll cuts," *Globe and Mail*, 21 May 1990, sec. B, p. 6; Madelaine Drohan, "Reforms take toll on Mexico," *Globe and Mail*, 21 November 1990, sec. B, p. 1; and Paul Knox, "Argentina binds the hand that feeds the economy," *Globe and Mail*, 28 May 1991, sec. B, p. 5.

68. See Nicole Bonnet, "Bearing the brunt of Fujishock," *Globe and Mail*, 6 December 1990, sec. B, p. 8; and Andrew Hurst, "Latin America's economy looks brighter," *Globe and Mail*, 1 December 1990, sec. B, p. 4.

69. Former DEA official, interviewed in confidence by author, 20 August 1991.

70. Note that the prevailing international climate in past years often worked against the possibility of OAS membership.

71. It is worth mentioning here that the Conservative government did not attempt to "educate" the public—through leaks, consultations with outside groups, or parliamentary hearings—before announcing its intentions to join the OAS.

CHAPTER VII

1. This chapter relies heavily on an article previously published by the author. See Peter McKenna, "How is Canada Doing in the OAS?," *Canadian Foreign Policy* 1 no.2 (spring 1993): 81-98.

2. J.C.M. Ogelsby, "Membership a waste of time, money unless Canada takes initiatives," *London Free Press*, 12 January 1990, sec. A, p. 11.

3. L. Ronald Scheman, "Canada joins the OAS: Great news," *Times of the Americas*, 15 November 1989, p. 11.

4. On Mulroney's response to the invasion, see Ross Howard, "Critics anticipate diplomatic problems after endorsement," *Globe and Mail,* 22 December 1989, sec. A, p. 4.

5. Colin MacKenzie, "Canada takes up dispute on first day as new member of OAS," *Globe and Mail,* 9 January 1990, Sec. A, p. 10.

6. Canada's then Secretary of State for External Affairs Joe Clark was unable to attend the gathering because he was preoccupied with developments in the Persian Gulf.

7. In addition to such things as election monitoring, the unit is designed to strengthen democratic institutions and principles within OAS member states. Department of External Affairs, Mme. M. Landry, Minister for External Relations and International Development, (statement at the OAS General Assembly in Asunción, Paraguay, 5 June 1990), 1-7. The unit was created within the General Secretariat by OAS Secretary-General João Baena Soares in mid-October.

8. Canada also contributed financially to the Haitian elections by providing $1 million in material and technical support. See, Department of External Affairs, *Annual Report 1990-1991,* April 1992, 30. For a closer examination of Canada's involvement in the OAS, see Department of External Affairs, *Canada's First Year in the Organization of American States,* January 1990, 1-14.

9. The April 1991 report of the Consultation Group on the Inter-American System called, *inter alia,* for a clearer definition of the organization's priorities—as a guide for the allocation of resources. The group also put forth a number of recommendations, including increased OAS involve- ment in the hemisphere's pressing economic and social problems; in the promotion and strengthening of democracy and human rights; in advancing such critical issues as development, the environment, and population growth, and in fostering greater co-operation and interchange between the OAS, the UN, and a host of other regional organizations. In addition, it indicated its support for a review of the topic of hemispheric security, the strengthening of arms control mechanisms, and investing the Secretary General with "greater initiative- and action-taking capacity." Simply put, it stressed the need for the OAS to be "updated and modern- ized" so as to meet the many new challenges facing the hemisphere. Organization of American States, *Report of the Consultation Group on the Inter-American System,* AG/CP/doc. 516/91 corr. 1, 3 May 1991, 1-12.

10. After joining the OAS, the then Secretary of State for External Affairs Joe Clark hinted at the fact that Canada might be prepared to act in some bridge-building capacity. Charlotte Montgomery, "Canada seeks to thaw frost in U.S.-Cuban relationship," *Globe and Mail,* 14 April 1990, sec. A, p. 7.

11. Department of External Affairs, Barbara McDougall, Secretary of State for External Affairs (notes for a speech to the General Assembly of the Organization of American States), Santiago, Chile, 3 June 1991, 1.

12. Ibid., 4.

13. The prevention of regional conflicts was a key element in the government's recent statement on future foreign policy priorities for Canada. Department of External Affairs, *Foreign Policy Themes and Priorities 1991-92 Update,* Policy Planning Staff, December 1991, 5-7.

14. This section relies extensively on interviews with officials in the Department of External Affairs.

15. Canada actually pushed for a reduction in the budget of the board and a reallocation of those funds to the Inter-American Commission of Women and the Inter-American Children's Institute.

16. Provincial foot-dragging can be explained, in part, by concerns about the convention's language on such thorny issues as capital punishment and the protection of life by law "from the moment of conception." For further elaboration of these points, see William A. Schabas, "Substantive and Procedural Hurdles to Canada's Ratification of the American Convention on Human Rights," *Human Rights Law Journal* 12 nos.11-12 (December 1991): 405-413. For a further discussion of the human rights question, see James C. Hathaway, *Canada and the Inter-American Human Rights System: What Contribution to Expect?* (unpublished paper, October 1991), 1-19. It is worth mentioning that Canada's inability to ratify the convention goes some way toward explaining why Wilson's candidacy for the Inter-American Court was turned down.

17. Department of External Affairs, *Canadian International Relations Chronicle,* October-December 1991, 14.

18. In late September, Canadian officials also participated in the Tenth Inter-American Conference of Ministers of Agriculture—sponsored by the OAS—which took place in Madrid, Spain. Besides offering support for agricultural trade liberalization, the final declaration, which was backed by Canada, called for further modernization of agriculture in the Americas. See Government of Canada, "Madrid Declaration Signals New Direction for Agriculture in Americas," *News Release,* 25 September 1991, 1-2.

19. Organization of American States, "Resolution on Representative Democracy," AG/RES. 1080 (XXI-0/91), Santiago, Chile, 5 June 1991, 4.

20. "Haiti leader ousted; More violence feared," Halifax *Mail Star,* 1 October 1991, sec. A, p. 9.

21. "Mulroney raps 'Bloody Disgrace'," Halifax *Daily News,* 2 October 1991, p. 11.

22. Organization of American States, "Support to the democratic government of Haiti," MRE/RES. 1/91 Washington DC, 3 October 1991, 1-3.

23. Colin MacKenzie, "OAS mission to Haiti ends without success," *Globe and Mail,* 7 October 1991, sec. A, p. 1.

24. Organization of American States, "Support for Democracy in Haiti," MRE/RES. 2/91, Washington DC, 8 October 1991, 1-2.

25. David Olive, "Canada steps right up to direct OAS help for a fledgling democracy," *Globe and Mail,* 29 February 1992, sec. D, p. 4.

26. Ross Howard, "PM links aid giving to policies on rights," *Globe and Mail*, 15 October 1991, sec. A, p. 1; and Rheal Seguin, "Haiti in spotlight at Francophonie," *Globe and Mail*, 19 November 1991, sec. A, p. 9.

27. Colin MacKenzie, "Leaders hold rare phone conversations over Haiti crisis," *Globe and Mail*, 20 December 1991, sec. A, p. 8.

28. DEA official, interviewed in confidence by author, 19 December 1991.

29. André Picard, "Defiant expatriates keep faith with Titid," *Globe and Mail*, 4 October 1991, sec. A, p. 7; and Picard, "Montreal Haitian leaders praise Mulroney," *Globe and Mail*, 15 October 1991, sec. A, p. 8.

30. Department of External Affairs, "McDougall Concerned by the Situation in Peru," *News Release* 66, 7 April 1992, 1.

31. The Permanent Council of the OAS did meet in an emergency session to "deplore the events that have taken place in Peru" and to "urge the authorities in that country to immediately reinstate democratic institutions and full respect for human rights under the rule of law." See Organization of American States, "The Situation in Peru," CP/RES. 579 (897/92), 6 April 1992, 1.

32. "Peru to hold elections within 18 months," Halifax *Mail-Star*, 8 April 1992, sec. D, p.19.

33. Department of External Affairs, Barbara McDougall, Secretary of State for External Affairs (notes for a statement at the Organization of American States headquarters on the crisis in Peru), *Statement*, 92/15, 13 April 1992, 2.

34. Organization of American States, "Restoration of Democracy in Haiti," MRE/RES. 3/92, 17 May 1991, 2-3.

35. It was also reported that both Canada and the United States were prepared to approach the twelve members of the EC on tightening their sanctions against Haiti. See Howard W. French, "Latin states back steps to restore President in Haiti," *New York Times*, 18 May 1992, sec. A, p. 1.

36. Department of External Affairs, Barbara McDougall, Secretary of State for External Affairs (address to the 22ND Annual General Assembly of the Organization of American States, Nassau, Bahamas, 19 May 1992), 3.

37. Ibid., 3.

38. By early June, Canada had passed regulations freezing the assets in Canada of the Government of Haiti. In mid-June Prime Minister Mulroney, after holding talks with Venezuelan President Carlos Andrés Pérez, hinted at the possibility of initiating new steps to facilitate the reinstatement of President Aristide. "New Haiti moves considered," *Globe and Mail*, 15 June 1992, sec. A, p. 1.

39. Organization of American States, "Restoration of Democracy in Peru," MRE/RES. 2/92, 18 May 1992, 1.

40. Ibid., 2.

41. "Fujimori promises elections," *Globe and Mail*, 19 May 1992, sec. A, p. 7.

42. McDougall, address to assembly of OAS, 73.

43. Ibid., 4.

44. See, for example, Canada-Caribbean-Central America Policy Alternatives, *Report Card on Canada's First Year in the OAS in the Light of Hemispheric Relations* (CAPA occasional paper, July 1990), 1-13.

45. Canada-Caribbean-Central America Policy Alternatives, *Report on Canada's Second Year in the OAS* (CAPA occasional paper, April 1992), 2.

46. Ibid., 14.

47. Ibid., 20.

48. Ibid., 21.

CONCLUSION

1. This writer has found no evidence that would suggest that the U.S. government played any direct role in pressing the Mulroney government to join the OAS.

2. Part of this growing significance of Latin America to Canada was the result of new realities in the area of trade relations. The region was becoming a sizeable market for Canadian exports (particularly manufactured goods)—amounting to almost $3 billion in 1989. James J.Guy, "Canada Joins the OAS: A New Dynamic in the Inter-American System," *Inter-American Review Of Bibliography* 39, no. 4 (1989): 508. The burgeoning economic importance of Latin America was also derived from the possible formation of a hemispheric-wide free trade area in the 1990s—possibly in response to the "Single Europe" of 1992-93. Still, the business lobby in Canada put no overt pressure on the government to join the OAS. Former senior DEA official, interviewed in confidence by author, 20 August 1991. In short, it did not appear to be a major issue of importance for Canadian business leaders.

3. Since Canada will be expected to vote on resolutions before the Permanent Council, the Canadian government will not only have to think about issues before the OAS, but also to accord sufficient analytical resources to make informed and intelligent judgments and decisions.

4. Canadian official in Washington, interviewed in confidence by author, 2 September 1994.

5. This reality will almost certainly pose some difficulties for Canadian officials seeking to fashion a truly independent posture within the hemispheric body.

6. Canada's inability to get Bertha Wilson elected to the Inter-American

Commission on Human Rights—when Canadian officials were privately assured of the support of some twenty-two countries—was partly a signal sent by member states that Canada should not try to move too quickly to change the hemispheric forum.

7. Quoted in Charlotte Montgomery, "Canada Seeks to Thaw Frost," *Globe and Mail,* 14 April 1990, sec. A, p. 7.

8. Ross Howard, "External Affairs Department cut 250 jobs," *Globe and Mail,* 29 June 1990, sec. A, p. 74.

9. Canada's mission in Washington is led by Ambassador Brian Dickson and staffed by three counsellors. By way of comparison, the Chilean mission at the OAS is comprised of more than twelve members. Heraldo Muñoz, Chile's Ambassador to the OAS, interviewed by author, 4 March 1991, Washington. Note, however, that there are two foreign service officers tasked with OAS affairs at headquarters in Ottawa.

10. If the new government's response to developments in Haiti and Cuba are any indication, it seems as though Canada will become more, not less, engaged in the Americas. On Haiti, the Chrétien government has maintained its steadfast commitment to facilitate the return of President Aristide. And in the wake of the Carter initiative, and the apparent return to Haiti of Aristide, Ottawa has tentatively offered to provide peacekeepers as well as training for a new police force. In terms of Cuba, the government decided in June of 1994 to resume development assistance (roughly $1.5 million) to the beleaguered island—mainly through non-governmental organizations operating in the country.

11. Although there have been few real signs of policy impetus toward the region, it does seem that the Liberal agenda for the Americas will be largely trade-driven.

12. In the summer of 1994 both John Labatt Ltd. and Reichmann International LP were engaged in substantial projects in Mexico.

13. The new Liberal government seems to be placing considerable emphasis on strengthening commercial linkages with the Asia-Pacific region—especially China. In November of 1994 Prime Minister Chrétien led the largest Canadian trade mission ever sent to China.

14. While no dramatic increase is likely in bureaucratic resources allocated to Latin American affairs, staff will probably not be reduced in this area either.

POSTSCRIPT

1. See Peter McKenna, "How is Canada Doing in the OAS?" *Canadian Foreign Policy* 1 no.2 (spring 1993): 81-98.

2. For a recent, albeit favourable, discussion of this dynamic, see Jean-Paul Hubert, "Canada and the OAS: Review and Outlook," *FOCAL Lecture Series* (Ottawa: Canadian Foundation for the Americas, March 1994): 1-4.

3. In assessing the effectiveness of the OAS in the Haitian crisis, it is worth noting that few, if any, previous military coups in Latin America have been successfully reversed.

4. Much of this section draws heavily upon Peter McKenna, "Canada and the Haitian Crisis," *American Review of Canadian Studies* (forthcoming).

5. Jeff Sallot and Graham Fraser, "Canadian team set to help Aristide," *Globe and Mail*, 16 September 1994, sec. A, p. 7. Notwithstanding U.S. pressure for Canada to participate in "phase 1" of the planned invasion, the Chrétien government decided to send in Canadians only after the "dirty work" had been almost completed. Foreign Minister André Ouellet, in a recent meeting with U.S. Secretary of State Warren Christopher, assured his counterpart that Canada would begin its commitment within hours, possibly before the invasion phase had been completed. However, after the recent agreement negotiated by former U.S. President Jimmy Carter, without the full backing of President Aristide, Canada will only commit Canadians after Aristide himself has been restored to power in Haiti. Moreover, there is some doubt as to just how many peacekeepers Canada can provide to the Haitian mission—given the country's dwindling number of available Canadian armed forces personnel. Jeff Sallot, "Ottawa may cut forces in Bosnia," *Globe and Mail*, 21 September 1994, sec. A, p. 1. There has been some valid criticism of the Liberal government's fainthearted handling of the crisis itself and its recent unwillingness to assume any "serious responsibilities" for militarily removing the junta. See, for example, Jeffrey Simpson, "The sound we make is moral outrage; The action we take is quibbling," *Globe and Mail*, 15 September 1994, sec. A., p. 20. By not participating in phase one, Canada lost a fair amount of credibility—since it had pledged its unwavering support for restoring President Aristide to power from the beginning.

6. Since October 1993, naval vessels from Canada, the United States, and France have been enforcing the sanctions against the military junta. They

have focused their energies mainly on preventing desperately-needed petroleum supplies from reaching the tiny country. In August 1994 Ottawa agreed to dispatch some ten Canadians to help in enforcing the embargo along the 330-kilometre border between Haiti and the Dominican Republic. With the military leadership agreeing to step down before 15 October, these observers have now been recalled to Canada.

7. Douglas Jehl, "No deadline is set, but President says junta faces U.S. attack," *New York Times,* 16 September 1994, sec. A, p. 1.

8. In early January the Inter-American Commission on Human Rights called upon the Canadian government to respond to a claim by a Kenyan dissident who was reportedly denied refugee status in the country and subsequently deported. See Estanislao Oziewics, "OAS agency asks Canada to explain deportation," *Globe and Mail,* 8 January 1993, sec. A, p. 5. More recently, Canada was accused by some of using heavy-handed tactics to get César Gaviria elected to the post of OAS Secretary General. See Larry Birns and Jeremy Latimer, "Canada's reputation jeopardized by support for U.S. bullying of OAS," *Ottawa Citizen,* 23 March 1994 and David Todd, "Canada denies it lobbied to keep Costa Rican from top OAS post," *Montreal Gazette,* 8 April 1994.

9. Note the appointment of a new Canadian Ambassador to the OAS, a changeover of staff at the mission in Washington, the addition of another officer—bringing the total to four. Additionally, a second foreign service officer has been added to cover OAS affairs at the renamed Department of Foreign Affairs and International Trade in Ottawa. Interestingly, other officials within Foreign Affairs now look upon positions dealing with the OAS as an area of rising importance and potential career enhancement.

10. Canada has had some problems in the area of OAS reform—including some from the former Secretary General, Baena Soares, and his personal staff. While some initiatives have been successful, this goal has proven to be more difficult than was initially anticipated.

11. For a "mixed," though critical, assessment of Canada's activities within the OAS, see Canada-Caribbean-Central America Policy Alternatives (CAPA), *Report on Canada's Third Year in the OAS* (CAPA Occasional Paper, June 1993), 1-33.

12. Perhaps one could argue that Canada, as the second largest contributor, could be more influential than officials currently believe.

13. For discussion of the coup, see Tim Golden, "Guatemala's counter-coup: A military about-face," *New York Times,* 3 June 1993, sec. A, p. 3; and

Edmond Mulet, "The palace coup that failed," *Globe and Mail*, 29 June 1993, sec. A, p. 17.

14. External Affairs and International Trade Canada, "Canada Applauds Guatemala's Return to Democracy," *This Week in Trade and Foreign Policy* 129, June 3-9, 1993.

15. Isabel Vincent, "Paraguay's election isn't all beer and skittles—There's voting, too," *Globe and Mail*, 17 May 1993, sec. A, p. 16.

16. Canadian official in Washington, interviewed in confidence by author, 8 January 1994.

17. In the main, electoral observation consists of a variety of activities, including talking to the respective political parties, speaking with electoral officials, checking voter lists, organizing polling stations, and visiting as many stations as possible on election day.

18. The new Liberal government appears to be committed to the work of the unit, although John Graham was not kept on as its Executive Coordinator.

19. There had been some suggestion that such a transfer was too complicated and, moreover, that Canada had already committed substantial funds for elections in both Ukraine and South Africa. Canadian official in Washington, interviewed in confidence by author, 20 September 1994.

20. This commitment was recently reconfirmed by Secretary of State Christine Stewart in her remarks to the June 1994 OAS General Assembly. See Government of Canada, Christine Stewart, Secretary Of State (Latin America and Africa) (address to the 24th General Assembly of the Organization of American States, Belem, Brazil, 7 June 1994), 1-9.

21. On 23 January 1995 Canada's Elizabeth Spehar, formerly of the Montreal-based International Centre for Human Rights and Democratic Development, assumed the position of Executive Co-ordinator of the Unit for the Promotion of Democracy.

22. Isabel Vincent, "Paraguay election receives plaudits," *Globe and Mail*, 11 May 1993, sec. A, p. 6.

23. Canadian official in Washington, interviewed in confidence by author, 19 November 1993.

24. While the new work-plan looks promising, its implementation will likely be difficult. Canadian official in Washington, letter to author, 28 September 1994.

25. This discussion relies heavily upon a recent piece by John W. Graham, then-Executive Coordinator of the unit, titled: "In Pursuit of Democracy:

The Case of the UPD," *Changing Americas Series: Report* (Ottawa: Canadian Foundation for the Americas, December 1993), pp. 1-4.

26. Funds were made available by the unit for an impartial non-governmental organization in Paraguay "to prepare and to transmit by radio information about the modalities of a forthcoming national election and about the responsibilities of those concerned, including the electorate." Graham, "In Pursuit Of Democracy," p. 4.

27. Ibid., p. 3.

28. Ibid., pp. 3-4.

29. Ibid., p. 4.

30. Canada continues to be active in general budgetary and administrative reform of the organization. Canadian officials urged the creation of working groups to deal with this important question—human resources, material, evaluation, and auditing. Canada will be chairing the group on auditing and has recently hired an outside consultant to review the body's practices.

31. As of the end of 1994 working groups have been established within the OAS to accelerate and manage the transition process. Some six member states have ratified the appropriate legislative instruments to date and thus there is some hope that two-thirds of the members will have completed their own ratification processes by the next OAS General Assembly.

32. The creation of this new technical assistance council required modifications to the OAS Charter. Canada deposited its instruments of ratification with the General Secretariat of the OAS in Washington on 4 October 1993. Secretary of State for External Affairs, "Canada Ratifies Protocols Strengthening the Organization Of American States," News Release 191, 5 October 1993.

33. Organization Of American States, "Amendment of the Charter of the Organization of American States as Regards Technical Cooperation," 19th Special Session, 7 June 1993, Managua, Nicaragua, 3.

34. This interest, however, has to be weighed against the Canadian government's continued inability to secure a seat on the Inter-American Commission on Human Rights. While it is true that Canada still has not signed the American Convention on Human Rights, this does not prevent it from running a candidate when a position becomes vacant. As for the American Convention, some of the provinces continue to have difficulty with its wording, particularly in the area of abortion and capital

punishment, although meetings of the Continuing Committee of Human Rights Officials are still ongoing. For the most part, the work at the official level has been completed, and the requisite reservations and statements of understanding have been agreed upon—which should further open the door to ratification. Some officials hope to have a final federal-provincial position by the end of 1994 and final cabinet approval early in the new year. This, of course, would allow Canada to announce its belated ratification at the June 1995 OAS General Assembly.

35. Organization of American States, "Declaration of Managua for the Promotion of Democracy and Development," 23rd Regular Session, 7 June 1993, Managua, Nicaragua, pp.4-5.

36. Stewart (address to 24th General Assembly), 4. Rather than any increase in the size of the commission, as advanced by the Nicaragua mission, Canada would like to see more resources allocated to the working side of the commission to improve services to the existing commissioners.

37. Opposition from Mexico and South American members stems in large part from the fact that the military authorities in these countries continue to view the IADB in a favourable light. The United States, for its part, is still interested in maintaining high-level linkages with Latin American militaries. Interestingly, some Caribbean members are also committed to maintaining the board—perhaps out of concern for their own security needs.

38. Canadian official in Washington, interviewed in confidence by author, 19 November 1993.

39. Organization of American States, "Inter-American Defense Board," 33rd regular Session, 9 June 1993, Managua, Nicaragua, 2.

40. McDougall (address to the Assembly of OAS), 5.

41. Christine Stewart (address to 24th General Assembly), 7. Canada now realizes that dismantling of the board entirely is a non-starter. It has resigned itself to reforming the institution and is now undertaking bilateral consultations with countries such as Mexico, Brazil, Argentina, Chile, and the United States. Canadian officials, in hinting at the possible cutting off of Ottawa's funding to the board, are continuing to garner support for restructuring the institution, modernizing its mandate, permitting universal membership, and clarifying the precise legal connections between the board and the OAS itself. Canadian official in Washington, interviewed by author, 1 September 1994.

42. Organization of American States, "Meeting of Experts on Security

Mechanisms and Measures to Promote Confidence in the Region," 23rd
Regular Session, 8 June 1993, Managua, Nicaragua, 3.

43. There will be a regional conference on CBMs in Chile scheduled for some
time in 1995. Canadian officials are working on organizing the conference and on setting the agenda. At the moment, the issue of landmines
and their dangers to civilian populations is likely to occupy a fair amount
of time of the conference participants. Questions about responsible use
and regulation, increased detectability, and ensuring better and more
accurate records on where they are located are also likely to dominate the
meetings.

44. For a recent treatment of the drug trade and its implications for Canada,
see Hal P. Klepak, "The Impact of the International Narcotics Trade on
Canada's Foreign and Security Policy," *International Journal* 49 no.1
(winter 1993-94): 66-92.

45. The final report, based on the compilation of the responses received, was
tabled in March of 1994 in Argentina. CICAD is now in the process of
assessing the effectiveness of the various strategies for dealing with the
drug problem.

46 Final papers from both Canada and Mexico will be tabled at an October
1994 meeting in Chile. It will be at this meeting that the final stamp of
approval will be placed on administrative reform and commission
priorities.

47. With the arrival of a new Secretary General to the OAS in mid-September
1994, Canadian officials hope that reforms to CICAD will be given new
impetus under the leadership of César Gaviria. There will be a new
Executive Secretary of CICAD and the introduction of one main commission meeting (instead of having two) to review the commission's work
and to look specifically at drug issues themselves.

48. With these changes, projects in member states will have to be approved
directly by the commission.

49. See Organization of American States, "Establishment of the Special
Committee on Trade (CEC)," 9th plenary session, 11 June 1993,
Managua, Nicaragua.

50. It is hoped that after the autumn meeting of the advisory group something will be ready for discussion at the December Summit of the
Americas in Miami.

51. At the November 1994 meeting of CIM, to be held in Washington,
Canada will not be seeking reelection to the executive committee of the

commission. This is largely because of the great interest on the part of other member states in having representatives on the executive committee.

52. Issues about the environment, including sustainable development, were on the agenda of the Summit of the Americas, chaired by U.S. President Bill Clinton.

53. Incorporating and utilizing the NGO network might be a useful means of embarrassing some member states into implementing measures they would not otherwise undertake.

54. Canadian official in Washington, interviewed by author, 2 September 1994.

55. Maureen Appel Molot, "Where Do We, Should We, or Can We Sit?: A Review of Canadian Foreign Policy Literature," *International Journal of Canadian Studies* 1 no.2 (spring-fall 1990):81.

56. See Cranford Pratt, ed., *Middle Power Internationalism: The North South Dimension* (Montreal: McGill-Queen's University Press, 1990).

57. For a sampling of this tradition, see John W. Holmes, *Canada: A Middle-Aged Power* (Toronto: McClelland and Stewart, 1976); and Carsten Holbraad, *Middle Powers in International Politics* (New York: St. Martin's Press, 1984).

58. On this point, see Kim Richard Nossal, *The Politics of Canadian Foreign Policy* (Scarborough, Ont: Prentice-Hall, 1989), p. 51.

59. For discussion of this point, see John W. Holmes, "Most Safely in the Middle," *International Journal* 39 (spring 1984): 366-88.

60. For an interesting discussion of this argument, see Tom Keating, *Canada and World Order* (Toronto: McClelland and Stewart, 1993), pp. 9-23.

61. While these countries have not struck a formal agreement to work on these issues together, this should not discourage Canada from engaging in coalition-building activities within the hemispheric body. Although Canada does have solid working relations with all of the member states, no "patterns" of coalition behaviour seem to have been formalized. Put another way, Canada's allies on a particular matter or problem will be more a function of the issue in question, and not the country itself. In fact, Canada has experienced some difficulties with both Mexico and Brazil on issues such as OAS reform, democratic development, and human rights.

62. For more on this additional space, see Andrew F. Cooper, Richard A. Higgott, and Kim Richard Nossal, *Relocating Middle Powers: Australia and Canada in a Changing World Order* (Vancouver: UBC Press, 1993), p. 21.

63. Clinton's foreign policy has emerged rather slowly since his inauguration—being driven and shaped largely by events in the external environment. Nevertheless, Anthony Lake, Clinton's security advisor, has articulated the organizing principle known as "enlargement" as an alternative to the long-standing policy of "containment." Graham Fraser, "Clinton, aides sculpt new foreign policy," *Globe and Mail,* 27 September 1993, sec. A, p. 7. This new, post-Cold War principle is based largely on strengthening and consolidating democratic governments and market economies, while countering those states which are hostile to democracy and free markets. Graham Fraser, "Bill Clinton's tightrope act," *Globe and Mail,* 5 October 1993, sec. A, p. 11. It is worth mentioning that U.S. support and commitments to reforming and strengthening the OAS have been less than firm.

64. For more on this point, see Cooper, Higgott, and Nossal, *Relocating Middle Powers,* p. 21.

65. See, for instance, Barbara McDougall, introduction to *Making A Difference: Canada's Foreign Policy in a Changing World Order,* ed. John English and Norman Hillmer (Toronto: Lester Publishing, 1992), pp. ix-xvi; and McDougall, "Canada and the New Internationalism," *Canadian Foreign Policy* 1 no.1 (winter 1992/93): 1-6.

66. External Affairs and International Trade Canada, Barbara McDougall, Secretary Of State For External Affairs (address to the 23rd OAS General Assembly, Managua, Nicaragua, 7 June 1993), p. 2.

67. Ibid., 6.

68. In mid-September 1994 Foreign Minister Ouellet, as an indication of this commitment—attended the inauguration of César Gaviria as the new Secretary General of the OAS.

69. Stewart (address to 24th General assembly), 2.

70. Canadian officials in both Ottawa and Washington, interviewed in confidence by author, 24 November 1993.

71. Canadian official in Washington, interviewed in confidence by author, 24 November 1993.

72. Canadian official in the Unit for the Promotion of Democracy, interviewed in confidence by author, 19 November 1993.

73. See Barbara McDougall, "Canada's Commitment to the Organization of American States," *North-South* (June-July 1992): 34.

74. Canadian official in Washington, interviewed in confidence by author, 25 November 1993. For an alternative view, see *Inter-Church Committee on*

Human Rights in Latin America, Critiques of the Department of External Affairs' Country Profiles (January 1992), pp. 1-16.

75. This raises the question, of course, of whether Canada's agenda at the OAS is, at least in part, driven by political considerations.

76 . Canadian officials in both Washington and Ottawa, interviewed in confidence by author, 24 November 1993. There is no evidence, however, to support the view that the Canadian business community, led arguably by the Business Council on National Issues (BCNI), has helped fashion Canada's OAS agenda. Representative of the Business Council, letter to author, 30 July 1992.

77. Officialdom in Ottawa might wish to be careful, especially if Canada wants to remain a member of good standing, about promoting Canadian interests rather than the interests of the OAS itself.

78. In September of 1994 at the official inauguration of César Gaviria as the new OAS Secretary General, Foreign Minister Ouellet indicated his support for Gaviria's formal address as well as Canada's desire to have John Graham stay on as Executive Co-ordinator of the UPD. Canadian official in Washington, interviewed by author, 22 September 1994. Gaviria's address focused on issues such as good governance and strengthening of democratic culture, respect for human rights, environmental conservation, and hemispheric integration. Organization of American States, César Gaviria-Trujillo (address given upon assuming office as Secretary General of the Organization of American States), Washington, DC, 15 September 1994, 1-11.

79. Liberal Party of Canada, *Creating Opportunity: The Liberal Plan for Canada* (Ottawa: The Liberal Party of Canada, 1993), p. 106. Also see Giles Gherson, "Lots of sound bites but no substance about where Canada's heading abroad," *Globe and Mail,* 12 January 1994, sec. A, p. 16.

80. Liberal Party, *Creating Opportunity.*

81. André Ouellet, "The Commitments of a Liberal Foreign Policy Agenda," *Canadian Foreign Policy* 1 no.3 (fall 1993): 1.

Bibliography

GOVERNMENT DOCUMENTS AND PUBLICATIONS

CANADA. 1965. Department of Foreign Affairs. Archives. "Dominican Miscellany." 16 December, File 20-4-OAS-4-1, vol. 4.

———. 1966. "Canada and the OAS." 31 May, File 20-4-OAS-4-1, vol. 4.

———. 1966. "Membership in the Organization of American States." 29 June, File 20-4-OAS-4, vol. 2.

———. 1964. "Mexico, Cuba and the OAS." 3 April, File 20-4-OAS-4-1, vol. 2.

———. 1964. "Canada and the OAS." 4 September, File 20-4-OAS-4-1, vol. 3.

———. 1964. "Possible Entry of Canada into the Organization of American States." 29 October, File 20-4-OAS-4-1, vol. 3.

———. 1964. "Possible Entry of Canada into the Organization of American States." 7 December, File 20-4-OAS-4-1, vol. 3.

———. 1966. "Notes for Minister's Statement on Canada and the OAS to the External Affairs Committee." 10 May, File 20-4-OAS-4-1, vol. 4.

———. 1965. "Canada and the OAS." 13 December, File 20-4-OAS-4-1, vol. 4.

———. 1967. "Summary of Main Points on Paper on 'Implications for Canada of Joining the OAS.'" 16 January, File 20-4-OAS-4-1, vol. 5.

———. 1967. "Implications for Canada of Joining the OAS." 20 January, File 20-4-OAS-4, vol. 2.

———. 1967. "Joint Study with Commonwealth Caribbean Countries of Implications of Joining the OAS." 23 January, File 20-4-OAS-4, vol. 2.

———. 1986. "General OAS Brief." 3 March, File 20-4-OAS-1, vol. 14.

———. 1963. "Excerpt from Statement on International Affairs Passed by the Fourth Constitutional Convention of the Canadian Labour Congress." October, File 20-4-OAS-4.

———. 1964. "Possible Entry of Canada into the Organization of American States." 24 August, File 20-4-OAS-4-1, vol. 3.

———. 1967. "Canadian Position re OAS Resolutions on Cuba." 29 November, File 20-4-OAS-1.

CANADA. 1967. "Political and Military Implications of Membership in the OAS." 27 January, File 20-4-OAS-4, vol. 2.

———. 1963. "Canada and the OAS." 1 November, File 20-4-OAS-4-1, vol. 1.

———. 1964. "Possible Entry of Canada into the Organization of American States." 21 August, File 20-4-OAS-4-1.

———. 1964. "Canada and the OAS." 4 September, File 20-4-OAS-4-1, vol. 3.

———. 1964. "Statements Concerning Canada's Joining the OAS made at Hyannisport Meeting." 8 January, File 20-4-OAS-4-1.

———. 1964. "Appointment of Liaison Officer to the OAS." 17 March, File 20-4-OAS-4.

DEPARTMENT OF EXTERNAL AFFAIRS. 1991. *Canada's First Year in the Organization of American States*. Ottawa: Supply and Services Canada.

———. 1986. *Canada's International Relations: Response of the Government of Canada to the Report of the Special Joint Committee of the Senate and House of Commons*. Ottawa: Minister of Supply and Services Canada.

———. 1985. *Competitiveness and Security: Directions in Canada's International Relations*. Ottawa: Minister of Supply and Services Canada.

———. 1970. *Foreign Policy for Canadians*. Ottawa: Queen's Printer.

———. 1972. "Permanent Observer Status to the Organization of American States." *Communiqué* 5, 2 February.

———. 1972. "Head of Canadian Delegation to the General Assembly of the Organization of American States." *Communiqué* 5, 2 February.

———. 1972. "Canadian Membership in the Inter-American Development Bank." *Communiqué* 31, 3 May.

———. 1972. "Canada Joins Inter-American Institute of Agricultural Sciences." *Communiqué* 72, 4 October.

———. 1973. "Notes for the Statement by Mr. Pierre de Bané, Parliamentary Secretary to the Secretary of State for External Affairs." *Communiqué* 43, 9 April.

———. Documents On Canadian External Relations, Ottawa: Information Canada.

———. 1963. "Canada Sends Observers to the Inter-American Conference of Ministers of Labour on the Alliance for Progress." *Press Release* A.18, 2 May.

———. 1964. "Signature of Agreement between Canada and Inter-American Development Bank." *Press Release* 89, 4 December.

———. 1972. "Notes for Statement by Mr. Paul St. Pierre Parliamentary Secretary to the Secretary of State for External Affairs." *Statements*, 15 April.

DEPARTMENT OF EXTERNAL AFFAIRS. 1947. "Canada in the Americas." *Statements and Speeches*, 47/7, 8 March.

———. 1967. "Canada and Latin America." *Statements and Speeches*, 67/21, 31 May.

———. 1968. "Canada and the World." *Statements and Speeches*, 68/17, 29 May.

———. 1970. "Canada and Latin America—A Period of Mutual Discovery." *Statements and Speeches*, 70/10, 30 June.

———. 1971. "Canada Seeks Closer Links with Latin America." *Statements and Speeches*, 71/14, 13 April.

———. 1972. "Canada Forges another Link with Latin America." *Statements and Speeches*, 72/9, 10 May.

GOVERNMENT OF CANADA. 1982. *Canada's Relations with Latin America and the Caribbean: Final Report to the House of Commons of the Subcommittee on Canada's Relations with Latin America and the Caribbean*. Ottawa: Queen's Printer.

NATIONAL ARCHIVES OF CANADA. 1954. "Tenth Inter-American Conference." 1 April. File RG-25 2226-40, vol. 28.

———. 1954. "Organization of American States." 28 April 1954, File RG-25 2226-40, vol. 28.

———. 1954. "Canadian Membership in the O.A.S." 13 May. File RG-25 2226-40, vol. 28.

———. 1954. "Organization of American States." 9 June. File RG-25 2226-40, vol. 28.

———. 1943. "The Attitude of the United States towards Canadian Entry into the Pan-American Union." 20 January. RG-25 B-3, File 148, vol. 2152.

———. 1943. "Pan-American Union: General File: 1943." 7 January. RG-25 B-3, File 148, vol. 2152.

———. 1942. "Canada and the Pan-American Union." 15 December. RG-25 B-3, File 148, vol. 2152.

———. 1928. "Pan-American Union: General File: 1928-1937." 9 January. RG-25 B-3, File 148, vol. 2152.

———. 1941. "Canadian Entry into Pan-American Union." 24 November. RG-25, File 2226-40, vol. 134.

———. 1943. "Pan-American Union: General File: 1943." 16 January. RG-25 B-3, File 148, vol. 2152.

———. 1941. "Canadian Entry into Pan-American Union." 24 November. RG-25, File 2226-40, vol. 134.

NATIONAL ARCHIVES OF CANADA. 1945. "Pan-American Union: Canadian Entry 1945." 17 March. RG-25 B-3, File 628, vol. 2127.

———. 1945. "Canada and the Inter-American System." 16 February. RG-25 B-3, File 628, vol. 2127.

———. 1942. "The Attitude of Canada to the Pan-American Union." 7 February. RG-25 B-3, File 148, vol. 2152.

———. 1942. "Canada and the Pan-American Union." 15 December. RG-25, File 4889-40, vol. 3182.

———. 1942. "Pan-American Union: General File: 1942." 15 December. RG-25 B-3, File 141, vol. 2128.

———. 1943. "Pan-American Union: General File: 1943." 24 February. RG-25 B-3, File 148, vol. 2152.

———. 1941. "Canadian Entry into the Pan-American Union." 31 October. RG-25, File 2226-40, vol. 134.

———. 1941. "Canada and the Pan-American Union: Summary." 21 November. RG-25, File 2226-40, vol. 134.

———. 1941. "Pan-American Union." 3 November. RG-25, File 2226-40, vol. 134.

———. 1941. "Pan-American Union." 21 November. RG-25, File 2226-40, vol. 134.

———. 1941. "Canada and the Pan-American Union." 21 November. RG-25, File 2226-40, vol. 134.

———. 1941. "Legation in Washington to SSEA." 16 December. RG-25 File 2226-40, vol. 134.

———. 1942. "Canada and the Pan-American Union." 15 December. RG-25 B-3, File 148, vol. 2152.

———. 1942. "Canada, the Pan-American Union and the United States." 13 April. RG-25, File 2226-40, vol. 134.

———. 1944. "Report on Canadian Representation in and Relations with Latin American States." 17 April. RG-25, File 7145-40, vol. 3291.

———. 1945. "Pan-American Union: Canadian Entry: 1945." RG-25 B-3, File 628, vol. 2127.

———. 1949. "Extract from Minutes of Press Conference Held by the Prime Minister." 12 February. RG-25, File 2226-40, vol. 11.

———. 1949. "Canada and the Organization of American States." 11 March. RG-25, File 4900-B-40.

———. 1956. "Canada and the Organization of American States." 9 October. RG-25, File 2228-40, vol. 28.

———. 1953. "The Organization of American States." 9 October. RG-25, File 2226-40, vol. 28.

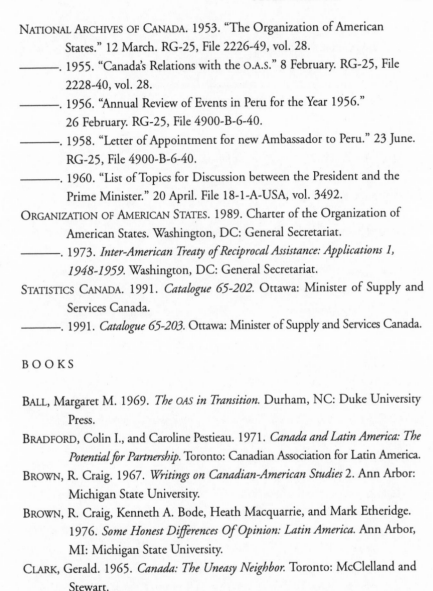

NATIONAL ARCHIVES OF CANADA. 1953. "The Organization of American States." 12 March. RG-25, File 2226-49, vol. 28.

———. 1955. "Canada's Relations with the O.A.S." 8 February. RG-25, File 2228-40, vol. 28.

———. 1956. "Annual Review of Events in Peru for the Year 1956." 26 February. RG-25, File 4900-B-6-40.

———. 1958. "Letter of Appointment for new Ambassador to Peru." 23 June. RG-25, File 4900-B-6-40.

———. 1960. "List of Topics for Discussion between the President and the Prime Minister." 20 April. File 18-1-A-USA, vol. 3492.

ORGANIZATION OF AMERICAN STATES. 1989. Charter of the Organization of American States. Washington, DC: General Secretariat.

———. 1973. *Inter-American Treaty of Reciprocal Assistance: Applications 1, 1948-1959*. Washington, DC: General Secretariat.

STATISTICS CANADA. 1991. *Catalogue 65-202*. Ottawa: Minister of Supply and Services Canada.

———. 1991. *Catalogue 65-203*. Ottawa: Minister of Supply and Services Canada.

BOOKS

BALL, Margaret M. 1969. *The OAS in Transition*. Durham, NC: Duke University Press.

BRADFORD, Colin I., and Caroline Pestieau. 1971. *Canada and Latin America: The Potential for Partnership*. Toronto: Canadian Association for Latin America.

BROWN, R. Craig. 1967. *Writings on Canadian-American Studies* 2. Ann Arbor: Michigan State University.

BROWN, R. Craig, Kenneth A. Bode, Heath Macquarrie, and Mark Etheridge. 1976. *Some Honest Differences Of Opinion: Latin America*. Ann Arbor, MI: Michigan State University.

CLARK, Gerald. 1965. *Canada: The Uneasy Neighbor*. Toronto: McClelland and Stewart.

CLARKSON, Stephen. 1982. *Canada and the Reagan Challenge*. Toronto: James Lorimer.

CONNELL-SMITH, Gordon. 1966. *The Inter-American System*. London: Oxford University Press.

———. 1974. *The United States and Latin America*. London: Heinemann Educational Books.

COOPER, Andrew F., Richard A. Higgott, and Kim Richard Nossal. 1993. *Relocating Middle Powers: Australia and Canada in a Changing World Order*. Vancouver: B.C. Press.

CRENNA, C. David, ed. 1987. *Pierre Elliot Trudeau: Lifting the Shadow of War.* Edmonton: Hurtig.

DE ONIS, Juan. 1970. *The Alliance That Lost Its Way.* Chicago: Quadrangle.

DIEFENBAKER, John G. 1976. *One Canada: The Years of Achievement, 1957-1962.* Toronto: Macmillan.

DOBELL, Peter C. 1972. *Canada's Search for New Roles: Foreign Policy in the Trudeau Era.* London: Oxford University Press.

DREIER, John C. 1962. *The Organization of American States and the Hemisphere Crisis.* New York: Harper and Row.

EAYRS, James.1980. *In Defence of Canada: Growing Up Allied.* Toronto: University of Toronto Press.

FENWICK, Charles G. 1963. *The Organization of American States: The Inter-American Regional System.* Washington, DC: Kauffman.

FONTAINE, Roger W., James D. Theberge, eds. 1976. *Latin America's New Internationalism: The End of Hemispheric Isolation.* New York, NY: Praeger Publishers.

FREEDMAN, Lawrence, and Virginia Gamba-Stonehouse. 1991. *Signals Of War: The Falklands Conflict of 1982.* Princeton, NJ: Princeton University Press.

GARCIA-AMADOR, Francisco V. 1966. *The Inter-American System: Its Development and Strengthening.* Dobbs Ferry, NY: Oceana.

GAROS, Casper. 1990. *Canada-United States Free Trade: Background, Issues, and Impact.* Amsterdam: VU University Press.

GILPIN, Robert. 1987. *The Political Economy of International Relations.* Princeton, NJ: Princeton University Press.

GLEIJESES, Piero. 1991. *Shattered Hope: The Guatemalan Revolution and the United States, 1944-1954.* Princeton, NJ: Princeton University Press,.

GRANATSTEIN, Jack. 1973. *Canadian Foreign Policy Since 1945: Middle Power or Satellite.* Toronto: Copp Clark.

————, and Robert Bothwell. 1990. *Piroutte: Pierre Trudeau and Canadian Foreign Policy.* Toronto: University of Toronto Press.

GREGG, Robert W., ed. 1968. *International Organization in the Western Hemisphere.* Syracuse, NY: Syracuse University Press.

GRIFFEN, Keith. 1969. *Underdevelopment in Spanish America: An Interpretation.* London: George Allen and Unwin.

GWYN, Richard. 1985. *The 49th Paradox: Canada in North America.* Toronto: Totem.

HAAR, Jerry and Edgar J. Dosman, eds. 1993. *A Dynamic Partnership: Canada's Changing Role in the Americas.* New Brunswick, NJ: Transaction.

HAM, Henry H. 1987. *Problems and Prospects of the Organization of American States.* New York: Peter Lang.

HARBRON, John D. 1963. *Canada and the Organization of American States.* N.P.: Canadian-American Committee.

HASTINGS, Max, and Simon Jenkins. 1983. *The Battle for the Falklands.* New York: Norton.

HAWES, Michael. 1984. *Principal Power, Middle Power, Or Satellite?* Toronto: York University Research Programme in Strategic Studies.

HILLIKER, John F. 1990. *Canada's Department of External Affairs.* vol. 1. *The Early Years, 1909-1946.* London: Institute of Public Administration of Canada.

HOLMES, John W. 1970. *The Better Part of Valour: Essays on Canadian Diplomacy.* Toronto: McClelland and Stewart.

———. 1982. The Shaping of Peace: *Canada and the Search for World Order, 1943-1957,* 2. Toronto: University of Toronto Press.

———, and John Kirton, eds. 1988. *Canada and the New Internationalism.* University of Toronto: Centre for International Studies.

HUMPHREY, John P. 1942. *The Inter-American System: A Canadian View.* Toronto: Macmillan.

KANE, William Everett. 1972. *Civil Strife in Latin America: A Legal History of U.S. Involvement.* Baltimore: Johns Hopkins University Press.

KEATING, Tom. 1993. *Canada and World Order.* Toronto: McClelland and Stewart.

KING, Mackenzie. 1980. *The Mackenzie King Diaries, 1932-1949.* Toronto: University of Toronto Press.

KINZER, Stephen and Stephen C. Schlesinger. 1982. *Bitter Fruit: The Untold Story of the American Coup in Guatemala.* Garden City, NY: Doubleday.

KLEPAK, H.P. 1990. *Security Considerations and Verification of a Central American Arms Control Regime.* Ottawa: Arms Control Verification Occasional Papers No. 5, Department of National Defense, June.

———. 1993. *Canada And Latin American Security.* Laval, QC: Meridien.

LECUÑA, Vicente. 1948. *Cartas del Libertador.* New York.

LLOYD, Trevor. 1968. *Canada in World Affairs, 1957-1959.* Toronto: Oxford University Press.

LOWENTHAL, Abraham F. 1972. *The Dominican Intervention.* Cambridge, MA.: Harvard University Press.

LYON, Peyton V. 1968. *Canada in World Affairs, 1961-1963.* Toronto: Oxford University Press.

MANGER, William. 1961. *Pan-America in Crisis: The Future of the OAS.* Dallas: Southern Methodist University Press.

MARTIN, Lawrence. 1983. *The Presidents and the Prime Ministers.* Markham: Paperjacks.

———. 1993. *Pledge Of Allegiance.* Toronto: McClelland and Stewart.

MARTIN, Paul. 1983. *A Very Public Life.* Ottawa: Deneau.

MCFARLANE, Peter. 1989. *Northern Shadows: Canadians and Central America.* Toronto: Between the Lines.

MECHAM, Lloyd J. 1965. *A Survey of United States-Latin American Relations.* Boston: Houghton Mifflin.

———. 1962. *The United States and Inter-American Security, 1889-1960.* Austin: University of Texas Press.

NASH, Knowlton. 1990. *Kennedy and Diefenbaker: The Feud that Helped Topple a Government.* Toronto: McClelland and Stewart.

NEF, Jorge. 1978. *Canada and the Latin American Challenge.* Guelph: Ontario Co-operative Programme in Caribbean and Latin American Studies.

NERVAL, Gaston. 1934. *Autopsy of the Monroe Doctrine: The Strange Story of Inter-American Relations.* New York.

NORTH, Liisa, ed. 1990. *Between War and Peace in Central America.* Toronto: Between the Lines.

NOSSAL, Kim Richard. 1985. *The Politics of Canadian Foreign Policy.* Scarborough, ON: Prentice-Hall.

OGELSBY, J.C.M. 1976. *Gringos From the Far North.* Toronto: Macmillan.

PERL, Raphael, ed. 1983. *The Falklands Dispute in International Law and Politics: A Documentary Source Book.* New York: Oceana.

PRATT, Cranford, ed. 1990. *Middle Power Internationalism: The North-South Dimension.* Montreal: McGill-Queen's University Press.

PRESTON, Richard A. 1965. *Canada In World Affairs, 1959 to 1961.* Toronto: Oxford University Press.

RADWANSKI, George. 1978. *Trudeau.* Scarborough: Signet.

ROBERTSON, William Spence. 1923. *Hispanic-American Relations with the United States.* New York: Oxford University Press,.

ROBINSON, Basil H. 1989. *Diefenbaker's World: A Populist in Foreign Affairs.* Toronto: University of Toronto Press.

ROCHLIN, James. 1994. *Discovering the Americas: The Evolution of Canadian Foreign Policy.* Vancouver: University of British Columbia Press.

ROUSSIN, Marcel. 1958. *Le Canada et le système interaméricain.* Ottawa: University of Ottawa Press.

SCHULZINGER, Robert D. 1984. *American Diplomacy in the Twentieth Century.* New York: Oxford University Press.

SLATER, Jerome. 1965. *A Revaluation of Collective Security: The OAS in Action.* Colombus: Ohio State University Press.

———. 1967. *The OAS and United States Foreign Policy.* Colombus: Ohio State University Press.

———. 1970. *Intervention and Negotiation: The United States and the Dominican Revolution.* New York: Harper and Row.

SOWARD, F.H., and A.M. Macaulay. 1948. *Canada and the Pan-American System.* Toronto: Ryerson.

STOETZER, O. Carlos. 1966. *The Organization of American States: An Introduction.* New York: Frederick A. Praegar.

SWIFT, Jeannine. 1978. *Economic Development in Latin America.* New York: St. Martin's.

TENNYSON, Brian Douglas, ed. 1990. *Canadian-Caribbean Relations: Aspects of a Relationship.* University College of Cape Breton: Centre for International Studies.

THOMAS, A.J., and Ann van Wynen Thomas. 1961. *The OAS.* Washington, DC: Public Affairs Press.

THORDARSON, Bruce. 1972. *Trudeau and Foreign Policy: A Study in Decision-Making.* Toronto: Oxford University Press.

THOMPSON, Dale C., and Roger F. Swanson. 1971. *Canadian Foreign Policy: Options And Perspectives.* Toronto: McGraw-Hill Ryerson.

WHITAKER, Arthur P. 1954. *The Western Hemisphere Idea: Its Rise and Decline.* Ithaca: Cornell University Press.

JOURNAL ARTICLES

ANGLIN, Douglas G. 1961. "United States Opposition to Canadian Membership in the Pan-American Union: A Canadian View." *International Organization* 15(winter 1961):1-20.

BANKER, Stephen. 1982. "The Changing OAS." *International Perspectives* (May-June 1982):23-26.

BLOOMFIELD, Richard, and Abraham F. Lowenthal. 1990. "Inter-American Institutions in a Time of Change." *International Journal* 64(autumn 1990):867-88.

BRECHER, Irving, and Richard A. Brecher. 1967. "Canada and Latin America: The Case for Canadian Involvement." *Queen's Quarterly* 74(autumn 1967):462-71.

BUERGENTHAL, Thomas. 1975. "The Revised OAS Charter and the Protection of Human Rights." *The American Journal of International Law* 69(October 1975):828-36.

CAMINOS, Hugo, and Roberto Lavalle. 1989. "New Departures in the Exercise of Inherent Powers by the UN and OAS Secretaries-General: The Central American Situation." *The American Journal Of International Law* 83(April 1989):395-402.

CHILD, Jack. 1989. "The 1889-1890 Washington Conference through Cuban Eyes: José Martí and the First International American Conference." *Inter-American Review of Bibliography* 39 no.4 (1989):443-56.

CLAUDE, Inis L. 1964. "The 'Try OAS First' Issue." *International Conciliation* 547(March 1964):21-63.

COHEN, Andrew. 1989. "Canada's Foreign Policy: The Outlook for the Second Mulroney Mandate." *Behind the Headlines* 46 no.4 (summer 1989):1-15.

CONNELL-SMITH, Gordon. 1982. "The OAS and the Falklands Conflict." *The World Today* 38 no.9 (September 1982):340-47.

———. 1984. "Latin America and the Falklands Conflict." *Year Book of World Affairs* 38 (1984): 73-88.

CORBETT, P.E. 1941. "Canada in the Western Hemisphere." *Foreign Affairs* 19 (July 1941):778-89.

DOSMAN, Edgar J. 1985. "Hemispheric Relations in the 1980s: A Perspective from Canada." *Journal of Canadian Studies* 19(winter 1984-85):42-60.

———. 1992. "Canada and Latin America: The New Look," *International Journal* 47 no.3 (summer 1992):529-54.

DOXEY, G.V. 1967. "Canada, and the Organisation of American States." Unpublished paper, March.

DREIER, John C. 1978. "New Wine and Old Bottles: The Changing Inter-American System." *International Organization* 22 no.2 (spring 1978):477-93.

DUPRAS, Maurice. 1984. "Canada and the OAS." *International Perspectives* (January-February 1984):15-17.

DURAND, Enrique. 1985. "Modernizing the OAS." *Americas* 10 no.1 (November-December 1985):53.

EDITORIAL. 1964. "Le Canada et L'OEA." *Cité Libre* 15(October 1964): 2-3.

FARER, Tom J. 1987. "The OAS at the Crossroads: Human Rights." *Iowa Law Review* 72 (1986-87):401-13.

FENWICK, C.G. 1957. "The Honduras-Nicaragua Boundary Dispute." *The American Journal of International Law* 51(1957):761-65.

———. 1949. "Application of the Treaty of Rio De Janeiro to the Controversy between Costa Rica and Nicaragua." *American Journal Of International Law* 43(April 1949):329-33.

FULFORD, Robert. 1990. "Canada: A Great Northern Paradox?" *Americas* 42 no.1 (1990):6-16.

FURNISS, Edgar S. 1950. "The Inter-American System And Recent Caribbean Disputes. "*International Organization* 4 no.4 (November 1950):585-97.

GANNON, Francis X. 1984. "Will the OAS Live to Be 100?" *Caribbean Review* 13 no.4 (fall 1984):12-15.

———. 1982. "Globalism Versus Regionalism: U.S. Policy and the OAS." *Orbis* 26 no.1 (spring 1982):195-221.

GARCÍA-MORA, Manuel R. 1951. "The Law of the Inter-American Treaty of Reciprocal Assistance." *Fordham Law Review* 20 no.1 (March 1951):1-22.

GRABENDORFF, Wolf. 1982. "Interstate Conflict Behaviour and Regional Potential for Conflict in Latin America." *Journal of Interamerican Studies and World Affairs* 24 no.3 (August 1982):267-94.

GUY, James John. 1989. "Canada Joins the OAS: A New Dynamic in the Inter-American System." *Inter-American Review of Bibliography* 34 no.4 (1989):500-11.

———. 1976. "Canada and Latin America." *The World Today* 32 no.10 (October 1976):376-86.

———. 1977. "The Growing Relationship of Canada and the Americas." *International Perspectives* (July-August 1977):3-6.

———. 1987. "Canada and the Caribbean: How 'Special' the Relationship?" *The Round Table* 304(1987):434-44.

HAFFA, Annegret, and Nikolaus Werz. 1983. "The Falklands Conflict and Inter-American Relations." *Aussenpolitik* 34 no.2 (1983):185-201.

HAGLUND, David G. 1987. "How is Canada Doing on Central America?" *International Perspectives* (September-October 1987):5-8.

Harbron, John D. 1972. "Canada and Latin America: Ending a Historic Isolation." *International Perspectives* (May-June 1972):25-29.

———. 1974. "Growing Pressures on Canada to Seek Hemispheric Identity." *International Perspectives* (May-June 1974):31-35.

HERMANN, Charles F. 1989. "Who Makes Foreign Policy Decisions and How: An Empirical Inquiry." *International Studies Quarterly* 33 no.4 (1989):361-87.

———. 1990. "Changing Course: When Governments Choose to Redirect Foreign Policy." *International Studies Quarterly* 34 no.2 (1990):3-21.

HOLMES, John W. 1962. "Our Other Hemisphere: Reflections on the Bahia Conference." *International Journal* 27 no.4 (autumn 1961-62):414-19.

———. 1986. "The United Nations in Perspective." *Behind the Headlines* 44 no.1 (October 1986): 1-24.

———. 1963. "Canadian External Policies since 1945." *International Journal* 18 no.2 (spring 1963):137-47.

HUARD, Victor. 1988. "Quiet Diplomacy or Quiet Acquiescence?" *Canadian Journal of Latin American and Caribbean Studies* 13 no.26 (1988):105-37.

HUBERT, Jean-Paul. 1994. "Canada and the OAS: Review and Outlook." *FOCAL Lecture Series* (March 1994):1-4.

ISBISTER, Claude. 1987. "Third World Debt: IMF and the World Bank." *Behind the Headlines* 44 no.4 (March 1987):1-17.

IRWIN, W. Arthur. 1965. "Should Canada Join the Organization of American States?" *Queen's Quarterly* 72 no.2 (summer 1965):289-303.

KILGOUR, David. 1986. "Canada and Latin America." *International Perspectives* (January-February 1986):19-21.

KIRTON, John. 1987. "Shaping the Global Order: Canada and the Francophone and Commonwealth Summits of 1987." *Behind the Headlines* 44 no.6 (June 1987):1-17.

———. 1988. "Canada's New Internationalism." *Current History* 87 no.527 (March 1988):101-04,134.

KLEPAK, Hal P. 1994. "The Impact of the International Narcotics Trade on Canada's Foreign and Security Policy," *International Journal* 49 no.1 (winter 1993-94):66-92.

KOS-RABCEWICZ-ZUBKOWSKI, Ludwik J. 1967. "Canada and the Organization of American States." *Air University Review* 18 (September-October 1967):61-69.

KUNZ, Josef. 1945. "The Inter-American Conference on Problems of War and Peace at Mexico City and the Problem of the Reorganization of the Inter-American System." *American Journal of International Law* 39 (July 1945):527-33.

LANDAU, G. 1990 "Canada Inside the OAS." *Peace and Security* 4 no.4 (winter 1989-1990):24.

LEIS, Raul. 1990. "Panama: The Other Side of Midnight." *NACLA Report on the Americas* 23 no.6 (April 1990):4-6.

LEMCO, Jonathan. 1986. "Canada and Central America: A Review of Current Issues." *Behind The Headlines* 42 no.5 (May 1986):1-19.

LIJPHART, Arend. 1971. "Comparative Politics and the Comparative Method." *The American Political Science Review* 65 no.3 (September 1971):682-93.

MACDONALD, Ronald St. John. 1964. "The OAS in Action." *The University of Toronto Law Journal* 15(1963-64):359-429.

MACKENZIE, David. 1991. "'The World's Greatest Joiner': Canada and the Organization of American States." *British Journal Of Canadian Studies* 6 no.1 (1991):203-20.

MACQUARRIE, Heath. 1968. "Canada and the O.A.S.: The Still Vacant Chair." *The Dalhousie Review* 48 no.1 (spring 1968):37-45.

MAECHLING, Charles. 1990. "Washington's Illegal Invasion." *Foreign Policy* 79 (summer 1990):113-31.

MANGER, William. 1928. "The Pan-American Union at the Sixth International Conference Of American States." *The American Journal of International Law* 22 no.4 (July 1928):764-75.

MARTZ, Mary Jeanne Reid. 1977. "OAS Reforms and the Future of Pacific Settlement." *Latin American Research Review* 12 no.2 (1977):176-86.

MASSE, Vincent. 1948. "Canada and the Inter-American System." *Foreign Affairs* 26 no.4 (July 1948):693-700.

McKENNA, Peter. 1993. "Needed: A Policy for Latin America." *Policy Options* 14 no.4 (May 1993):27-28.

———. 1993. "Canada and the OAS: Opportunities and Constraints," *The Round Table* 327(July 1993):323-39.

———. 1993. "How Is Canada Doing in the OAS?" *Canadian Foreign Policy* 1 no.2 (spring 1993):81-98.

McNAUGHT, Kenneth. 1962. "Canada's Pan-American Hot Seat." *Saturday Night* 76 no.16 (August 1962):15-17.

MILLER, Eugene H. 1948. "Canada and the Pan-American Union." *International Journal* 3 no.1 (winter 1947-48):24-38.

MILLER, Robert and David Pollock, 1991. "Canada y America Latina." *Integracíon Latinoamericana* 165(marzo 1991):16-26.

MILLET, Richard L. 1990. "The Aftermath of Intervention: Panama 1990." *Journal of Interamerican Studies and World Affairs* 32 no.1 (spring 1990):1-15.

MOÍSES, José Alváro. 1991. "Democracy Threatened: The Latin American Paradox," *Alternatives* 16(1991):141-60.

MOORE, John Norton. 1982. "The Inter-American System Snarls in Falklands War." *American Journal Of International Law* 76(1982):830-31.

MOUNT, Graeme S. and Edelgard E. Mahant. 1985. "Review of Recent Literature on Canadian-Latin American Relations." *Journal of Interamerican Studies and World Affairs* 27 no.2 (summer 1985):127-51.

MURRAY, D.R. 1982. "The Bilateral Road: Canada and Latin America in the 1980s." *International Journal* 37 no.2 (winter 1981-82):108-31.

———. 1984. "Hard Realities: Canadian-Latin American Relations at the End of the Trudeau Era." Unpublished paper, presented at the National Defence College, Kingston, 1984.

———. 1974. "Canada's First Diplomatic Missions in Latin America." *Journal of Interamerican Studies and World Affairs* 16 no.2 (May 1974):153-72.

———. 1983. "Difficult Choices: Canadian-Latin American Relations in the mid-1980s." Unpublished paper, presented at the National Defence College, Kingston, May 1983.

———. 1981. "New Developments in Canadian-Latin American Relations." Unpublished paper, February 1981.

———. 1979. "The Present and Future Significance of Latin America for Canada." Unpublished paper, December 1979.

NOSSAL, Kim Richard. 1984. "Analyzing the Domestic Sources of Canadian Foreign Policy." *International Journal* 39 no.1 (winter 1983-84):1-22.

OGELSBY, J.C.M. 1969. "Canada and the Pan-American Union: Twenty Years On." *International Journal* 24 no.3 (summer 1969):571-89.

———. 1979. "A Trudeau Decade: Canadian-Latin American Relations 1968-1978." *Journal of Interamerican Studies and World Affairs* 21(May 1979):187-208.

———. 1978. "Latin America." *International Journal* 33(spring 1978):401-07.

OUELLET, André. 1993. "The Commitments of a Liberal Foreign Policy Agenda," *Canadian Foreign Policy* 1 no.3 (fall 1993):1-6.

PÉREZ, Carlos Andrés. 1990. "OAS Opportunities." *Foreign Policy* 80(Fall 1990):52-55.

PHARAND, Donat. 1986. "Canada and the OAS: The Vacant Chair Revisited." *Revue générale de droit* 17(1986):429-54.

PICK, Alfred. 1975. "Protocol Signed at San José Provides Reform of Rio Treaty." *International Perspectives* (September-October 1975):25-30.

PODEA, Iris S. 1948. "Pan-American Sentiment in French Canada." *International Journal* 3 no.4 (autumn 1948):334-48.

POITRAS, Guy and Raymond Robinson. 1994. "The Politics of NAFTA in Mexico," *Journal of Interamerican Studies and World Affairs* 36 no.1

(spring 1994):1-35.

RADWANSKI, George. 1976. "Trudeau in Latin America Set Stage for Closer Relations." *International Perspectives* (May-June 1976):6-10.

REDEKOP, Clarence G. 1986. "The Mulroney Government and South Africa: Constructive Disengagement." *Behind the Headlines* 44 no.2 (December 1986):1-16.

ROBERTSON, A.H. 1968. "Revision of the Charter of the Organization of American States." *The International and Comparative Law Quarterly* 17(1968):346-67.

ROBINSON, P. Stuart. 1994. "Reason, Meaning, and the Institutional Context of Foreign Policy Decision-making," *International Journal* 49 no.2 (Spring 1994):408-33.

ROCHLIN, James. 1988. "The Political Economy of Canadian Relations with Central America." *Canadian Journal of Latin American and Caribbean Studies* 13 no.25 (1988):45-70.

———. 1990. "The Evolution of Canada as an Actor in Inter-American Affairs." *Millennium* 19 no.2 (1990):229-48.

———. 1991. "Canada, the Pan-American Union and the Organization of American States: An Historical Overview." Unpublished paper, May 1991.

ROPP, Steve C. 1991. "Panama: The United States Invasion and its Aftermath." *Current History* 90 no.554 (March 1991):113-16,130.

ROUSSIN, Marcel. 1964. "Latin America: Challenge and Response." Unpublished paper, August 1964.

———. 1953. "Canada: The Case of the Empty Chair." *World Affairs* 116 no.1 (spring 1953):15-16.

———. 1953. "Evolution of the Canadian Attitude towards the Inter-American System." *The American Journal of International Law* 47 no.2 (1953):296-300.

RUBIN, Seymour J. 1982. "The Falklands (Malvinas), International Law, and the OAS." *The American Journal of International Law* 76(1982):594-95.

RUIZ, Wilson. 1988. "A View from the South: Canadian/Latin American Links." *Briefing* 19(March 1988):1-14.

SCHEMAN, L.Ronald. 1987. "Rhetoric and Reality: The Inter-American System's Second Century." *Journal of Interamerican Studies and World Affairs* 29 no.3 (fall 1987):1-31.

———. 1987. "Institutional Reform in the Organization of American States, 1975-1983: A Case Study in Problems of International Cooperation." *Public Administration and Development* 7 no.2 (April-June 1987): 215-36.

SCHEMAN, L.Ronald. 1985. "OAS Charter Reform." *LASA Forum* 16 no.3 (Fall 1985):10-11.

———. 1986. "The OAS and Political Action." *LASA Forum* 16 no.4 (winter 1986):34-36.

———. 1986. "The OAS and Technical Cooperation." *LASA Forum* 16 no.4 (spring 1986):22-24.

SCHUYLER, George W. 1991. "Perspectives on Canada and Latin America: Changing Context ... Changing Policy?" *Journal of Interamerican Studies and World Affairs* 33 no.1 (spring 1991):19-58.

SCLANDERS, Ian. 1963 "The Case against Canadian Membership in the OAS." *Maclean's Magazine.* 15 June 1963:4.

SEPULVEDA, César. 1972. "The Reform of the Charter of the Organization of American States." *The Hague Academy Of International Law* 3(1972):91-140.

SHARP, Mitchell. 1972. "Canada-U.S. Relations: Options for the Future." *International Perspectives* (September-October 1972):1-24.

SLATER, Jerome. 1969. "The Decline of the OAS." *International Journal* 24 no.3 (summer 1969):497-506.

———. 1969. "The Limits of Legitimation in International Organizations: The Organization of American States and the Dominican Crisis." *International Organization* 23 no.1 (winter 1969):48-72.

SMITH, David Edward. 1966. "Should Canada Join the Organization of American States? A Rejoinder to W. Arthur Irwin." *Queen's Quarterly* 73(spring 1966):100-14.

SMITH, Peter H. 1991. "Crisis and Democracy In Latin America." *World Politics* 43 no.4 (July 1991):608-34.

SOKOL, John. 1962. "Latin America Wants Canada in the OAS." *The Commentator* 6 no.5 (May 1962):19-20.

STAIRS, Denis. 1982. "The Political Culture of Canadian Foreign Policy." *Canadian Journal of Political Science* 15 no.4 (December 1982):669-90.

STEVENSON, Brian J.R. 1991. "Entering the Inter-American System: Canada and the OAS in the 1990s." Unpublished paper.

———. 1991. "Canada and the OAS: A New Era Emerges?" Canada-Caribbean-Central America Policy alternatives (CAPA) working paper:1-21.

TAYLOR, Philip B. 1956. "The Guatemalan Affair: A Critique of United States Foreign Policy." *The American Political Science Review* 50 no.3 (September 1956):787-806.

TOMASEK, Robert D. 1974. "Caribbean Exile Invasions: A Special Regional Type of Conflict." *Orbis* 17 no.4 (winter 1974):1354-82.

TOMASEK, Robert D. 1989. "The Organization of American States and Dispute Settlement from 1948 to 1981: An Assessment." *Inter-American Review of Bibliography* 39 no.4 (1989):461-76.

TRAVIS, Martin B. 1957. "The Organization of American States: A Guide to the Future." *The Western Political Quarterly* 10(1957):491-511.

TRINDADE, A.A. Cancado. 1982. "The Inter-American Juridicial Committee: An Overview." *The World Today* 38 no.11 (November 1982):437-42.

WHITAKER, Arthur P. 1959. "The Organization Of American States." *The Year Book of World Affairs 1959* 13(1959):115-39.

WILL, R.M. 1960. "Economic Aspects of Canadian-Latin American Relations." *International Journal* 15 no.4 (autumn 1960):346-54.

WILLIAMSON, Kenneth B. 1983. "Canada and the Inter-American System: A Matter Of Choice." Unpublished paper, 1983.

BOOK CHAPTERS

BELL, George. 1986. "Canada and the OAS: Going Around the Buoy Again?" In *Canada, the Caribbean, and Central America*, ed. Brian MacDonald. Toronto: Canadian Institute of Strategic Studies, 97-117.

BRIGAGAO, Clovis. 1988. "The Institutional System and the Management of the Crisis." In *Latin America: Peace, Democratization and Economic Crisis*, ed. José Silva-Michelena. Tokyo: United Nations University, 151-86.

BURNS, Bradford E. 1984. "The Continuity of the National Period." In *Latin America: Its Problems and its Promise*, ed. Jan Kippers Black. Boulder CO: Westview Press, 61-80.

CAMERON, Maxwell A. 1991. "Canada And Latin America." In *Canada Among Nations, 1990-91*, ed. Brian W. Tomlin and Maureen Appel Molot. Ottawa: Carleton University Press, 109-23.

CHILD, Jack. 1986. "War in the South Atlantic." In *United States Policy in Latin America: A Quarter Century of Crisis and Challenge, 1961-1986*, ed. John D. Martz. Lincoln: University of Nebraska Press, 202-34.

CLARK, Joe. 1988. "Canada's New Internationalism." In *Canada and the New Internationalism*, ed. John Holmes and John Kirton. University of Toronto: Centre for International Studies, 3-11.

DOSMAN, Edgar, and David H. Pollock. 1990. "Canada, Mexico and the North-South Dialogue: The Need for Audacity." In *Relations Between Mexico And Canada*, ed. Omar Martínez Legorreta. El Colegio De México: Centro De Estudios Internacionales, 269-83.

GLADE, William P. 1984. "Economic Aspects Of Latin America." In *Latin America: Its Problems and Its Promise*, ed. Jan Kippers Black. Boulder, CO: Westview Press, 133-47.

GRAHAM, John. 1988. "Shaping Stability in Central America." In *Canada and the New Internationalism*, ed. John Holmes and J. Kirton. University of Toronto: Centre for International Studies, 35-40.

GUY, James. 1990. "The Caribbean: A Canadian Perspective." In *Canadian-Caribbean Relations: Aspects of a Relationship*, ed. Brian Douglas Tennyson. University College of Cape Breton: Centre for International Studies, 257-99.

HARBRON, John D. 1976. "Canada Draws Closer to Latin America: A Cautious Involvement." In *Latin America's New Internationalism*, ed. Roger R. Fontaine and James D. Theberge. New York: Praegar, 109-42.

JACKSON, Robert. 1983. "Canadian Foreign Policy and the Western Hemisphere." In *Governance in the Western Hemisphere*, ed. Viron P. Vaky. New York: Praegar, 119-34.

KEATING, Tom. 1991. "In Search of a Foreign Policy." In *Social Democracy Without Illusions*, ed. J. Richards, R. Cairns and L. Pratt. Toronto: McClelland and Stewart, 158-81.

KIRTON, John. 1986. "The Foreign Policy Decision Process." In *Canada Among Nations*, ed. Maureen Appel Molot and Brian W. Tomlin. Toronto: James Lorimer, 24-45.

KRYZANEK, Michael J. 1986. "The Dominican Intervention Revisited: An Attitudinal and Operational Analysis." In *United States Policy in Latin America: A Quarter Century of Crisis and Challenge, 1961-1986*, ed. John D. Martz. Lincoln: University of Nebraska Press, 135-56.

KURTH, James R. 1990. "The Rise and Decline of the Inter-American System: A u.s. View." In *A New U.S.-Latin American Security Relationship*, ed. Richard J. Bloomfield and Gregory F. Treverton. Boulder, CO: Lynne Rienner, 9-25.

LUMSDEN, Ian. 1968. "The 'Free World' of Canada and Latin America." In *An Independent Foreign Policy for Canada?* ed. Stephen Clarkson. Toronto: McClelland and Stewart, 198-211.

MANGER, William. 1971. "Reform of the OAS: The 1967 Buenos Aires Protocol of Amendment to the 1948 Charter of Bogotá: An Appraisal." In *Regional International Organizations: Structures and Functions*, ed. Paul A. Tharp. New York: St. Martin's Press, 141-51.

MUÑOZ, Heraldo. 1990. "The Rise and Decline of the Inter-American System: A Latin American View." In *Alternative to Intervention: A New U.S.-*

Latin American Security Relationship, ed. Richard J. Bloomfield and
Gregory F. Treverton. Boulder, CO: Lynne Rienner, 27-37.

MURRAY, David R. 1978. "On Diplomatic Unrelations." In *Canada and the
Latin American Challenge,* ed. Jorge Nef. Guelph: Ontario Co-operative
Programme in Latin American Studies, 170-77.

OGELSBY, J.C.M. 1976. "Canada and Latin America." In *Canada and the Third
World,* ed. Peyton V. Lyon and Tareq Y. Ismael. Toronto: Macmillan,
162-99.

PETRAS, James F., and Morris H. Morley. 1987. "The United States and Canada:
State Policy and Strategic Perspectives on Capital in Central America."
In *Frontyard Backyard: The Americas in the Global Crisis,* ed. John
Holmes and Colin Leys. Toronto: Between the Lines, 149-79.

PRATT, Cranford. 1990. "Middle Power Internationalism and Global Poverty."
In *Middle Power Internationalism: The North-South Dimension,* ed.
Cranford Pratt. Montreal: McGill-Queen's University Press, 1990, 3-24.

RANDALL, Stephen. 1977 "Canadian Policy and the Development of Latin
America." In *A Foremost Nation: Canadian Foreign Policy and a
Changing World,* ed. Norman Hillmer and Garth Stevenson. Toronto:
McClelland and Stewart, 202-29.

ROUSSIN, Marcel. 1963. "The Inter-American Regional System." In *The Alliance
For Progress: A Critical Appraisal,* ed. William Manger. Washington,
DC: Public Affairs Press, 129-31.

SCHEMAN, L. Ronald, and John W. Ford. 1985. "The Organization of American
States as Mediator." In *International Mediation in Theory and Practice,*
ed. Saadia Touval and I. William Zartman. Boulder, CO: Westview
Press, 197-232.

SLATER, James. 1984. "United States Policy In Latin America." In *Latin
America: Its Problems and Its Promise,* ed. Jan Knippers Black. Boulder,
CO: Westview Press, 221-42.

THOMAS, A.J. and Ann Van Wynen Thomas. 1967. "The Dominican Republic
Crisis 1965: Legal Aspects." In *The Dominican Republic Crisis 1965,*
ed. John Carey. Dobbs Ferry, NY: Oceana, 1-81.

————. 1971. "The Rule-Making System of the OAS." In *Regional International
Organizations: Structures and Functions,* ed. Paul A. Tharp. New York:
St. Martin's, 109-40.

VON RIEKHOFF, Harald. 1987. "The Structure of Foreign Policy Decision
Making and Management." In *Canada Among Nations,* ed. Brian W.

Tomlin and Maureen Appel Molot. Toronto: James Lorimer, 14-30.

WILLIAMSON, K.B., and D.H. Pollock. 1989. "Canada's Role In Selected
Intergovernmental Organizations." In *Conference Proceedings*, ed.
A.R.M. Ritter. Canadian Association of Latin American and Caribbean
Studies, 418-41.

WILSON, Larman C. 1975. "Multilateral Policy and the Organization of
American States: Latin American-U.S. Convergence and Divergence."
In *Latin American Foreign Policies: An Analysis,* ed. Harold Eugene
Davis and Larman C. Wilson. Baltimore: Johns Hopkins University
Press, 47-84.

WINKS, Robin W. 1989. "Canada and the Three Americas: Her Hemispheric
Role." In *Friends So Different,* ed. Lansing Lamont and J. Duncan
Edmonds. Ottawa: University of Ottawa Press, 251-61.